Object-Oriented JavaScript

Create scalable, reusable high-quality JavaScript applications, and libraries

Stoyan Stefanov

BIRMINGHAM - MUMBAI

Object-Oriented JavaScript

Create scalable, reusable high-quality JavaScript applications, and libraries

Copyright © 2008 Packt Publishing

First published: July 2008

Production Reference: 1160708

Published by Packt Publishing Ltd.
32 Lincoln Road
Olton
Birmingham, B27 6PA, UK.

ISBN 978-1-847194-14-5

www.packtpub.com

Cover Image by Nilesh Mohite (nilpreet2000@yahoo.co.in)

Credits

Author

Stoyan Stefanov

Reviewers

Dan Wollman

Douglas Crockford

Gamaiel Zavala

Jayme Cousins

Julie London

Nicolas Zakas

Nicole Sullivan

Philip Tellis

Ross Harmes

Tenni Theurer

Wayne Shea

Yavor Paunov

Senior Acquisition Editor

Douglas Paterson

Development Editor

Nikhil Bangera

Technical Editor

Gagandeep Singh

Editorial Team Leader

Akshara Aware

Project Manager

Abhijeet Deobhakta

Project Coordinator

Patricia Weir

Indexer

Monica Ajmera

Proofreader

Dirk Manuel

Production Coordinator

Rajni Thorat

Cover Designer

Rajni Thorat

About the Author

Stoyan Stefanov is a Yahoo! web developer, Zend Certified Engineer, and book author. He talks regularly about JavaScript, PHP, and other web development topics at conferences and on his blog at www.phpied.com, and also runs a number of other sites, including JSPatterns.com—a site dedicated to exploring JavaScript patterns. Stoyan is the engineering lead of Yahoo!'s performance optimization tool YSlow, and contributes to other open-source projects such as Firebug and PEAR.

A "citizen of the world", Stoyan was born and raised in Bulgaria, but is also a Canadian citizen, and is currently residing in Los Angeles, California. In his rare offline moments, he enjoys playing the guitar and going to the Santa Monica beaches and pools with his family.

About the Reviewers

Dan Wellman lives with his wife and three children in his home town of Southampton on the south coast of England. By day his mild-mannered alter-ego works for a small yet accomplished e-commerce production agency. By night he battles the forces of darkness and fights for truth, justice, and less intrusive JavaScript.

He has been writing computer-related articles, tutorials, and reviews for around five years and is rarely very far from a keyboard of some description.

Douglas Crockford is a product of the US public education system. A registered voter, he owns his own car. He is the world's foremost living authority on JavaScript. He is the author of *JavaScript: The Good Parts*. He has developed office automation systems. He did research in games and music at Atari. He was Director of Technology at Lucasfilm. He was Director of New Media at Paramount.

He was the founder and CEO of Electric Communities/Communities.com. He was founder and CTO of State Software, where he discovered JSON, the data interchange standard. He is now an architect at Yahoo!

Gamaiel Zavala is a frontend engineer at Yahoo! in Santa Monica, California. He enjoys writing all types of code and strives to understand the big picture, from protocols and packets to the wide gamut of technologies delivering user experience to the front end. Aside from the geeky stuff, he is enjoying a new family with his lovely wife and baby boy.

Jayme Cousins started creating commercial websites once released from University with a degree in Geography. His projects include marketing super-niche spatial analysis software, preparing online content overnight for his city's newspaper, printing road names on maps, painting houses, and teaching College tech courses to adults. He currently lives behind a keypad in London, Canada with his wife Heather and newborn son Alan. Jayme previously reviewed *Learning Mambo* from Packt Publishing. He enjoys matching technology with real-world applications for real-world people and often feels that his primary role is that of a translator of technobabble for entrepreneurs.

Jayme now provides web development, consulting, and technical training through his business, In House Logic (www.inhouselogic.com).

Julie London is a software engineer with over eight years of experience in building enterprise-level web applications. A Flash developer for many years, she now concentrates on other client-side technologies including CSS, JavaScript, and XSL. She currently lives in Los Angeles where she works as a frontend engineer for Yahoo!

Nicholas C. Zakas is principal frontend engineer for the Yahoo! front page, a contributor to YUI, and JavaScript teacher at Yahoo! He is the author of two books, *Professional JavaScript for Web Developers* and *Professional Ajax*, as well as over a dozen online articles on JavaScript.

Nicholas began his career as webmaster of a small software company, transitioning into a user interface designer and prototyper before moving fully into software engineering. He moved to Silicon Valley from Massachusetts in 2006 to join Yahoo! Nicholas can be contacted through his website at www.nczonline.net.

Nicole Sullivan is a CSS performance guru living in California. She began her professional career in 2000, when her future husband (then a W3C employee) told her that if her website didn't validate he wouldn't be able to sleep at night. She thought she'd better figure out what this 'validator' thing was all about, and a love for standards was born.

She began building Section 508 compliant, accessible websites. As her appreciation for performance and large-scale sites grew, she went on to work in the online marketing business, building CSS framework solutions for many well-known European and world-wide brands, such as SFR, Club Med, SNCF, La Poste, FNAC, Accor Hotels, and Renault.

Nicole now works for Yahoo! in the Exceptional Performance group. Her role involves researching and evangelizing performance best practices and building tools like YSlow that help other F2E's create better sites. She writes about standards, her dog, and her obsession with object oriented CSS at `www.stubbornella.org`.

Philip Tellis is a lazy geek working with Yahoo! He likes letting the computer do his work for him, and if it can't, he'll just reprogram it.

When he isn't hacking code, Philip rides his bike around Silicon Valley, and tries his hand at food hacking, but not at the same time.

Ross Harmes works as a frontend engineer for Flickr in San Francisco, California. He's also an author of the book Pro JavaScript Design Patterns. Some of his technical writings and online projects, such as the YUI Bundle for TextMate, can be found at `www.techfoolery.com`.

Tenni Theurer joined Yahoo! in early 2006 as a technical evangelist in Yahoo!'s Exceptional Performance group. She then took the reins as manager and grew the engineering team to lead the global effort in making Yahoo! products faster and accelerating the user experience worldwide. Tenni is currently a Sr. Product Manager in Yahoo!'s Search Distribution group. Tenni has spoken at several conferences including Web 2.0 Expo, Ajax Experience, Rich Web Experience, AJAXWorld, BlogHer, WITI, and CSDN-DrDobbs. She is a featured guest blogger on Yahoo! Developer Network and Yahoo! User Interface Blog. Prior to Yahoo!, Tenni worked in IBM's Pervasive Computing group on enterprise mobile solutions where she worked directly with high profile customers on large-scale deployments.

Wayne Shea is a software engineer at Yahoo!. His projects at Yahoo! include research on improving mobile web performances and developing scalable high-performance web services. Before joining Yahoo!, he had been busy creating mobile web browsers for cell phones at Openwave and Access.

Yavor Paunov is a product of the joined efforts of the Computer Science departments of the Technical University, Sofia, Bulgaria, and Concordia University in Montreal, Canada. His experience spans from two-person startups to multi-national companies. Outside work, Yavor's habits include listening to live music and extended walks with his charming shoe-eating cocker spaniel.

Table of Contents

Preface

This book explores JavaScript for what it is: a highly expressive and flexible prototype-based object-oriented programming language. Once dismissed as a toy for designers to make things such as rollover buttons, today this interesting and unique language is back, stronger than ever. Today's Web 2.0 world of AJAX, fat-client programming, desktop-like rich Internet applications, drag-and-drop maps and webmail clients, rely heavily on JavaScript to provide a highly interactive user experience. And if we never had the chance to properly explore JavaScript before, now is the time to sit down and (re-)learn it.

This book doesn't assume any prior knowledge of JavaScript and works from the ground up to give you a thorough understanding of the language.

What This Book Covers

Chapter 1 talks briefly about the history, present, and future of JavaScript, and then moves on to explore the basics of object-oriented programming (OOP) in general. You then learn how to set up your training environment (Firebug) in order to dive into the language on your own, using the book examples as a base.

Chapter 2 discusses the language basics: variables, data types, arrays, loops, and conditionals.

Chapter 3 covers functions. JavaScript has many uses for functions and here you learn to master them all. You also learn about the scope of variables and JavaScript's built-in functions. An interesting, but often misunderstood feature of the language—closures—is demystified at the end of the chapter.

Chapter 4 introduces objects: how to work with properties and methods, and the various ways to create your objects. There's also an overview of the built-in objects in JavaScript, such as Math and Date (just an overview, Appendix C has all the details).

Chapter 5 is dedicated to the all-important concept of prototypes in JavaScript.

Chapter 6 expands your "thinking in JavaScript" horizon, discussing a dozen ways to implement inheritance in JavaScript.

Chapter 7 is the browser chapter. In this chapter, you learn about BOM (Browser Object Model), DOM (W3C's Document Object Model), browser events, and AJAX.

Chapter 8 dives into various unique JavaScript coding patterns, as well as several language-independent design patterns, translated to JavaScript from the Book of Four, the most influential work of software design patterns.

Appendix A lists the reserved words in JavaScript.

Appendix B is a reference to the built-in JavaScript functions, together with sample uses.

Appendix C is a reference that provides detail and provides examples of the use of every method and property of every built-in object in JavaScript.

Appendix D is a regular expressions pattern reference.

Conventions

In this book, you will find a number of styles of text that distinguish between different kinds of information. Here are some examples of these styles, and an explanation of their meaning.

Code words in text are shown as follows: " The key/value pairs are divided by colons, in the format `key: value` ."

A block of code will be set as follows:

```
var book = {
  name: 'Catch-22',
  published: 1961,
  author: {
    firstname: 'Joseph',
    lastname: 'Heller'
  }
};
```

When we wish to draw your attention to a particular part of a code block, the relevant lines or items will be shown in bold:

```
function TwoDShape(){}
// take care of inheritance
TwoDShape.prototype = Shape.prototype;
TwoDShape.prototype.constructor = TwoDShape;
```

New terms and **important words** are introduced in a bold-type font. Words that you see on the screen, in menus or dialog boxes for example, appear in our text like this: "clicking the **Next** button moves you to the next screen".

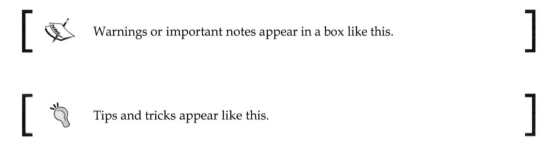

Warnings or important notes appear in a box like this.

Tips and tricks appear like this.

Reader Feedback

Feedback from our readers is always welcome. Let us know what you think about this book— what you liked or may have disliked. Reader feedback is important for us to develop titles that you really get the most out of.

To send us general feedback, simply send an email to feedback@packtpub.com, and mention the book title in the subject of your message.

If there is a book that you need and would like to see us publish, please send us a note in the **SUGGEST A TITLE** form on www.packtpub.com or email suggest@packtpub.com.

If there is a topic that you have expertise in and you are interested in either writing or contributing to a book, see our author guide on www.packtpub.com/authors.

Customer Support

Now that you are the proud owner of a Packt book, we have a number of things to help you to get the most from your purchase.

Errata

Although we have taken every care to ensure the accuracy of our contents, mistakes do happen. If you find a mistake in one of our books—maybe a mistake in text or code—we would be grateful if you would report this to us. By doing this you can save other readers from frustration, and help to improve subsequent versions of this book. If you find any mistakes, report them by visiting http://www.packtpub.com/support, selecting your book, clicking on the **let us know** link, and entering the details of the error. Once your comments have been verified, your submission will be accepted and added to the list of existing errata for the book. Any existing errata can be viewed by selecting your book from http://www.packtpub.com/support.

Questions

If you are having a problem with some aspect of the book you can contact us at questions@packtpub.com, and we will do our best to address it.

I'd like to dedicate this book to my wife Eva and my daughters Zlatina and Nathulie. Thank you for your patience, support, and encouragement.

To my reviewers who volunteered their time reviewing drafts of this book and whom I deeply respect and look up to: a big thank you for your invaluable input.

1
Introduction

What do Yahoo! Maps, Google Maps, Yahoo! Mail, My Yahoo!, Gmail, Digg,
YouTube and a plethora of other popular "Web 2.0" applications have in common?
They all offer rich and responsive user interfaces, heavily employing code written
in the JavaScript language. JavaScript started with simple one-liners embedded in
HTML, but is now used in much more sophisticated ways. Developers leverage the
object-oriented nature of the language to build scalable code architectures made up
of reusable pieces. JavaScript provides behavior, the third pillar in today's paradigm
that sees web pages as consisting of three clearly distinguishable parts: content
(HTML), presentation (CSS), and behavior (JavaScript).

JavaScript programs run inside a host environment. The web browser is the most
common environment, but it is not the only one. Using JavaScript, you can create
all kinds of widgets, application extensions, and other pieces of software. Learning
JavaScript is a pretty good deal: you learn one language and can then code all kinds
of different applications.

This book is about JavaScript and focuses on its object-oriented nature. The book
starts from zero, and does not assume any prior programming knowledge. Although
there is one chapter dedicated to the web browser environment, the rest of the book
is about JavaScript in general, so is applicable to all environments.

Let's start with the first chapter, which gives you an overview of the story behind
JavaScript. It also introduces the basic concepts you'll encounter in discussions on
object-oriented programming.

A Bit of History

Initially, the Web was conceived as a collection of static HTML documents, tied together with hyperlinks. Soon, as the Web grew in popularity and size, the webmasters who were creating static HTML web pages felt they needed something more. They wanted the opportunity for richer user interaction, mainly driven by desire to save server round-trips for simple tasks such as form validation. Two options came up: Java applets (they failed) and LiveScript, which was conceived by Netscape in 1995 and later included in the Netscape 2.0 browser under the name of JavaScript.

The ability to alter otherwise static elements of a web page was very well received and other browsers followed suit. Microsoft's Internet Explorer (IE) 3.0 shipped with JScript, which was a copy of the same language plus some IE-specific features. Eventually there was an effort to standardize the various implementations of the language and this is how ECMAScript (European Computer Manufacturers Association) was born. Today we have the standard, called ECMA-262, and JavaScript is just one implementation of this standard, albeit the most popular one.

For better or for worse, JavaScript's instant popularity happened during the period of the Browser Wars I (approximately 1996-2001). Those were the times of the initial Internet boom when the two major browser vendors—Netscape and Microsoft, were competing for market share. These two vendors were constantly adding more bells and whistles to their browsers and their versions of JavaScript. This situation, together with the lack of agreed-upon standards brought a lot of bad opinions of JavaScript. More often than not, development was a pain: you write a script while working in one browser. Once you're done with development, you test in the other browser and it simply doesn't work. At the same time, the browser vendors were busy adding features, but falling behind on providing proper development tools.

Browser vendors were introducing incompatibilities that annoyed the web developers, but this was only one part of the problem. The other part of the problem were the web developers themselves, who were adding too many features to their web pages. Developers were eager to make use of every new possibility that the browsers provided and ended up "enhancing" their web pages with things like animations in the status bar, flashing colors, blinking texts, shaking browser windows, snowflakes, objects stalking your mouse cursor, and so on, often at the expense of usable pages. These various ways to abuse JavaScript was the other reason why the language got its bad reputation. This caused "the real programmers" (developers with background in more established languages such as Java or C/C++) to dismiss JavaScript as nothing but a toy for front-end designers to play around with.

The JavaScript backlash caused some web projects to completely ban any client-side programming and trust only their predictable and reliable server. And really, why would you double the time to deliver a project and spend this additional time debugging problems with the different browsers?

The Winds of Change

Everything changed in the years following the end of the Browser Wars I. A number of processes reshaped the web development landscape in a very positive way.

- Microsoft won the war, and for about five years (which is more or less forever in Internet time), they stopped adding features to Internet Explorer and JScript. This allowed time for other browsers as well as developers to catch up and even surpass IE's capabilities.

- The movement for web standards was embraced by developers and browser vendors alike. Naturally, developers didn't like having to code everything two (or more) times to account for browsers' differences; therefore they liked the idea of having agreed-upon standards that everyone would follow. We're still far from being able to develop in a fully standards-compliant environment, but ideally, this will happen in the future.

- Developers and technologies matured and more people started caring about things like usability, progressive enhancement techniques, and accessibility.

In this healthier environment, developers started finding out new and better ways to use the instruments that were already available. After the public release of applications such as Gmail and Google Maps, which were rich on client-side programming, it became clear that JavaScript is a mature, unique in certain ways, and powerful prototypal object-oriented language. The best example of it's rediscovery is the wide adoption of the functionality provided by the XMLHttpRequest object, which was once an IE-only innovation, but was then implemented by most other browsers. XMLHttpRequest allows JavaScript to make HTTP requests and get fresh content from the server in order to update some parts of a page, without a full page reload. Due to the wide use of XMLHttpRequest, a new breed of desktop-like web applications, dubbed AJAX applications, was born.

The Present

An interesting thing about JavaScript is that it always runs inside a *host environment*. The browser is the most popular host environment, but it is not the only one. JavaScript can run on the server, on the desktop, and in rich media. Today, you can use JavaScript to do all of this:

- Create rich and powerful web applications (the kind of applications that run inside the web browser, such as Gmail)

- Write server-side code such as ASP scripts or, for example, code that is run using Rhino (a JavaScript engine written in Java)

- Create rich media applications (Flash, Flex) using ActionScript, which is based on ECMAScript

- Write scripts that automate administrative tasks on your Windows desktop, using Windows Scripting Host
- Write extensions/plugins for a plethora of desktop application such as Firefox, Dreamweaver, and Fiddler
- Create web applications that store information in an off-line database on the user's desktop, using Google Gears
- Create Yahoo! Widgets, Mac Dashboard widgets, or Adobe Air applications that run on your desktop

This is by no means an extensive list. JavaScript started inside web pages, but today it's safe to say it is practically everywhere.

The Future

We can only speculate what the future will be, but it's quite certain that it will include JavaScript. For quite some time JavaScript may have been underestimated and underused (or rather overused in the wrong ways), but every day we witness new uses of JavaScript in much more interesting and creative ways. Where they once wrote simple one-liners, often embedded in-line in HTML tag attributes (such as `onclick`), developers nowadays ship sophisticated, well-designed and architected, extensible applications, and libraries. JavaScript is indeed taken seriously and developers are starting to rediscover and enjoy its unique object-oriented features more and more.

Once listed in the "nice to have" sections of job postings, these days the knowledge of JavaScript is a yes/no factor when it comes to hiring web developers. Common job interview questions you can hear today include: "Is JavaScript an object-oriented language? Good. Now how do you implement inheritance in JavaScript?" After reading this book, you'll be prepared to ace your JavaScript job interview and even impress your interviewers with some bits that maybe they didn't know.

Object-Oriented Programming

Before diving into JavaScript let's take a moment to review what people mean when they say "object-oriented", and what the main features of this programming style are. Here's a list of concepts that are most often used when talking about object-oriented programming (OOP):

- Object, method, property
- Class
- Encapsulation

- Aggregation
- Reusability/inheritance
- Polymorphism

Let's take a closer look into each one of these concepts.

Objects

As the name *object-oriented* suggests, objects are quite important. An object is a representation of a "thing" (someone or something), and this representation is expressed with the help of a programming language. The thing can be anything—a real-life object, or some more convoluted concept. Taking a common object like a cat for example, you can see that it has certain characteristics (color, name, weight) and can perform some actions (meow, sleep, hide, escape). The characteristics of the object are called *properties* in OOP and the actions are called *methods*.

There is also an analogy with the spoken language:

- Objects are most often named using nouns (book, person)
- Methods are verbs (read, run)
- Values of the properties are adjectives

Let's take, for example, the sentence "The black cat sleeps on my head". "The cat" (a noun) is the object ,"black" (adjective) is the value of the `color` property, and "sleep" (a verb) is an action, or a method in OOP. For the sake of the analogy, we can go a step further and say that "on my head" specifies something about the action "sleep", so it's acting as a parameter passed to the `sleep` method.

Classes

In real life, similar objects can be grouped based on some criteria. A hummingbird and an eagle are both birds, so they can be classified as belonging to the Birds class. In OOP, a class is a blueprint, or recipe for an object. Another name for "object" is "instance", so we say that the eagle is an instance of the Birds class. You can create different objects using the same class, because a class is just a template, while the objects are concrete instances, based on the template.

There's a difference between JavaScript and the "classic" OO languages like C++ and Java. You should understand right from the start that in JavaScript there are no classes; everything is based on objects. JavaScript has the notion of prototypes, which are also objects (we'll discuss them later in detail). In a classic OO language, you'd say something like "create me a new object called Bob which is of class Person". In a prototypal OO language, you'd say, "I'm going to take this object Person that I have lying around and reuse it as a prototype for a new object that I'll call Bob".

Encapsulation

Encapsulation is another OOP-related concept, which illustrates the fact that an object contains (encapsulates) both:

- Data (stored in properties) and
- The means to do something with the data (using methods)

One other term that goes together with encapsulation is *information hiding*. This is a rather broad term and can mean different things, but let's see what people usually mean when they use it in the context of OOP.

Imagine an object, say an MP3 player. You, as a user of the object, are given some interface to work with, such as buttons, the display, and so on. You use the interface in order to get the object to do something useful for you, like playing a song. Exactly how it is working on the inside, you don't know and, most often, don't care. In other words, the implementation of the interface is hidden from you. The same thing happens in OOP, when your code uses an object by calling its methods. It doesn't matter if you coded the object yourself or it came from some third party library; your code doesn't need to know how the methods work internally. In compiled languages, you can't actually read the code that makes an object work. In JavaScript, because it's an interpreted language, you can see the source code, but the concept is still the same—you work with the object's interface, without worrying about its implementation.

Another aspect of information hiding is the visibility of methods and properties. In some languages, objects can have *public*, *private*, and *protected* methods and properties. This categorization defines the level of access the users of the object have. For example, only the internal implementation of the object has access to the private methods, while anyone has access to the public ones. In JavaScript, all methods and properties are public, but we'll see that there are ways to protect the data inside an object and achieve privacy.

Aggregation

Combining several objects into a new one is known as *aggregation* or *composition*. The aggregation concept illustrates the ability to combine several objects into a new one. Aggregation is a powerful way to separate a problem into smaller and more manageable parts (divide and conquer). When a problem scope is so complex that it's impossible to think about it at a detailed level in its entirety, you can separate the problem into several smaller areas, and possibly then separate each of these into even smaller chunks. This allows you to think about the problem on several levels of *abstraction*. A personal computer is a very complex object. You cannot think about all the things that need to happen when you start your computer. But you can abstract the problem saying that you need to initialize the objects it consists of: the Monitor object, the Mouse object, the Keyboard object, and so on. Then you can dive deeper into each of the sub-objects. This way you are composing complex objects by assembling reusable parts.

To use another analogy, a Book object could can contain (aggregate) one or more author objects, a publisher object, several chapter objects, a table of contents, and so on.

Inheritance

Inheritance is a very elegant way to reuse code that has already been written. For example, you can have a generic object Person, which has properties such as name and date of birth, and that implements the functionality walk, talk, sleep, eat. Then you figure out that you need an object Programmer. You could re-implement all the methods and properties that Person has, but it would be smarter to just say that Programmer *inherits* Person, and save yourself some work. The Programmer object only needs to implement more-specific functionality, such as the method "write code", while reusing all of the Person's functionality.

In classical OOP, classes inherit from other classes, but in JavaScript, because there are no classes, objects inherit from other objects.

When an object inherits from another object, it usually adds new methods to the inherited ones, thus *extending* the old object. Often the following phrases can be used interchangeably: "B inherits from A" and "B extends A". Also, the object that inherited a number of methods, can pick one or more methods and redefine them, customizing them for its own needs. This way the interface stays the same, the method name is the same, but when called on the new object, the method behaves differently. This way of redefining how an inherited method works is known as *overriding*.

Polymorphism

In the example above, we had a Programmer object that inherited all of the methods of the parent Person object. This means that both objects provide a "talk" method, among others. Now imagine that somewhere in our code, there's a variable called Bob and it so happens that we don't know if Bob is a Person, or a Programmer object. We can still call the "talk" method on the Bob object and the code will work. This ability to call the same method on different objects and have each of them respond in their own way is called *polymorphism*.

OOP Summary

If you are new to the OO programming lingo and you're not sure you've fully grasped the concepts above, don't worry. We'll look at some code and you'll see that, although they may seem complicated when just talking about high-level concepts, things are much simpler in practice.

Thus said, let's rehash the concepts once more.

Feature	Illustrates concept
Bob is a man (an object).	objects
Bob's date of birth is June 1st, 1980, gender: male, hair: black.	properties
Bob can eat, sleep, drink, dream, talk and calculate his age.	methods
Bob is an instance of class Programmer.	class (in classical OOP)
Bob is based on another object, called Programmer.	prototype (in prototypal OOP)
Bob holds data (such as *birth date*) and methods that work with the data (such as *calculate age*).	encapsulation
We don't need to know how the calculation method works internally. The object might have some private data, such as the number of days in February in a leap year, we don't know, nor do we want to know.	information hiding
Bob is part of a Web Dev Team object, together with Jill, a Designer object and Jack, a Project Manager object.	aggregation, composition

Feature	Illustrates concept
Designer, Project Manager and Programmer are all based on and extend a Person object.	inheritance
You can call the methods *Bob:talk*, *Jill:talk* and *Jack:talk* and they'll all work fine, albeit producing different results (Bob will probably talk more about performance, Jill about beauty and Jack about deadlines). Each object inherited the method *talk* from Person and customized it.	polymorphism, method overriding

Setting up Your Training Environment

This book takes a "do it yourself" approach when it comes to writing code, because the author firmly believes that the best way to really learn a programming language is by writing code. So there's no cut-and-paste-ready code downloads, which you can simply put in your pages. On the contrary, you're expected to type in code, see how it works and then tweak it and play around with it. When trying out the code examples, you're encouraged to enter the code into Firebug's console. Let's see how you go about doing this.

Getting the Tools You Need

As a developer, you most likely already have Firefox installed and use it for your daily web browsing pleasure. If not, do yourself a favor and install it right now. It's free and runs on any platform—Windows, Linux, or Mac. Download it from `http://www.mozilla.com/firefox/`.

The Firefox browser is extensible and there are lots of useful extensions out there (all written in JavaScript!). A popular extension is Firebug—an indispensable tool for web development, with lots of useful features. Download Firebug from `http://www.getfirebug.com/`, install it, and try it out by starting Firefox and going to any page and pressing *F12* (on Windows) or clicking on the little bug icon at the bottom right corner of the Firefox screen. This will open the Firebug feature we're most interested in—the console.

Using the Firebug Console

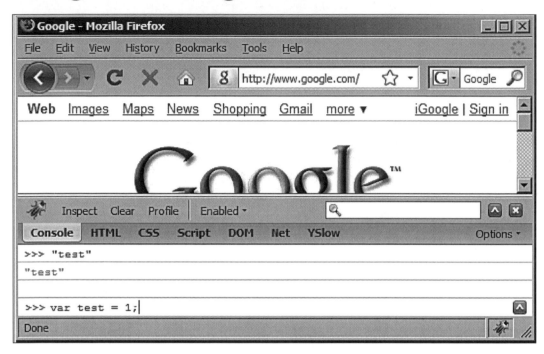

You can type code directly into the Firebug console, and when you press *Enter*, the code is evaluated and executed. The return value of the code is printed in the console. The code is executed in the context of the currently-loaded page, so for example if you type document.location.href it will return the URL of the current page.

The console also has an auto-complete feature. It works similarly to the normal command line prompt in your operating system. If, for example, you type **docu** and hit the *Tab* key, **docu** will be auto-completed to **document**. Then if you type . (the dot operator), you can press *Tab* several times and it will iterate through all the available properties and methods you can call on the document object.

By using the *UP* and *DOWN* arrow keys, you can go through the list of already-executed commands and bring them back in the console.

The console gives you only one line to type in, but you can execute several JavaScript statements by separating them with semi-colons. If you need more space or more lines, you can open the console in a multi-line mode, by clicking the upward-facing arrow on the far right of the input line. An example of multi-line mode is shown in the next screenshot.

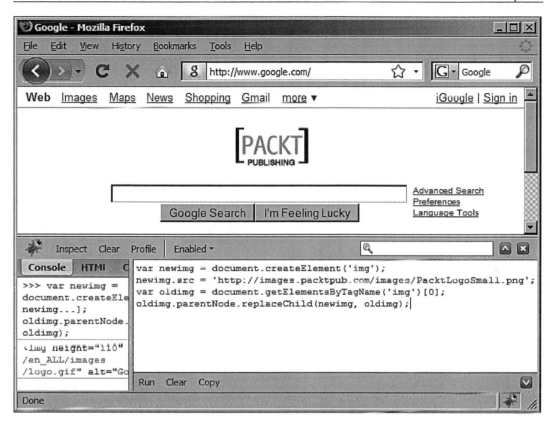

This example shows how you can use the console to type in some code that swaps the logo on the `google.com` home page with an image of your choice. As you see, you can test your JavaScript code live on any page.

One configuration option you should set in Firefox is the strictness of JavaScript warnings you will see in the console. This will help you make sure that the code you write is of better quality. Although warnings are not errors, you should aim at writing code that doesn't throw any warnings. For example using an undeclared variable is not an error, but it's not a good idea, so Firefox's JavaScript engine will generate a warning, which will be displayed in the console if the strict setting is turned on. To set the "strict" setting, do this:

1. Type **about:config** in Firefox's address bar.
2. Search for **strict** by typing it in the **Filter** field and pressing *Enter*.
3. Double-click the line that says **javascript.options.strict**. This should set its **Value** to **true**.

Summary

In this chapter, you learned about how JavaScript came to be and where it is today. You were also introduced to Object-oriented programming concepts and saw how JavaScript is not a classic OO language, but a prototypal one. Finally, you learned how to set up and use your training environment—the Firebug console. Now you're ready to dive into JavaScript and learn how to use its powerful OO features. For additional information on the topics discussed in this chapter, take a look at the following web pages.

- On the YUI Theater (`http://developer.yahoo.com/yui/theater/`), there are several talks by Douglas Crockford that are highly recommended. Part 1 of the "Theory of the DOM" talks about browser history, and Part 1 of "The JavaScript Programming Language" talks about history of JavaScript (amongst other things).

- For OOP concepts see the Wikipedia article (`http://en.wikipedia.org/wiki/Object-oriented_programming`) and Sun's Java documentation (`http://java.sun.com/docs/books/tutorial/java/concepts/index.html`), although the latter talks about OOP using classes.

- For examples of what's possible today with JavaScript, take a look at the Yahoo! Widgets page (`http://widgets.yahoo.com/`), Google Maps (`http://maps.google.com`), or the JavaScript version of the Processing visualization language (`http://ejohn.org/blog/processingjs/`).

2
Primitive Data Types, Arrays, Loops, and Conditions

Before diving into the object-oriented features of JavaScript, let's first take a look at some of the basics. This chapter walks you through:

- The primitive data types in JavaScript, such as strings and numbers
- Arrays
- Common operators, such as +, -, `delete`, and `typeof`
- Flow control statements, such as loops and if-else conditions

Variables

Variables are used to store data. When writing programs, it is convenient to use variables instead of the actual data, as it's much easier to write `pi` instead of 3.141592653589793 especially when it happens several times inside your program. The data stored in a variable can be changed after it was initially assigned, hence the name "variable". Variables are also useful for storing data that is unknown to the programmer when the code is written, such as the result of later operations.

There are two steps required in order to use a variable. You need to:

- Declare the variable
- Initialize it, that is, give it a value

In order to *declare* a variable, you use the var statement, like this:

```
var a;
var thisIsAVariable;
var _and_this_too;
var mix12three;
```

For the names of the variables, you can use any combination of letters, numbers, and the underscore character. However, you can't start with a number, which means that this is invalid:

```
var 2three4five;
```

To *initialize* a variable means to give it a value for the first (initial) time. You have two ways to do so:

- Declare the variable first, then initialize it, or
- Declare and initialize with a single statement

An example of the latter is:

```
var a = 1;
```

Now the variable named a contains the value 1.

You can declare (and optionally initialize) several variables with a single var statement; just separate the declarations with a comma:

```
var v1, v2, v3 = 'hello', v4 = 4, v5;
```

Variables are Case Sensitive

Variable names are case-sensitive. You can verify this statement using the Firebug console. Try typing this, pressing *Enter* after each line:

```
var case_matters = 'lower';
var CASE_MATTERS = 'upper';
case_matters
CASE_MATTERS
```

To save keystrokes, when you enter the third line, you can only type **ca** and press the *Tab* key. The console will auto-complete the variable name to case_matters. Similarly, for the last line—type **CA** and press *Tab*. The end result is shown on the following figure.

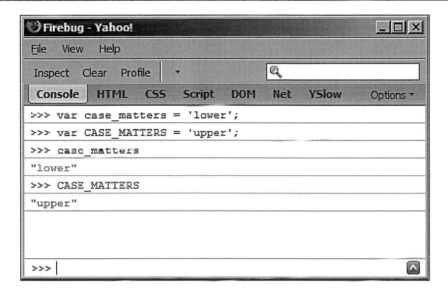

Throughout the rest of this book, only the code for the examples will be given, instead of a screenshot:

```
>>> var case_matters = 'lower';
>>> var CASE_MATTERS = 'upper';
>>> case_matters
```

"lower"

```
>>> CASE_MATTERS
```

"upper"

The three consecutive greater-than signs (**>>>**) show the code that you type, the rest is the result, as printed in the console. Again, remember that when you see such code examples, you're strongly encouraged to type in the code yourself and experiment tweaking it a little here and there, so that you get a better feeling of how it works exactly.

Operators

Operators take one or two values (or variables), perform an operation, and return a value. Let's check out a simple example of using an operator, just to clarify the terminology.

```
>>> 1 + 2
```

3

In this code:

- + is the *operator*
- The *operation* is addition
- The input values are 1 and 2 (the input values are also called *operands*)
- The *result* value is **3**

Instead of using the values 1 and 2 directly in the operation, you can use variables. You can also use a variable to store the result of the operation, as the following example demonstrates:

```
>>> var a = 1;
>>> var b = 2;
>>> a + 1
```

2

```
>>> b + 2
```

4

```
>>> a + b
```

3

```
>>> var c = a + b;
>>> c
```

3

The following table lists the basic arithmetic operators:

Operator symbol	Operation	Example
+	Addition	```>>> 1 + 2``` **3**
-	Substraction	```>>> 99.99 - 11``` **88.99**
*	Multiplication	```>>> 2 * 3``` **6**
/	Division	```>>> 6 / 4``` **1.5**

Operator symbol	Operation	Example

%	Modulo, the reminder of a division	```>>> 6 % 3```
		0
		```>>> 5 % 3```
		2
		
		It's sometimes useful to test if a number is even or odd. Using the modulo operator it's easy. All odd numbers will return **1** when divided by 2, while all even numbers will return **0**.
		```>>> 4 % 2```
		0
		```>>> 5 % 2```
		1

++	Increment a value by 1	*Post-increment* is when the input value is incremented *after* it's returned.
		```>>> var a = 123; var b = a++;```
		```>>> b```
		123
		```>>> a```
		124
		
		The opposite is *pre-increment*; the input value is first incremented by 1 and then returned.
		```>>> var a = 123; var b = ++a;```
		```>>> b```
		124
		```>>> a```
		124

--	Decrement a value by 1	*Post-decrement*
		```>>> var a = 123; var b = a--;```
		```>>> b```
		123
		```>>> a```
		122
		
		Pre-decrement
		```>>> var a = 123; var b = --a;```
		```>>> b```
		122
		```>>> a```
		122

When you type `var a = 1;` this is also an operation; it's the *simple assignment operation* and `=` is the *simple assignment operator*.

There is also a family of operators that are a combination of an assignment and an arithmetic operator. These are called *compound operators*. They can make your code more compact. Let's see some of them with examples.

```
>>> var a = 5;
>>> a += 3;
```

8

In this example `a += 3;` is just a shorter way of doing `a = a + 3;`

```
>>> a -= 3;
```

5

Here `a -= 3;` is the same as `a = a - 3;`

Similarly:

```
>>> a *= 2;
```

10

```
>>> a /= 5;
```

2

```
>>> a %= 2;
```

0

In addition to the arithmetic and assignment operators discussed above, there are other types of operators, as you'll see later in this and the following chapters.

Primitive Data Types

Any value that you use is of a certain *type*. In JavaScript, there are the following *primitive* data types:

1. Number—this includes floating point numbers as well as integers, for example 1, 100, 3.14.

2. String—any number of characters, for example "a", "one", "one 2 three".

3. Boolean—can be either `true` or `false`.

4. Undefined—when you try to access a variable that doesn't exist, you get the special value undefined. The same will happen when you have declared a variable, but not given it a value yet. JavaScript will initialize it behind the scenes, with the value undefined.

5. Null—this is another special data type that can have only one value, the null value. It means no value, an empty value, nothing. The difference with undefined is that if a variable has a value null, it is still defined, it only happens that its value is nothing. You'll see some examples shortly.

Any value that doesn't belong to one of the five primitive types listed above is an object. Even null is considered an object, which is a little awkward—having an object (something) that is actually nothing. We'll dive into objects in Chapter 4, but for the time being just remember that in JavaScript the data types are either:

- Primitive (the five types listed above), or
- Non-primitive (objects)

Finding out the Value Type —the typeof Operator

If you want to know the data type of a variable or a value, you can use the special typeof operator. This operator returns a string that represents the data type. The return values of using typeof can be one of the following—"number", "string", "boolean", "undefined", "object", or "function". In the next few sections, you'll see typeof in action using examples of each of the five primitive data types.

Numbers

The simplest number is an integer. If you assign 1 to a variable and then use the typeof operator, it will return the string **"number"**. In the following example you can also see that the second time we set a variable's value, we don't need the var statement.

```
>>> var n = 1;
>>> typeof n;
```

"number"

```
>>> n = 1234;
>>> typeof n;
```

"number"

Numbers can also be floating point (decimals):

```
>>> var n2 = 1.23;
>>> typeof n;
```

"number"

You can call `typeof` directly on the value, without assigning it to a variable first:

```
>>> typeof 123;
```

"number"

Octal and Hexadecimal Numbers

When a number starts with a 0, it's considered an *octal* number. For example, the octal `0377` is the decimal **255**.

```
>>> var n3 = 0377;
>>> typeof n3;
```

"number"

```
>>> n3;
```

255

The last line in the example above prints the decimal representation of the octal value. While you may not be very familiar with octal numbers, you've probably used *hexadecimal* values to define, for example, colors in CSS stylesheets.

In CSS, you have several options to define a color, two of them being:

- Using decimal values to specify the amount of R (red), G (green) and B (blue) ranging from 0 to 255. For example `rgb(0, 0, 0)` is black and `rgb(255, 0, 0)` is red (maximum amount of red and no green or blue).
- Using hexadecimals, specifying two characters for each R, G and B. For example, `#000000` is black and `#ff0000` is red. This is because `ff` is the hexadecimal for 255.

In JavaScript, you put `0x` before a hexadecimal value (also called *hex* for short).

```
>>> var n4 = 0x00;
>>> typeof n4;
```

"number"

```
>>> n4;
```

0

```
>>> var n5 = 0xff;
>>> typeof n5;
```

"number"

```
>>> n5;
```

255

Exponent Literals

`1e1` (can also be written as `1e+1` or `1E1` or `1E+1`) represents the number one with one zero after it, or in other words 10. Similarly, `2e+3` means the number 2 with 3 zeros after it, or 2000.

```
>>> 1e1
```

10

```
>>> 1e+1
```

10

```
>>> 2e+3
```

2000

```
>>> typeof 2e+3;
```

"number"

`2e+3` means moving the decimal point 3 digits to the *right* of the number 2. There's also `2e-3` meaning you move the decimal point 3 digits to the *left* of the number 2.

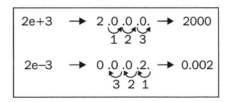

```
>>> 2e-3
```

0.002

```
>>> 123.456E-3
```

0.123456

```
>>> typeof 2e-3
```

"number"

Infinity

There is a special value in JavaScript called `Infinity`. It represents a number too big for JavaScript to handle. `Infinity` is indeed a number, as typing `typeof Infinity` in the console will confirm. You can also quickly check that a number with 308 zeros is ok, but 309 zeros is too much. To be precise, the biggest number JavaScript can handle is `1.7976931348623157e+308` while the smallest is `5e-324`.

```
>>> Infinity
```

Infinity

```
>>> typeof Infinity
```

"number"

```
>>> 1e309
```

Infinity

```
>>> 1e308
```

1e+308

Dividing by 0 will give you infinity.

```
>>> var a = 6 / 0;
>>> a
```

Infinity

Infinity is the biggest number (or rather a little bigger than the biggest), but how about the smallest? It's infinity with a minus sign in front of it, minus infinity.

```
>>> var i = -Infinity;
>>> i
```

-Infinity

```
>>> typeof i
```

"number"

Does this mean you can have something that's exactly twice as big as `Infinity` —
from 0 up to infinity and then from 0 down to minus infinity? Well, this is purely for
amusement and there's no practical value to it. When you sum infinity and minus
infinity, you don't get 0, but something that is called **NaN** (Not A Number).

```
>>> Infinity - Infinity
```

NaN

```
>>> -Infinity + Infinity
```

NaN

Any other arithmetic operation with `Infinity` as one of the operands will give you
`Infinity`:

```
>>> Infinity - 20
```

Infinity

```
>>> -Infinity * 3
```

-Infinity

```
>>> Infinity / 2
```

Infinity

```
>>> Infinity - 9999999999999999
```

Infinity

NaN

What was this **NaN** you saw in the example above? It turns out that despite its name,
"Not A Number", NaN is a special value that is also a number.

```
>>> typeof NaN
```

"number"

```
>>> var a = NaN;
>>> a
```

NaN

You get **NaN** when you try to perform an operation that assumes numbers but the
operation fails. For example, if you try to multiply 10 by the character "f", the result
is **NaN**, because "f" is obviously not a valid operand for a multiplication.

```
>>> var a = 10 * "f";
>>> a
```

NaN

NaN is contagious, so if you have even only one **NaN** in your arithmetic operation, the whole result goes down the drain.

```
>>> 1 + 2 + NaN
```

NaN

Strings

A *string* is a sequence of characters used to represent text. In JavaScript, any value placed between single or double quotes is considered a string. This means that 1 is a number but "1" is a string. When used on strings, typeof returns the string "string".

```
>>> var s = "some characters";
>>> typeof s;
```

"string"

```
>>> var s = 'some characters and numbers 123 5.87';
>>> typeof s;
```

"string"

Here's an example of a number used in string context:

```
>>> var s = '1';
>>> typeof s;
```

"string"

If you put nothing in quotes, it's still a string (an empty string):

```
>>> var s = ""; typeof s;
```

"string"

As you saw before, when you use the plus sign with two numbers, this is the arithmetic operation addition. However, if you use the plus sign on strings, this is a *string concatenation* operation and it returns the two strings glued together.

```
>>> var s1 = "one"; var s2 = "two"; var s = s1 + s2; s;
```

"onetwo"

```
>>> typeof s;
```

"string"

The dual function of the + operator can be a source of errors. Therefore, it is always best to make sure that all of the operands are strings if you intend to concatenate them, and are all numbers if you intend to add them. You will learn various ways to do so further in the chapter and the book.

String Conversions

When you use a number-like string as an operand in an arithmetic operation, the string is converted to a number behind the scenes. (This works for all operations except addition, because of addition's ambiguity)

```
>>> var s = '1'; s = 3 * s; typeof s;
```

"number"

```
>>> s
```

3

```
>>> var s = '1'; s++; typeof s;
```

"number"

```
>>> s
```

2

A lazy way to convert any number-like string to a number is to multiply it by 1 (a better way is to use a function called parseInt(), as you'll see in the next chapter):

```
>>> var s = "100"; typeof s;
```

"string"

```
>>> s = s * 1;
```

100

```
>>> typeof s;
```

"number"

If the conversion fails, you'll get NaN:

```
>>> var d = '101 dalmatians';
>>> d * 1
```

NaN

A lazy way to convert anything to a string is to concatenate it with an empty string.

```
>>> var n = 1;
>>> typeof n;
```

"number"

```
>>> n = "" + n;
```

"1"

```
>>> typeof n;
```

"string"

Special Strings

Some strings that have a special meaning, as listed in the following table:

String	Meaning	Example

\
 \\
 \'
 \"
	\ is the escape character.
	
	 When you want to have quotes inside your string, you escape them, so that JavaScript doesn't think they mean the end of the string.
	
	 If you want to have an actual backslash in the string, escape it with another backslash.
		`>>> var s = 'I don't know';`
		
		 This is an error, because JavaScript thinks the string is "I don" and the rest is invalid code. The following are valid:
		 `>>> var s = 'I don\'t know';`
		 `>>> var s = "I don\'t know";`
		 `>>> var s = "I don't know";`
		 `>>> var s = '"Hello", he said.';`
		 `>>> var s = "\"Hello\", he said.";`
		 Escaping the escape:
		 `>>> var s = "1\\2"; s;`
		
		 "1\2"

\n	End of line	`>>> var s = '\n1\n2\n3\n';`
		 `>>> s`
		 `"`
		
		 1
		 2
		 3
		
		 `"`

String	Meaning	Example

\r	Carriage return	All these:
		
		`>>> var s = '1\r2';`
		`>>> var s = '1\n\r2';`
		`>>> var s = '1\r\n2';`
		
		Result in:
		
		`>>> s`
		"1
		
		2"

\t	Tab	`>>> var s = "1\t2"`
		`>>> s`
		"1 2"

\u	\u followed by a character code allows you to use Unicode	Here's my name in Bulgarian written with Cyrillic characters: `>>> "\u0421\u0442\u043E\u044F\u043D"` **"Стоян"**

There are some additional characters which are rarely used: \b (backspace), \v (vertical tab), and \f (form feed).

Booleans

There are only two values that belong to the boolean data type: the values `true` and `false`, used without quotes.

```
>>> var b = true; typeof b;
```

"boolean"

```
>>> var b = false; typeof b;
```

"boolean"

If you quote `true` or `false`, they become strings.

```
>>> var b = "true"; typeof b;
```

"string"

Logical Operators

There are three operators, called *logical operators,* that work with boolean values. These are:

- `!` —logical NOT (negation)
- `&&` —logical AND
- `||` —logical OR

In everyday meaning, if something is not true, it is false. Here's the same statement expressed using JavaScript and the logical `!` operator.

```
>>> var b = !true;
>>> b;
```

false

If you use the logical NOT twice, you get the original value:

```
>>> var b = !!true;
>>> b;
```

true

If you use a logical operator on a non-boolean value, the value is converted to boolean behind the scenes.

```
>>> var b = "one";
>>> !b;
```

false

In the case above, the string value `"one"` was converted to a boolean `true` and then negated. The result of negating `true` is `false`. In the next example, we negate twice so the result is `true`.

```
>>> var b = "one";
>>> !!b;
```

true

Using double negation is an easy way to convert any value to its boolean equivalent. This is rarely useful, but on the other hand understanding how any value converts to a boolean is important. Most values convert to `true` with the exception of the following (which convert to `false`):

- The empty string `""`
- `null`

- undefined
- The number 0
- The number NaN
- The boolean false

These six values are sometimes referred to as being *falsy*, while all others are *truthy* (including, for example, the strings "0", " ", and "false").

Let's see some examples of the other two operators—the logical AND and the logical OR. When you use AND, the result is true only if *all* of the operands are true. When using OR, the result is true if *at least one* of the operands is true.

```
>>> var b1 = true; var b2 = false;
>>> b1 || b2
```

true

```
>>> b1 && b2
```

false

Here's a table that lists the possible operations and their results:

Operation	Result
true && true	true
true && false	false
false && true	false
false && false	false
true || true	true
true || false	true
false || true	true
false || false	false

You can use several logical operations one after the other:

```
>>> true && true && false && true
```

false

```
>>> false || true || false
```

true

You can also mix && and || in the same expression. In this case, you should use parentheses to clarify how you intend the operation to work. Consider these:

```
>>> false && false || true && true
```

true

```
>>> false && (false || true) && true
```

false

Operator Precedence

You might wonder why the expression above (false && false || true && true) returned true. The answer lies in *operator precedence*. As you know from mathematics:

```
>>> 1 + 2 * 3
```

7

This is because multiplication has precedence over addition, so 2 * 3 is evaluated first, as if you've typed:

```
>>> 1 + (2 * 3)
```

7

Similarly for logical operations, ! has the highest precedence and is executed first, assuming there are no parentheses that demand otherwise. Then, in the order of precedence, comes && and finally ||. In other words:

```
>>> false && false || true && true
```

true

is the same as:

```
>>> (false && false) || (true && true)
```

true

Best Practice
Use parentheses instead of relying on operator precedence. This makes your code easier to read and understand.

Lazy Evaluation

If you have several logical operations one after the other, but the result becomes clear at some point before the end, the final operations will not be performed, because they can't affect the end result. Consider this:

```
>>> true || false || true || false || true
```

true

Since these are all OR operations and have the same precedence, the result will be true if at least one of the operands is true. After the first operand is evaluated, it becomes clear that the result will be true, no matter what values follow. So the JavaScript engine decides to be lazy (ok, efficient) and not do unnecessary work by evaluating code that doesn't affect the end result. You can verify this behavior by experimenting in the console:

```
>>> var b = 5;
>>> true || (b = 6)
```

true

```
>>> b
```

5

```
>>> true && (b = 6)
```

6

```
>>> b
```

6

This example also shows another interesting behavior — if JavaScript encounters a non-boolean expression as an operand in a logical operation, the non-boolean is returned as a result.

```
>>> true || "something"
```

true

```
>>> true && "something"
```

"something"

This behavior is something to watch out for and avoid, because it makes the code harder to understand. Sometimes you might see this behavior being used to define variables when you're not sure whether they were previously defined. In the next example, if the variable v is defined, its value is kept; otherwise, it's initialized with the value 10.

```
var mynumber = mynumber || 10;
```

This is simple and looks elegant, but be aware that it is not completely bulletproof. If mynumber is defined and initialized to 0 (or to any of the six falsy values), this code might not behave in exactly the way it was designed to work.

Comparison

There's another set of operators that all return a boolean value as a result of the operation. These are the *comparison operators*. The following table lists them, together with some examples.

Operator symbol	Description	Example

==	Equality comparison:
	
	 Returns true when both operands are equal. The operands are converted to the same type before being compared.
		>>> 1 == 1
		 true
		 >>> 1 == 2
		 false
		 >>> 1 == '1'
		 true

===	Equality and type comparison:
	
	 Returns true if both operands are equal *and* of the same type. It's generally better and safer if you compare this way, because there's no behind-the-scenes type conversions.
		>>> 1 === '1'
		 false
		 >>> 1 === 1
		 true

!=	Non-equality comparison:
	
	 Returns true if the operands are not equal to each other (after a type conversion)
		>>> 1 != 1
		 false
		 >>> 1 != '1'
		 false
		 >>> 1 != '2'
		 true

!==	Non-equality comparison without type conversion:
	
	 Returns true if the operands are not equal OR they are different types.
		>>> 1 !== 1
		 false
		 >>> 1 !== '1'
		 true

Operator symbol	Description	Example

>	Returns `true` if the left operand is *greater than* the right one.	`>>> 1 > 1`
		false
		`>>> 33 > 22`
		true

>=	Returns `true` if the left operand is *greater than or equal to* the right one.	`>>> 1 >= 1` **true**

<	Returns `true` if the left operand is *less than* the right one.	`>>> 1 < 1`
		false
		`>>> 1 < 2`
		true

<=	Returns `true` if the left operand is *less than or equal to* the right one.	`>>> 1 <= 1`
		true
		`>>> 1 <= 2`
		true

An interesting thing to note is that NaN is not equal to anything, not even itself.

```
>>> NaN == NaN
```

false

Undefined and null

You get the `undefined` value when you try to use a variable that doesn't exist, or one that hasn't yet been assigned a value. When you declare a variable without initializing it, JavaScript automatically initializes it to the value `undefined`.

If you try using a non-existing variable, you'll get an error message.

```
>>> foo
```

foo is not defined

If you use the `typeof` operator on a non-existing variable, you get the string **"undefined"**.

```
>>> typeof foo
```

"undefined"

If you declare a variable without giving it a value, you won't get an error when you use that variable. But the `typeof` still returns **"undefined"**.

```
>>> var somevar;
>>> somevar
>>> typeof somevar
```

"undefined"

The `null` value, on the other hand, is not assigned by JavaScript behind the scenes; it can only be assigned by your code.

```
>>> var somevar = null
```

null

```
>>> somevar
```

null

```
>>> typeof somevar
```

"object"

Although the difference between `null` and `undefined` is small, it may be important at times. For example, if you attempt an arithmetic operation, you can get different results:

```
>>> var i = 1 + undefined; i;
```

NaN

```
>>> var i = 1 + null; i;
```

1

This is because of the different ways `null` and `undefined` are converted to the other primitive types. Below are examples that show the possible conversions.

Conversion to a number:

```
>>> 1*undefined
```

NaN

```
>>> 1*null
```

0

Conversion to a boolean:

```
>>> !!undefined
```

false

```
>>> !!null
```

false

Conversion to a string:

```
>>> "" + null
```

"null"

```
>>> "" + undefined
```

"undefined"

Primitive Data Types Recap

Let's quickly summarize what has been discussed so far:

- There are five primitive data types in JavaScript:
    - number
    - string
    - boolean
    - undefined
    - null

- Everything that is not a primitive is an object
- The number data type can store positive and negative integers or floats, hexadecimal numbers, octal numbers, exponents, and the special numbers NaN, Infinity, and -Infinity
- The string data type contains characters in quotes
- The only values of the boolean data type are true and false
- The only value of the null data type is the value null
- The only value of the undefined data type is the value undefined

- All values become `true` when converted to a boolean, with the exception of the six falsy values:

  ○ `""`

  ○ `null`

  ○ `undefined`

  ○ `0`

  ○ `NaN`

  ○ `false`

Arrays

Now that you know the basic primitive data types in JavaScript, it's time to move to a more interesting data structure—the array.

To declare a variable that contains an empty array, you use square brackets with nothing between them:

```
>>> var a = [];
>>> typeof a;
```

"object"

`typeof` returns **"object"**, but don't worry about this for the time being, we'll get to that when we take a closer look at objects.

To define an array that has three elements, you do this:

```
>>> var a = [1,2,3];
```

When you simply type the name of the array in the Firebug console, it prints the contents of the array:

```
>>> a
```

[1, 2, 3]

So what is an array exactly? It's simply a list of values. Instead of using one variable to store one value, you can use one array variable to store any number of values as *elements* of the array. Now the question is how to access each of these stored values?

The elements contained in an array are indexed with consecutive numbers starting from zero. The first element has index (or position) 0, the second has index 1 and so on. Here's the three-element array from the previous example:

Index	Value
0	1
1	2
2	3

In order to access an array element, you specify the index of that element inside square brackets. So a[0] gives you the first element of the array a, a[1] gives you the second, and so on.

```
>>> a[0]
```

1

```
>>> a[1]
```

2

Adding/Updating Array Elements

Using the index, you can also update elements of the array. The next example updates the third element (index 2) and prints the contents of the new array.

```
>>> a[2] = 'three';
```

"three"

```
>>> a
```

[1, 2, "three"]

You can add more elements, by addressing an index that didn't exist before.

```
>>> a[3] = 'four';
```

"four"

```
>>> a
```

[1, 2, "three", "four"]

If you add a new element, but leave a gap in the array, those elements in between are all assigned the undefined value. Check out this example:

```
>>> var a = [1,2,3];
>>> a[6] = 'new';
```

"new"

```
>>> a
```

[1, 2, 3, undefined, undefined, undefined, "new"]

Deleting Elements

In order to delete an element, you can use the delete operator. It doesn't actually remove the element, but sets its value to undefined. After the deletion, the length of the array does not change.

```
>>> var a = [1, 2, 3];
>>> delete a[1];
```

true

```
>>> a
```

[1, undefined, 3]

Arrays of arrays

An array can contain any type of values, including other arrays.

```
>>> var a = [1, "two", false, null, undefined];
>>> a
```

[1, "two", false, null, undefined]

```
>>> a[5] = [1,2,3]
```

[1, 2, 3]

```
>>> a
```

[1, "two", false, null, undefined, [1, 2, 3]]

Let's see an example where you have an array of two elements, each of them being an array.

```
>>> var a = [[1,2,3],[4,5,6]];
>>> a
```

[[1, 2, 3], [4, 5, 6]]

The first element of the array is `a[0]` and it is an array itself.

```
>>> a[0]
```

[1, 2, 3]

To access an element in the nested array, you refer to the element index in another set of square brackets.

```
>>> a[0][0]
```

1

```
>>> a[1][2]
```

6

Note also that you can use the array notation to access individual characters inside a string.

```
>>> var s = 'one';
>>> s[0]
```

"o"

```
>>> s[1]
```

"n"

```
>>> s[2]
```

"e"

There are more ways to have fun with arrays (and we'll get to that in Chapter 4), but let's stop here for now, remembering that:

- An array is a data store
- An array contains indexed elements
- Indexes start from zero and increment by one for each element in the array
- To access array elements we use the index in square brackets
- An array can contain any type of data, including other arrays

Conditions and Loops

Conditions provide a simple but powerful way to control the flow of execution through a piece of code. *Loops* allow you to perform repeating operations with less code. Let's take a look at:

- `if` conditions,
- `switch` statements,
- `while`, `do-while`, `for`, and `for-in` loops.

Code Blocks

Let's start by clarifying what a block of code is, as blocks are used extensively when constructing conditions and loops.

A block of code consists of zero or more expressions enclosed in curly brackets.

```
{
  var a = 1;
  var b = 3;
}
```

You can nest blocks within each other indefinitely:

```
{
  var a = 1;
  var b = 3;
  var c, d;
  {
    c = a + b;
    {
      d = a - b;
    }
  }
}
```

Best Practice Tips

- Use end-of-line semicolons. Although the semicolon is optional when you have one expression per line, it's good to develop the habit of using them. For best readability, the individual expressions inside a block should be placed one per line and separated by semi-colons.

- Indent any code placed within curly brackets. Some people use one tab indentation, some use four spaces, and some use two spaces. It really doesn't matter, as long as you're consistent. In the example above the outer block is indented with two spaces, the code in the first nested block is indented with four spaces and the innermost block is indented with six spaces.

- Use curly brackets. When a block consists of only one expression, the curly brackets are optional, but for readability and maintainability, you should get into the habit of always using them, even when they're optional.

Ready to jump into loops and ifs? Note that the examples in the following sections require you to switch to the multi-line Firebug console.

if Conditions

Here's a simple example of an `if` condition:

```
var result = '';
if (a > 2) {
  result = 'a is greater than 2';
}
```

The parts of the `if` condition are:

- The `if` statement
- A condition in parentheses — "is a greater than 2?"
- Code block to be executed if the condition is satisfied

The condition (the part in parentheses) always returns a boolean value and may contain:

- A logical operation: `!`, `&&` or `||`
- A comparison, such as `===`, `!=`, `>`, and so on
- Any value or variable that can be converted to a boolean
- A combination of the above

There can also be an optional `else` part of the `if` condition. The else statement is followed by a block of code to be executed if the condition was evaluated to `false`.

```
if (a > 2) {
  result = 'a is greater than 2';
} else {
  result = 'a is NOT greater than 2';
}
```

In between the `if` and the `else`, there can also be an unlimited number of `else if` conditions. Here's an example:

```
if (a > 2 || a < -2) {
  result = 'a is not between -2 and 2';
} else if (a === 0 && b === 0) {
  result = 'both a and b are zeros';
} else if (a === b) {
  result = 'a and b are equal';
} else {
  result = 'I give up';
}
```

You can also nest conditions by putting new conditions within any of the blocks.

```
if (a === 1) {
  if (b === 2) {
    result = 'a is 1 and b is 2';
  } else {
    result = 'a is 1 but b is not 2';
  }
} else {
  result = 'a is not 1, no idea about b';
}
```

Checking if a Variable Exists

It's often useful to check whether a variable exists. The laziest way to do this is simply putting the variable in the condition part of the `if`, for example `if (somevar) {...}`, but this is not necessarily the best method. Let's take a look at an example that tests whether a variable called `somevar` exists, and if so, sets the `result` variable to `yes`:

```
>>> var result = '';
>>> if (somevar){result = 'yes';}
```

somevar is not defined

```
>>> result;
""
```

This code obviously works, because at the end `result` was not "yes". But firstly, the code generated a warning: **somevar is not defined** and as a JavaScript whiz you don't want your code to do anything like that. Secondly, just because `if (somevar)` returned `false` doesn't mean that `somevar` is not defined. It could be that `somevar` is defined and initialized but contains a falsy value, like `false` or 0.

A better way to check if a variable is defined is to use `typeof`.

```
>>> if (typeof somevar !== "undefined"){result = 'yes';}
>>> result;
```

""

`typeof` will always return a string and you can compare this string with `"undefined"`. Note that the variable `somevar` may have been declared but not assigned a value yet and you'll still get the same result. So when testing with `typeof` like this, you're really testing whether the variable has any value (other than the value `undefined`).

```
>>> var somevar;
>>> if (typeof somevar !== "undefined"){result = 'yes';}
>>> result;
```

""

```
>>> somevar = undefined;
>>> if (typeof somevar !== "undefined"){result = 'yes';}
>>> result;
```

""

If a variable is defined and initialized with any value other than `undefined`, its type returned by `typeof` is no longer "undefined".

```
>>> somevar = 123;
>>> if (typeof somevar !== "undefined"){result = 'yes';}
>>> result;
```

"yes"

Alternative if Syntax

When you have a very simple condition you can consider using an alternative `if` syntax. Take a look at this:

```
var a = 1;
var result = '';
if (a === 1) {
  result = "a is one";
} else {
  result = "a is not one";
}
```

The `if` condition can be expressed simply as:

```
var result = (a === 1) ? "a is one" : "a is not one";
```

You should only use this syntax for very simple conditions. Be careful not to abuse it, as it can easily make your code unreadable.

The `?` is called *ternary operator*.

Switch

If you find yourself using an `if` condition and having too many `else` `if` parts, you could consider changing the `if` to a `switch`.

```
var a = '1';
var result = '';
switch (a) {
  case 1:
    result = 'Number 1';
    break;
  case '1':
    result = 'String 1';
    break;
  default:
    result = 'I don\'t know';
    break;
}
result;
```

The result of executing this will be **"String 1"**. Let's see what the parts of a `switch` are:

- The `switch` statement.
- Some expression in parentheses. The expression most often contains a variable, but can be anything that returns a value.

- A number of *case blocks* enclosed in curly brackets.

- Each `case` statement is followed by an expression. The result of the expression is compared to the expression placed after the `switch` statement. If the result of the comparison is `true`, the code that follows the colon after the `case` is executed.

- There is an optional `break` statement to signal the end of the case block. If this `break` statement is reached, we're all done with the switch. Otherwise, if the `break` is missing, we enter the next `case` block, which should be avoided.

- There's an optional `default` statement, which is followed by a block of code that is executed if none of the previous cases evaluated to `true`.

In other words, the step-by-step procedure for executing a `switch` statement is as follows:

1. Evaluate the switch expression found in parentheses, remember it.

2. Move to the first case, compare its value with the one from step 1.

3. If the comparison in step 2 returns `true`, execute the code in the `case` block.

4. After the `case` block is executed, if there's a `break` statement at the end of it, exit the switch.

5. If there's no `break` or step 2 returned `false`, move on to the next `case` block.
    Repeat steps 2 to 5.

6. If we're still here (we didn't exit in step 4), execute the code following the `default` statement.

Best Practice Tips

- Indent the `case` line, and then further indent the code that follows it.

- Don't forget to `break`.
  Sometimes you may want to omit the break intentionally, but that's rare. It's called a *fall-through* and should always be documented because it may look like an accidental omission. On the other hand, sometimes you may want to omit the whole code block following a case and have two cases sharing the same code. This is fine, but doesn't change the rule that if there's code that follows a `case` statement, this code should end with a `break`. In terms of indentation, aligning the `break` with the `case` or with the code inside the case is a personal preference; again, being consistent is what matters.

- Use the `default` case. This will help you make sure you have a meaningful result after the switch, even if none of the cases matched the value being switched.

Loops

`if-else` and `switch` statements allow your code to take different paths, as if you're at a crossroads and decide which way to go depending on a condition. Loops, on the other hand, allow your code to take a few roundabouts before merging back into the main road. How many repetitions? That depends on the result of evaluating a condition before (or after) each iteration.

Let's say you are (your program execution is) traveling from A to B. At some point, you reach a place where you evaluate a condition C. The result of evaluating C tells you if you should go into a loop L. You make one iteration. Then you evaluate the condition once again to see if another iteration is needed. Eventually, you move on your way to B.

An *infinite loop* is when the condition is always true and your code gets stuck in the loop "forever". This is, of course, is a logical error and you should look out for such scenarios.

In JavaScript, there are four types of loops:

- `while` loops
- `do-while` loops
- `for` loops
- `for-in` loops

While Loops

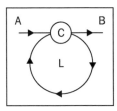

`while` loops are the simplest type of loop. They look like this:

```
var i = 0;
while (i < 10) {
  i++;
}
```

The `while` statement is followed by a condition in parentheses and a code block in curly brackets. As long as the condition evaluates to `true`, the code block is executed over and over again.

Do-while loops

do-while loops are a slight variation of the while loops. An example:

```
var i = 0;
do {
  i++;
} while (i < 10)
```

Here, the do statement is followed by a code block and a condition after the block. This means that the code block will always be executed, at least once, before the condition is evaluated.

If you initialize i to 11 instead of 0 in the last two examples, the code block in the first example (the while loop) will not be executed and i will still be 11 at the end, while in the second (do-while loop), the code block will be executed once and i will become 12.

For Loops

for is the most widely used type of loop and you should make sure you're comfortable with this one. It requires a just little bit more in terms of syntax.

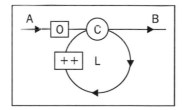

In addition to the condition C and the code block L, you have the following:

- Initialization — some code that is executed *before* you even enter the loop (marked with 0 in the diagram)

- Increment — some code that is executed *after every iteration* (marked with ++ in the diagram)

The most widely used pattern of using a for loop is:

- In the initialization part you define a variable, most often called i, like this: var i = 0;

- In the condition part you compare i to a boundary value, like i < 100

- In the increment part, you increase i by 1, like i++

Here's an example:

```
var punishment = '';
for (var i = 0; i < 100; i++) {
  punishment += 'I will never do this again, ';
}
```

All three parts (initialization, condition, increment) can contain multiple expressions separated by commas. You can rewrite the example and define the variable punishment inside the initialization part of the loop.

```
for (var i = 0, punishment = ''; i < 100; i++) {
  punishment += 'I will never do this again, ';
}
```

Can you move the body of the loop inside the increment part? Yes, you can, especially as it's a one-liner. This will give you a loop that looks a little awkward, as it has no body:

```
for (var i = 0, punishment = '';
     i < 100;
     i++, punishment += 'I will never do this again, ')
{
  // nothing here
}
```

These three parts are actually all optional. Here's another way of rewriting the same example:

```
var i = 0, punishment = '';
for (;;) {
  punishment += 'I will never do this again, ';
  if (++i == 100) {
    break;
  }
}
```

Although the last rewrite works exactly the same way as the original, it is longer and harder to read. It's also possible to achieve the same result by using a while loop. But for loops make the code tighter and more robust, because the mere syntax of the for loop makes you think about the three parts (initialization, condition, increment) and thus, helps you reconfirm your logic and avoid situations such as being stuck in an infinite loop.

`for` loops can be nested within each other. Here's an example of a loop that is nested inside another loop and assembles a string containing 10 rows and 10 columns of asterisks. Think of `i` being the row and `j` being the column of an "image".

```
var res = '\n';
for(var i = 0; i < 10; i++) {
  for(var j = 0; j < 10; j++) {
    res += '* ';
  }
  res+= '\n';
}
```

The result is a string like:

```
"

* * * * * * * * * *
* * * * * * * * * *
* * * * * * * * * *
* * * * * * * * * *
* * * * * * * * * *
* * * * * * * * * *
* * * * * * * * * *
* * * * * * * * * *
* * * * * * * * * *
* * * * * * * * * *

"
```

Here's another example that uses nested loops and a modulus operation in order to draw a little snowflake-like result.

```
var res = '\n', i, j;
for(i = 1; i <= 7; i++) {
  for(j = 1; j <= 15; j++) {
    res += (i * j) % 8 ? ' ' : '*';
  }
  res+= '\n';
}
```

```
"
             *
    *    *       *
             *
*  *  *  *  *  *  *
             *
    *    *       *
             *
"
```

For-in Loops

The for-in loop is used to iterate over the elements of an array (or an object, as we'll see later). This is its only use; it cannot be used as a general-purpose repetition mechanism that replaces for or while. Let's see an example of using a for-in to loop through the elements of an array. But bear in mind that this is for informational purposes only, as for-in is mostly suitable for objects, and the regular for loop should be used for arrays.

In this example, we'll iterate over all of the elements of an array and print out the index (the key) and the value of each element:

```
var a = ['a', 'b', 'c', 'x', 'y', 'z'];
var result = '\n';
for (var i in a) {
  result += 'index: ' + i + ', value: ' + a[i] + '\n';
}
```

The result is:

```
"
```

index: 0, value: a

index: 1, value: b

index: 2, value: c

index: 3, value: x

index: 4, value: y

index: 5, value: z

"

Comments

One last thing for this chapter: comments. Inside your JavaScript code you can put comments. These are ignored by the JavaScript engine and don't have any effect on how the program works. But they can be invaluable when you revisit your code after a few months, or transfer the code to someone else for maintenance.

Two types of comments are allowed:

- Single line comments — start with // and end at the end of the line
- Multi-line comments — start with /* and end with */ on the same line or any subsequent line. Note that any code in between the comment start and the comment end will be ignored.

Some examples:

```
// beginning of line
var a = 1; // anywhere on the line
/* multi-line comment on a single line */
/*
    comment
    that spans
    several lines
 */
```

There are even utilities, such as JSDoc, that can parse your code and extract meaningful documentation based on your comments.

Summary

In this chapter, you learned a lot about the basic building blocks of a JavaScript program. Now you know the primitive data types:

- number
- string
- boolean
- undefined
- null

You also know quite a few operators:

- Arithmetic operators: +, -, *, /, and %.
- Increment operators: ++ and --.
- Assignment operators: =, +=, -=, *=, /=, and %=.
- Special operators: `typeof` and `delete`.
- Logical operators: &&, ||, and !.
- Comparison operators: ==, ===, !=, !==, <, >, >=, and <=.

Then you learned how to use arrays to store and access data, and finally you saw different ways to control the flow of your program—using conditions (`if-else` or `switch`) and loops (`while`, `do-while`, `for`, `for-in`).

This is quite a bit of information and it is recommended that you now go through the exercises below, then give yourself a well-deserved pat on the back before diving into the next chapter. More fun is coming up!

Exercises

1. What is the result of executing each of these lines in the console? Why?

   - ```
     var a; typeof a;
     ```
   - ```
     var s = '1s'; s++;
     ```
   - ```
     !!"false"
     ```
   - ```
     !!undefined
     ```
   - ```
     typeof -Infinity
     ```
   - ```
     10 % "0"
     ```
   - ```
     undefined == null
     ```
   - ```
     false === ""
     ```
   - ```
     typeof "2E+2"
     ```
   - ```
     a = 3e+3; a++;
     ```

2. What is the value of v after the following?
   ```
   >>> var v = v || 10;
   ```

   Experiment by first setting v to 100, 0, `null`, or unset it (`delete v`).

3. Write a script that prints out the multiplication table. **Hint**: use a loop nested inside another loop.

3
Functions

Mastering functions is an important skill when you learn any programming language and even more so when it comes to JavaScript. This is because JavaScript has many uses for functions, and much of the language's flexibility and expressiveness comes from them. Where most programming languages have a special syntax for some object-oriented features, JavaScript just uses functions. This chapter will cover:

- How to define and use a function
- Passing parameters to a function
- Pre-defined functions that are available to you "for free"
- The scope of variables in JavaScript
- The concept that functions are just data, albeit a special type of data

Understanding these topics will provide a solid base that will allow you to dive into the second part of the chapter, which shows some interesting applications of functions:

- Using anonymous functions
- Callbacks
- Self-invoking functions
- Inner functions (functions defined inside functions)
- Functions that return functions
- Functions that redefine themselves
- Closures

What is a Function?

Functions allow you group together some code, give this code a name, and reuse it later, addressing it by name. Let's see an example:

```
function sum(a, b) {
    var c = a + b;
    return c;
}
```

What are the parts that make up a function?

- The `function` statement.
- The *name* of the function, in this case `sum`.
- Expected parameters (arguments), in this case `a` and `b`. A function can accept zero or more arguments, separated by commas.
- A code block, also called the *body* of the function.
- The `return` statement. A function always returns a value. If it doesn't return value explicitly, it implicitly returns the value `undefined`.

Note that a function can only return a single value. If you need to return more values, then simply return an array that contains all of the values as elements of this array.

Calling a Function

In order to make use of a function, you need to *call* it. You call a function simply by using its name followed by any parameters in parentheses. "To *invoke*" a function is another way of saying "to call".

Let's call the function `sum()`, passing two parameters and assigning the value that the function returns to the variable `result`:

```
>>> var result = sum(1, 2);
>>> result;
```

3

Parameters

When defining a function, you can specify what parameters the function expects to receive when it is called. A function may not require any parameters, but if it does and you forget to pass them, JavaScript will assign the value `undefined` to the ones you skipped. In the next example, the function call returns `NaN` because it tries to sum 1 and `undefined`:

```
>>> sum(1)
```

NaN

JavaScript is not picky at all when it comes to parameters. If you pass more parameters than the function expects, the extra parameters will be silently ignored:

```
>>> sum(1, 2, 3, 4, 5)
```

3

What's more, you can create functions that are flexible about the number of parameters they accept. This is possible thanks to the arguments array that is created automatically inside each function. Here's a function that simply returns whatever parameters are passed to it:

```
>>> function args() { return arguments; }
>>> args();
```

[]

```
>>> args( 1, 2, 3, 4, true, 'ninja');
```

[1, 2, 3, 4, true, "ninja"]

By using the arguments array you can improve the sum() function to accept any number of parameters and add them all up.

```
function sumOnSteroids() {
  var i, res = 0;
  var number_of_params = arguments.length;
  for (i = 0; i < number_of_params; i++) {
    res += arguments[i];
  }
  return res;
}
```

If you test this function by calling it with a different number of parameters (or even no parameters at all), you can verify that it works as expected:

```
>>> sumOnSteroids(1, 1, 1);
```

3

```
>>> sumOnSteroids(1, 2, 3, 4);
```

10

```
>>> sumOnSteroids(1, 2, 3, 4, 4, 3, 2, 1);
```

20

```
>>> sumOnSteroids(5);
```

5

```
>>> sumOnSteroids();
```

0

The expression `arguments.length` returns the number of parameters passed when the function was called. Don't worry if the syntax is unfamiliar, we'll examine it in detail in the next chapter. We'll also see that `arguments` is technically not an array, but an array-like object.

Pre-defined Functions

There are a number of functions that are built into the JavaScript engine and available for you to use. Let's take a look at them. While doing so, you'll have a chance to experiment with functions, their parameters and return values , and become comfortable in working with them. The list of the built-in functions is:

- `parseInt()`
- `parseFloat()`
- `isNaN()`
- `isFinite()`
- `encodeURI()`
- `decodeURI()`
- `encodeURIComponent()`
- `decodeURIComponent()`
- `eval()`

The Black Box Function

Often, when you invoke functions, your program doesn't need to know how these functions work internally. You can think of a function as a black box: you give it some values (as input parameters) and then you take the output result it returns. This is true for any function—one that's built into the JavaScript engine, one that you create, or one that a co-worker or someone else created.

parseInt()

`parseInt()` takes any type of input (most often a string) and tries to make an integer out of it. If it fails, it returns NaN.

```
>>> parseInt('123')
```

123

```
>>> parseInt('abc123')
```

NaN

```
>>> parseInt('1abc23')
```

1

```
>>> parseInt('123abc')
```

123

The function accepts an optional second parameter, which is the *radix*, telling the function what type of number to expect—decimal, hexadecimal, binary, and so on. For example trying to extract a decimal number out of the string FF makes no sense, so the result is **NaN**, but if you try FF as a hexadecimal, then you get 255.

```
>>> parseInt('FF', 10)
```

NaN

```
>>> parseInt('FF', 16)
```

255

Another example would be parsing a string with a base 10 (decimal) and base 8 (octal).

```
>>> parseInt('0377', 10)
```

377

```
>>> parseInt('0377', 8)
```

255

If you omit the second parameter when calling `parseInt()`, the function will assume 10 (a decimal), with these exceptions:

- If you pass a string beginning with 0x as a first parameter, then the second is assumed to be 16 (a hexadecimal number is assumed)

- If the first parameter starts with 0, the function assumes 8 as a second parameter (an octal number is assumed)

```
>>> parseInt('377')
```

377

```
>>> parseInt('0377')
```

255

```
>>> parseInt('0x377')
```

887

The safest thing to do is to always specify the radix. If you omit the radix, your code will probably still work in 99% of cases (because most often you parse decimals), but every once in a while it might cause you a bit of hair loss while debugging some problems. For example, imagine you have a form field that accepts calendar days and the user types **08**; if you omit the radix you might get unexpected results.

parseFloat()

`parseFloat()` is the same as `parseInt()` but it also looks for decimals when trying to figure out a number from your input. This function takes only one parameter.

```
>>> parseFloat('123')
```

123

```
>>> parseFloat('1.23')
```

1.23

```
>>> parseFloat('1.23abc.00')
```

1.23

```
>>> parseFloat('a.bc1.23')
```

NaN

As with `parseInt()`, `parseFloat()` gives up at the first occurrence of an unexpected character, even though the rest of the string might have usable numbers in it.

```
>>> parseFloat('a123.34')
```

NaN

```
>>> parseFloat('12a3.34')
```

12

parseFloat() understands exponents in the input (unlike parseInt()).

```
>>> parseFloat('123e-2')
```

1.23

```
>>> parseFloat('123e2')
```

12300

```
>>> parseInt('1e10')
```

1

isNaN()

Using isNaN() you can check if an input value is a valid number that can safely be used in arithmetic operations. This function is also a convenient way to check whether parseInt() or parseFloat() succeeded.

```
>>> isNaN(NaN)
```

true

```
>>> isNaN(123)
```

false

```
>>> isNaN(1.23)
```

false

```
>>> isNaN(parseInt('abc123'))
```

true

The function will also try to convert the input to a number:

```
>>> isNaN('1.23')
```

false

```
>>> isNaN('a1.23')
```

true

The isNaN() function is useful because NaN is not equal to itself. So, surprisingly, NaN === NaN is **false**.

isFinite()

isFinite() checks whether the input is a number that is neither Infinity nor NaN.

```
>>> isFinite(Infinity)
```

false

```
>>> isFinite(-Infinity)
```

false

```
>>> isFinite(12)
```

true

```
>>> isFinite(1e308)
```

true

```
>>> isFinite(1e309)
```

false

If you wonder about the results returned by last two calls, remember from the previous chapter that the biggest number in JavaScript is 1.7976931348623157e+308.

Encode/Decode URIs

In a URL (Uniform Resource Locator) or a URI (Uniform Resource Identifier), some characters have special meanings. If you want to "escape" those characters, you can use the functions encodeURI() or encodeURIComponent(). The first one will return a usable URL, while the second one assumes you're only passing a part of the URL, like a query string for example, and will encode all applicable characters.

```
>>> var url = 'http://www.packtpub.com/scr ipt.php?q=this and that';
>>> encodeURI(url);
```

"http://www.packtpub.com/scr%20ipt.php?q=this%20and%20that"

```
>>> encodeURIComponent(url);
```

"http%3A%2F%2Fwww.packtpub.com%2Fscr%20ipt.php%3Fq%3Dthis%20and%20that"

The opposites of encodeURI() and encodeURIComponent() are decodeURI() and decodeURIComponent() respectively. Sometimes, in older code, you might see the similar functions escape() and unescape() but these functions have been deprecated and should not be used.

eval()

`eval()` takes a string input and executes it as JavaScript code:

```
>>> eval('var ii = 2;')
>>> ii
```

2

So `eval('var ii = 2;')` is the same as simply `var ii = 2;`

`eval()` can be useful sometimes, but should be avoided if there are other options. Most of the time there will be alternatives and, in most cases, the alternatives are more elegant and easier to write and maintain. "Eval is evil" is a mantra you can often hear from seasoned JavaScript programmers. The drawbacks of using `eval()` are:

- Performance—it is slower to evaluate "live" code, than to have the code directly in the script.
- Security—JavaScript is powerful, which also means it can cause damage. If you don't trust the source of the input you pass to `eval()`, just don't use it.

A Bonus—the alert() Function

Let's take a look at one very common function—`alert()`. This is not part of the core JavaScript (it is not in the ECMA specification), but it is provided by the host environment—the browser. It shows a string of text in a message box. It can also be useful for debugging sometimes, although the Firebug debugger is a much better tool for this purpose.

Here's a screenshot showing the result of executing the code `alert("hello!")`

Before using this function, bear in mind that it blocks the browser thread, meaning that no other code will be executed until the user closes the alert. If you have a busy AJAX-type application, it is generally not a good idea to use `alert()`.

Scope of Variables

It is important to note, especially if you have come to JavaScript from another language, that variables in JavaScript are not defined in a block scope, but in a *function scope*. This means that if a variable is defined inside a function, it's not visible outside of the function. However, a variable defined inside an `if` or a `for` code block is visible outside the code block. The term "global variables" describes variables you define outside of any function, as opposed to "local variables" which are defined inside a function. The code inside a function has access to all global variables as well as to its own local variables.

In the next example:

- The function `f()` has access to the variable `global`
- Outside of the function `f()`, the variable `local` doesn't exist

```
var global = 1;
function f() {
  var local = 2;
  global++;
  return global;
}
>>> f();

2

>>> f();

3

>>> local
```

local is not defined

It is also important to note that if you don't use `var` to declare a variable, this variable is automatically assigned global scope. Let's see an example:

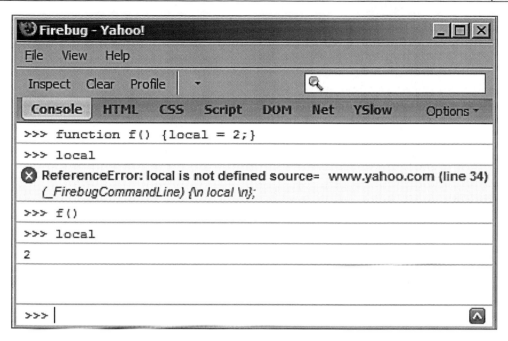

What happened? The function `f()` contains the variable `local`. Before calling the function, the variable doesn't exist. When you call the function for the first time, the variable `local` is created with a global scope. FThen if you access `local` outside the function, it's available.

Best Practice Tips

- Minimize the number of global variables. Imagine two people working on two different functions in the same script and they both decide to use the same name for their global variable. This could easily lead to unexpected results and hard-to-find bugs.
- Always declare your variables with the `var` statement.

Here's an interesting example that shows an important aspect of the local versus global scoping.

```
var a = 123;
function f() {
  alert(a);
  var a = 1;
  alert(a);
}
f();
```

You might expect that the first `alert()` will display 123 (the value of the global variable a) and the second will display 1 (the local a). This is not the case. The first alert will show **"undefined"**. This is because inside the function the local scope is more important than the global scope. So a local variable overwrites any global variable with the same name. At the time of the first `alert()` a was not yet defined (hence the value **undefined**) but it still existed in the local space.

Functions are Data

This is an important concept that we'll need later on — functions in JavaScript are actually data. This means that the following two ways to define a function are exactly the same:

```
function f(){return 1;}
var f = function(){return 1;}
```

The second way of defining a function is known as *function literal notation*.

When you use the `typeof` operator on a variable that holds a function value, it returns the string "function".

```
>>> function f(){return 1;}
>>> typeof f
```

"function"

So JavaScript functions are data, but a special kind of data with two important features:

- They contain code
- They are executable (can be invoked)

As you saw before, the way to execute a function is by adding parentheses after its name. As the next example demonstrates, this works regardless of how the function was defined. In the example, you can also see how a function is treated as a normal variable — it can be copied to a different variable and even deleted.

```
>>> var sum = function(a, b) {return a + b;}
>>> var add = sum;
>>> delete sum
```

true

```
>>> typeof sum;
```

"undefined"

```
>>> typeof add;
```

"function"

```
>>> add(1, 2);
```

3

Because functions are data assigned to variables, the same rules for naming functions apply as for naming variables—a function name cannot start with a number and it can contain any combination of letters, numbers, and the underscore character.

Anonymous Functions

In JavaScript, it's ok to have pieces of data lying around your program. Imagine you have the following in your code.

```
>>> "test"; [1,2,3]; undefined; null; 1;
```

This code may look a little odd, because it doesn't actually do anything, but the code is valid and is not going to cause an error. You can say that this code contains *anonymous* data—anonymous because the data pieces are not assigned to any variable and therefore don't have a name.

As you now know, functions are like any other variable so they can also be used without being assigned a name:

```
>>> function(a){return a;}
```

Now, these anonymous pieces of data scattered around your code are not really useful, except if they happen to be functions. In this case, there can be two elegant uses for them:

- You can pass an anonymous function as a parameter to another function. The receiving function can do something useful with the function that you pass.
- You can define an anonymous function and execute it right away.

Let's see these two applications of the anonymous functions in more detail.

Callback Functions

Because a function is just like any other data assigned to a variable, it can be defined, deleted, copied, and why not also *passed as an argument* to other functions?

Here's an example of a function that accepts two functions as parameters, executes them, and returns the sum of what each of them returns.

```
function invoke_and_add(a, b){
   return a() + b();
}
```

Now let's define two simple additional functions that only return hardcoded values:

```
function one() {
   return 1;
}
function two() {
   return 2;
}
```

Now we can pass those functions to the original function add() and get the result:

```
>>> invoke_and_add(one, two);
```

3

Another example of passing a function as a parameter is to use anonymous functions. Instead of defining one() and two(), you can simply do:

```
invoke_and_add(function(){return 1;}, function(){return 2;})
```

When you pass a function A to another function B and B executes A, it's often said that A is a *callback function*. If A doesn't have a name, then you can say that it's an *anonymous callback* function.

When are the callback functions useful? Let's see some examples that demonstrate the benefits of the callback functions, namely:

- They let you pass functions without the need to name them (which means there are less global variables)
- You can delegate the responsibility of calling a function to another function (which means there is less code to write)
- They can help with performance

Callback Examples

Take a look at this common scenario: you have a function that returns a value, which you then pass to another function. In our example, the first function, multiplyByTwo(), accepts three parameters, loops through them, multiplying them by two and returns an array containing the result. The second function, addOne(), takes a value, adds one to it and returns it.

```
function multiplyByTwo(a, b, c) {
  var i, ar = [];
  for(i = 0; i < 3; i++) {
    ar[i] = arguments[i] * 2;
  }
  return ar;
}
function addOne(a) {
  return a + 1;
}
```

Testing the functions we have so far:

```
>>> multiplyByTwo(1, 2, 3);
```

[2, 4, 6]

```
>>> addOne(100)
```

101

Now let's say we want to have an array `myarr` that contains three elements, and each of the elements is to be passed through both functions. First, let's start with a call to `multiplyByTwo()`.

```
>>> var myarr = [];
>>> myarr = multiplyByTwo(10, 20, 30);
```

[20, 40, 60]

Now loop through each element, passing it to `addOne()`.

```
>>> for (var i = 0; i < 3; i++) {myarr[i] = addOne(myarr[i]);}
>>> myarr
```

[21, 41, 61]

As you see everything works fine, but there's still room for improvement. One thing is that there were two loops. Loops can be expensive if they go through a lot or repetitions. We can achieve the result we want with one loop only. Here's how to modify `multiplyByTwo()` so that it accepts a `callback` function and invokes callback on every iteration:

```
function multiplyByTwo(a, b, c, callback) {
  var i, ar = [];
  for(i = 0; i < 3; i++) {
    ar[i] = callback(arguments[i] * 2);
  }
  return ar;
}
```

By using the modified function, the whole work is now done with just one function call, which passes the start values and the `callback`.

```
>>> myarr = multiplyByTwo(1, 2, 3, addOne);
```

[3, 5, 7]

Instead of defining `addOne()` we can use an anonymous function, this way saving an extra global variable.

```
>>> myarr = multiplyByTwo(1, 2, 3, function(a){return a + 1});
```

[3, 5, 7]

Anonymous functions are easy to change should the need arise:

```
>>> myarr = multiplyByTwo(1, 2, 3, function(a){return a + 2});
```

[4, 6, 8]

Self-invoking Functions

So far we have discussed using anonymous functions as callbacks. Let's see another application of an anonymous function—calling this function right after it was defined. Here's an example:

```
(
  function(){
    alert('boo');
  }
)()
```

The syntax may look a little scary at first, but it's actually easy—you simply place an anonymous function definition inside parentheses followed by another set of parentheses. The second set basically says "execute now" and is also the place to put any parameters that your anonymous function might accept.

```
(
  function(name){
    alert('Hello ' + name + '!');
  }
)('dude')
```

One good reason for using self-invoking anonymous functions is to have some work done without creating global variables. A drawback, of course, is that you cannot execute the same function twice (unless you put it inside a loop or another function). This makes the anonymous self-invoking functions best suited for one-off or initialization tasks.

Inner (Private) Functions

Bearing in mind that a function is just like any other value, there's nothing that stops you from defining a function inside another function.

```
function a(param) {
  function b(theinput) {
    return theinput * 2;
  };
  return 'The result is ' + b(param);
};
```

Using the function literal notation, this can also be written as:

```
var a = function(param) {
  var b = function(theinput) {
    return theinput * 2;
  };
  return 'The result is ' + b(param);
};
```

When you call the global function a(), it will internally call the local function b(). Since b() is local, it's not accessible outside a(), so we can say it's a *private* function.

```
>>> a(2);
```

"The result is 4"

```
>>> a(8);
```

"The result is 16"

```
>>> b(2);
```

b is not defined

The benefit of using private functions are as follows:

- You keep the global namespace clean (smaller chance of naming collisions).
- Privacy — you expose only the functions you decide to the "outside world", keeping to yourself functionality that is not meant to be consumed by the rest of the application.

Functions that Return Functions

As mentioned earlier, a function always returns a value, and if it doesn't do it explicitly with `return`, then it it does so implicitly by returning `undefined`. A function can return only one value and this value could just as easily be another function.

```
function a() {
  alert('A!');
  return function(){
    alert('B!');
  };
}
```

In this example the function `a()` does its job (says A!) and returns another function that does something else (says B!). You can assign the return value to a variable and then use this variable as a normal function:

```
>>> var newFunc = a();
>>> newFunc();
```

Here the first line will alert **A!** and the second will alert **B!**.

If you want to execute the returned function immediately, without assigning it to a new variable, you can simply use another set of parentheses. The end result will be the same.

```
>>> a()();
```

Function, Rewrite Thyself!

Because a function can return a function, you can use the new function to replace the old one. Continuing with the previous example, you can take the value returned by the call to `a()` to overwrite the actual `a()` function:

```
>>> a = a();
```

The above alerts **A!**, but the next time you call `a()` it alerts **B!**.

This is useful when a function has some initial one-off work to do. The function overwrites itself after the first call in order to avoid doing unnecessary repetitive work every time it's called.

In the example above, we redefined the function from the outside—we got the returned value and assigned it back to the function. But the function can actually rewrite itself from the inside.

```
function a() {
  alert('A!');
  a = function(){
    alert('B!');
  };
}
```

If you call this function for the first time, it will:

- Alert **A!** (consider this as being the one-off preparatory work)
- Redefine the global variable a, assigning a new function to it

Every subsequent time that the function is called, it will alert **B!**

Here's another example that combines several of the techniques discussed in the last few sections of this chapter:

```
var a = function() {
  function someSetup(){
    var setup = 'done';
  }
  function actualWork() {
    alert('Worky-worky');
  }
  someSetup();
  return actualWork;
}();
```

In this example:

- You have private functions — someSetup() and actualWork().
- You have a self-invoking function — the function a() calls itself using the parentheses following its definition.
- The function executes for the first time, calls someSetup() and then returns a reference to the variable actualWork, which is a function. Notice that there are no parentheses in the return, because it is returning a function reference, not the result of invoking this function.
- Because the whole thing starts with var a =..., the value returned by the self-invoked function is assigned to a.

If you want to test your understanding of the topics just discussed, answer the following questions. What will the code above alert when:

- It is initially loaded?
- You call a() afterwards?

These techniques could be really useful when working in the browser environment. Because different browsers can have different ways of achieving the same thing and you know that the browser features don't change between function calls, you can have a function determine the best way to do the work in the current browser, then redefine itself, so that the "browser feature sniffing" is done only once. You'll see concrete examples of this scenario later in this book.

Closures

The rest of the chapter is about closures (what better way to close a chapter?). Closures could be a little hard to grasp initially, so don't feel discouraged if you don't "get it" during the first read. You should go through the rest of the chapter and experiment with the examples on you own, but if you feel you don't fully understand the concept, you can come back to it later when the topics discussed previously in this chapter have had a chance to sink in.

Before we get to closures, let's review and expand on the concept of scope in JavaScript.

Scope Chain

As you know, in JavaScript, unlike many other languages, there is no curly braces scope, but there is function scope. A variable defined in a function is not visible outside the function, but a variable defined in a code block (an `if` or a `for` loop) is visible outside the block.

```
>>> var a = 1; function f(){var b = 1; return a;}
>>> f();
```

1

```
>>> b
```

b is not defined

The variable a is in the global space, whereas b is in the scope of the function `f()`. So:

- Inside `f()`, both a and b are visible
- Outside `f()`, a is visible, but b is not

If you define a function n() nested inside f(), n() will have access to variables in its own scope, plus the scope of its "parents". This is known as *scope chain*, and the chain can be as long (deep) as you need it to be.

```
var a = 1;
function f(){
  var b = 1;
  function n() {
    var c = 3;
  }
}
```

Lexical Scope

In JavaScript, functions have *lexical scope*. This means that functions create their environment (scope) when they are defined, not when they are executed. Let's see an example:

```
>>> function f1(){var a = 1; f2();}
>>> function f2(){return a;}
>>> f1();
```

a is not defined

Inside the function f1() we call the function f2(). Because the local variable a is also inside f1(), one might expect that f2() will have access to a, but that's not the case. At the time when f2() was *defined* (as opposed to *executed*), there was no a in sight. f2(), just like f1(), only has access to its own scope and the global scope. f1() and f2() don't share their local scopes.

When a function is defined, it "remembers" its environment, its scope chain. This doesn't mean that the function also remembers every single variable that is in scope. Just the opposite—you can add, remove or update variables inside the scope of the function and the function will see the latest, up-to-date state of the variables. If you continue with the example above and declare a global variable a, f2() will see it, because f2() knows the path to the global environment and can access everything in that environment. Also notice how f1() includes a call to f2(), and it works- even though although f2() is not yet defined. All f1() needs to know is its scope, so that everything that shows up in scope becomes immediately available to f1().

```
>>> function f1(){var a = 1; return f2();}
>>> function f2(){return a;}
>>> f1();
```

a is not defined

```
>>> var a = 5;
>>> f1();
```

5

```
>>> a = 55;
>>> f1();
```

55

```
>>> delete a;
```

true

```
>>> f1();
```

a is not defined

This behavior gives JavaScript great flexibility—you can add and remove variables and add them again, and it's totally fine. You can keep experimenting and delete the function f2(), then redefine it again with a different body. In the end, f1() will still work, because all it needs to know is how to access its scope and not what this scope used to contain at some point in time. Continuing with the example above:

```
>>> delete f2;
```

true

```
>>> f1()
```

f2 is not defined

```
>>> var f2 = function(){return a * 2;}
>>> var a = 5;
```

5

```
>>> f1();
```

10

Breaking the Chain with a Closure

Let's introduce closures with an illustration.

There is the global scope. Think of it as the Universe, as if it contains everything.

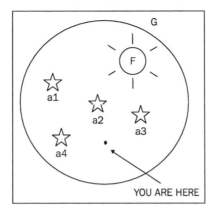

It can contain variables such as a and functions such as F.

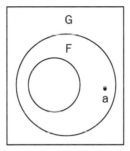

Functions have their own private space and can use it to store other variables (and functions). At some point, you end up with a picture like this:

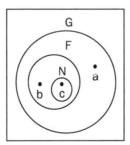

If you're at point a, you're inside the global space. If you're at point b, which is inside the space of the function F, then you have access to the global space and to the F-space. If you're at point c, which is inside the function N, then you can access the global space, the F-space and the N-space You cannot reach from a to b, because b is invisible outside F. But you can get from c to b if you want, or from N to b. The interesting thing—the closure—happens when somehow N breaks out of F and ends up in the global space.

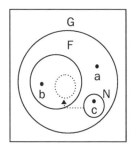

What happens then? N is in the same global space as a. And since functions remember the environment in which they were defined, N will still have access to the F-space, and hence can access b. This is interesting, because N is where a is and yet N does have access to b, but a doesn't.

And how does N break the chain? By making itself global (omitting `var`) or by having F deliver (or `return`) it to the global space. Let's see how this is done in practice.

Closure #1

Take a look at this function:

```
function f(){
  var b = "b";
  return function(){
    return b;
  }
}
```

This function contains a variable b, which is local, and therefore inaccessible from the global space:

```
>>> b
```

b is not defined

Check out the return value of `f()`: it's another function. Think of it as N in the illustrations above. This new function has access to its private space, to `f()`'s space and to the global space. So it can see `b`. Because `f()` is callable from the global space (it's a global function), you can call it and assign the returned value to another global variable. The result—a new global function that has access to `f()`'s private space.

```
>>> var n = f();
>>> n();
```

```
"b"
```

Closure #2

The final result of the next example will be the same as the previous example, but the way to achieve it is a little different. `f()` doesn't return a function, but instead it creates a new global function `n()` inside its body.

Let's start by declaring a placeholder for the global function-to-be. This is optional, but it's always good to declare your variables. Then you can define the function `f()` like this:

```
var n;
function f(){
  var b = "b";
  n = function(){
    return b;
  }
}
```

Now what happens if you invoke `f()`?

```
>>> f();
```

A new function is defined inside `f()` and since it's missing the `var` statement, it becomes global. During definition time, `n()` was inside `f()`, so it had access to `f()`'s scope. `n()` will keep its access to `f()`'s scope, even though `n()` becomes part of the global space.

```
>>> n();
```

```
"b"
```

A Definition and Closure #3

Based on what we have discussed so far, you can say that a closure is created when a function keeps a link to its parent's scope even after the parent has returned.

When you pass an argument to a function it becomes available as a local variable. You can create a function that returns another function, which in turn returns its parent's argument.

```
function f(arg) {
  var n = function(){
    return arg;
  };
  arg++;
  return n;
}
```

You use the function like this:

```
>>> var m = f(123);
>>> m();
```

124

Notice how `arg++` was incremented after the function was defined and yet, when called, `m()` returned the updated value. This demonstrates how the function binds to its scope, not to the current variables and their values found in the scope.

Closures in a Loop

Here's something that can easily lead to hard-to-spot bugs, because, on the surface, everything looks normal.

Let's loop three times, each time creating a new function that returns the loop sequence number. The new functions will be added to an array and we'll return the array at the end. Here's the function:

```
function f() {
  var a = [];
  var i;
  for(i = 0; i < 3; i++) {
    a[i] = function(){
      return i;
    }
  }
  return a;
}
```

Let's run the function, assigning the result to the array a.

```
>>> var a = f();
```

Now you have an array of three functions. Let's invoke them by adding parentheses after each array element. The expected behavior is to see the loop sequence printed out: 0, 1, and 2. Let's try:

```
>>> a[0]()
3
>>> a[1]()
3
>>> a[2]()
3
```

Hmm, not quite what we expected. What happened here? We created three closures that all point to the same local variable i. Closures don't remember the value, they only link (reference) the i variable and will return its current value. After the loop, i's value is **3**. So all the three functions point to the same value.

(Why 3 and not 2 is another good question to think about, for better understanding the for loop.)

So how do you implement the correct behavior? You need three different variables. An elegant solution is to use another closure:

```
function f() {
  var a = [];
  var i;
  for(i = 0; i < 3; i++) {
    a[i] = (function(x){
      return function(){
        return x;
      }
    })(i);
  }
  return a;
}
```

This gives the expected result:

```
>>> var a = f();
>>> a[0]();
0
```

```
>>> a[1]();
```

1

```
>>> a[2]();
```

2

Here, instead of just creating a function that returns i, you pass i to another self-executing function. For this function, i becomes the local value x, and x has a different value every time.

Alternatively, you can use a "normal" (as opposed to self-invoking) inner function to achieve the same result. The key is to use the middle function to "localize" the value of i at every iteration.

```
function f() {
  function makeClosure(x) {
    return function(){
      return x;
    }
  }
  var a = [];
  var i;
  for(i = 0; i < 3; i++) {
    a[i] = makeClosure(i);
  }
  return a;
}
```

Getter/Setter

Let's see two more examples of using closures. The first one involves the creation of *getter* and *setter* functions. Imagine you have a variable that will contain a very specific range of values. You don't want to expose this variable because you don't want just any part of the code to be able to alter its value. You protect this variable inside a function and provide two additional functions—one to get the value and one to set it. The one that sets it could contain some logic to validate a value before assigning it to the protected variable (let's skip the validation part for the sake of keeping the example simple).

You place both the getter and the setter functions inside the same function that contains the secret variable, so that they share the same scope:

```
var getValue, setValue;
(function() {
  var secret = 0;
  getValue = function(){
    return secret;
  };
  setValue = function(v){
    secret = v;
  };
})()
```

In this case, the function that contains everything is a self-invoking anonymous function. It defines setValue() and getValue() as global functions, while the secret variable remains local and inaccessible directly.

```
>>> getValue()
```

0

```
>>> setValue(123)
>>> getValue()
```

123

Iterator

The last closure example (also the last example in the chapter) shows the use of a closure to accomplish *Iterator* functionality.

You already know how to loop through a simple array, but there might be cases where you have a more complicated data structure with different rules as to what the sequence of values is. You can wrap the complicated "who's next" logic into an easy-to-use next() function. Then you simply call next() every time you need the consecutive value. For this example, we'll just use a simple array, and not a complex data structure.

Here's an initialization function that takes an input array and also defines a private pointer i that will always point to the next element in the array.

```
function setup(x) {
  var i = 0;
  return function(){
    return x[i++];
  };
}
```

Calling the `setup()` function with a data array will create the `next()` function for you.

```
>>> var next = setup(['a', 'b', 'c']);
```

From there it's easy and fun: calling the same function over and over again gives you the next element.

```
>>> next();
```

"a"

```
>>> next();
```

"b"

```
>>> next();
```

"c"

Summary

You have now completed the introduction to the fundamental concepts related to functions in JavaScript. You've been laying the groundwork that will allow you to quickly grasp the concepts of object-oriented JavaScript and the patterns that are in use in modern JavaScript programming. So far, we've been avoiding the OO features, but as you have reached this point in the book, it is only going to get more interesting from here on in. Let's take a moment and review the topics discussed in this chapter:

- The basics of how to define and invoke (call) a function
- Function parameters and their flexibility
- Built-in functions—`parseInt()`, `parseFloat()`, `isNaN()`, `isFinite()`, `eval()`, and the four functions to encode/decode a URL
- The scope of variables in JavaScript—no curly braces scope, variables have only function scope; functions have lexical scope and follow a scope chain

- Functions as data—a function is like any other piece of data that you assign to a variable and a lot of interesting applications follow from this, such as:
  ○ Private functions and private variables
  ○ Anonymous functions
  ○ Callbacks
  ○ Self-invoking functions
  ○ Functions overwriting themselves

- Closures

Exercises

1. Write a function that converts a hexadecimal color, for example blue "#0000FF", into its RGB representation **"rgb(0, 0, 255)"**. Name your function getRGB() and test it with this code:

```
>>> var a = getRGB("#00FF00");
>>> a;
```

   "rgb(0, 255, 0)"

2. What does each of these lines print in the console?

```
>>> parseInt(1e1)
>>> parseInt('1e1')
>>> parseFloat('1e1')
>>> isFinite(0/10)
>>> isFinite(20/0)
>>> isNaN(parseInt(NaN));
```

3. What does this following code alert()?

```
var a = 1;
function f() {
  var a = 2;
  function n() {
    alert(a);
  }
  n();
}
f();
```

4. All these examples alert **"Boo!"**. Can you explain why?

4.1.
```
var f = alert;
eval('f("Boo!")');
```

4.2.
```
var e;
var f = alert;
eval('e=f')('Boo!');
```

4.3.
```
(
  function(){
    return alert;
  }
)()('Boo!');
```

4
Objects

Now that you've mastered JavaScript's primitive data types, arrays, and functions, it is time for the best part—objects. In this chapter, you will learn:

- How to create and use objects
- What are the constructor functions
- What types of built-in JavaScript objects exist and what they can do for you

From Arrays to Objects

As you already know from Chapter 2, an array is just a list of values. Each value has an index (a numeric key) starting from zero and incrementing by one for each value.

```
>>>> var myarr = ['red', 'blue', 'yellow', 'purple'];
>>> myarr;
```

["red", "blue", "yellow", "purple"]

```
>>> myarr[0]
```

"red"

```
>>> myarr[3]
```

"purple"

If you put the indexes in one column and the values in another, you'll end up with a table of key/value pairs like this:

Key	Value
0	red
1	blue
2	yellow
3	purple

An object is very similar to an array but with the difference that you define the keys yourself. You're not limited to using only numeric indexes but can use friendlier keys, such as `first_name`, `age`, and so on.

Let's take a look at a simple object and examine its parts:

```
var hero = {
  breed: 'Turtle',
  occupation: 'Ninja'
};
```

You can see that:

- The name of the variable that contains the object is `hero`
- Instead of [and] which you use to define an array, you use { and } for objects
- You separate the elements (called properties) contained in the object with commas
- The key/value pairs are divided by colons, as `key: value`

The keys (names of the properties) can optionally be placed in quotation marks. For example these are all the same:

```
var o = {prop: 1};
var o = {"prop": 1};
var o = {'prop': 1};
```

It's recommended that you don't quote the names of the properties (it is also less typing!), but there are some cases when you have must use quotes:

- If the property name is one of the reserved words in JavaScript (see Appendix A)
- If it contains spaces or special characters (anything other than letters, numbers, and the underscore character)
- If it starts with a number

Basically, if the name you have chosen for a property is not a valid name for a variable in JavaScript, then you need to in place in quotes.

Have a look at this bizarre-looking object:

```
var o = {
  something: 1,
  'yes or no': 'yes',
  '!@#$%^&*': true
};
```

This is a valid object. The quotes are required for the second and the third properties, otherwise you will get an error.

Later in this chapter you will see other ways to define objects and arrays, in addition to [] and {}. But first, let's introduce this bit of terminology: defining an array with [] is called *array literal* notation and defining an object using the curly braces {} is called *object literal* notation.

Elements, Properties, Methods

When talking about arrays, you say that they contain *elements*. When talking about objects, you say that they contain *properties*. There isn't any significant difference in JavaScript; it is just the terminology that people are used to, probably from other programming languages.

A property of an object can contain a function, because functions are just data. In this case, you say that this property is a *method*.

```
var dog = {
  name: 'Benji',
  talk: function(){
    alert('Woof, woof!');
  }
};
```

It's also possible to store functions as array elements and invoke them, but you will not see much code like this in practice:

```
>>> var a = [];
>>> a[0] = function(what){alert(what);};
>>> a[0]('Boo!');
```

Hashes, Associative Arrays

In some programming languages, there is distinction between:

- A normal array, also called *indexed* or *enumerated* (the keys are numbers) and
- An associative array, also called a *hash* (the keys are strings)

JavaScript uses arrays to represent indexed arrays and objects to represent associative arrays. If you want a hash in JavaScript, you use an object.

Accessing Object's Properties

There are two ways to access a property of an object:

- Using square bracket notation, for example `hero['occupation']`
- Using the dot notation, for example `hero.occupation`

The dot notation is easier to read and write but it cannot always be used. The same rules apply as for quoting property names: if the name of the property is not a valid variable name, you cannot use the dot notation.

Let's take this object:

```
var hero = {
  breed: 'Turtle',
  occupation: 'Ninja'
};
```

Accessing a property with the dot notation:

```
>>> hero.breed;
```

"Turtle"

Accessing a property with the bracket notation:

```
>>> hero['occupation'];
```

"Ninja"

Accessing a non-existing property returns `undefined`:

```
>>> 'Hair color is ' + hero.hair_color;
```

"Hair color is undefined"

Objects can contain any data, including other objects.

```
var book = {
  name: 'Catch-22',
  published: 1961,
  author: {
    firstname: 'Joseph',
    lastname: 'Heller'
  }
};
```

To get to the `firstname` property of the object contained in the `author` property of the `book` object, you use:

```
>>> book.author.firstname
```

"Joseph"

Or using the square braces notation:

```
>>> book['author']['lastname']
```

"Heller"

It works even if you mix both:

```
>>> book.author['lastname']
```

"Heller"

```
>>> book['author'].lastname
```

"Heller"

One other case where you need square brackets is if the name of the property you need to access is not known beforehand. During runtime, it is dynamically stored in a variable:

```
>>> var key = 'firstname';
>>> book.author[key];
```

"Joseph"

Calling an Object's Methods

Because a method is just a property that happens to be a function, you can access methods in the same way as you would access properties: using the dot notation or using square brackets. Calling (invoking) a method is the same as calling any other function: just add parentheses after the method name, which effectively say "Execute!".

```
var hero = {
  breed: 'Turtle',
  occupation: 'Ninja',
  say: function() {
    return 'I am ' + hero.occupation;
  }
}
>>> hero.say();
```

"I am Ninja"

If there are any parameters that you want to pass to a method, you proceed as with normal functions:

```
>>> hero.say('a', 'b', 'c');
```

Because you can use the array-like square brackets to access a property, this means you can also use brackets to access and invoke methods, although this is not at a common practice:

```
>>> hero['say']();
```

[**Best Practice Tip: No quotes**
1. Use the dot notation to access methods and properties
2. Don't quote properties in your object literals]

Altering Properties/Methods

JavaScript is a dynamic language; it allows you to alter properties and methods of existing objects at any time. This includes adding new properties or deleting them. You can start with a blank object and add properties later. Let's see how you can go about doing this.

An empty object:

```
>>> var hero = {};
```

Accessing a non-existing property:

```
>>> typeof hero.breed
```

"undefined"

Adding some properties and a method:

```
>>> hero.breed = 'turtle';
>>> hero.name = 'Leonardo';
>>> hero.sayName = function() {return hero.name;};
```

Calling the method:

```
>>> hero.sayName();
```

"Leonardo"

Deleting a property:

```
>>> delete hero.name;
```

true

Calling the method again will no longer work:

```
>>> hero.sayName();
```

reference to undefined property hero.name

Using this Value

In the previous example, the method `sayName()` used `hero.name` to access the `name` property of the `hero` object. When you're inside a method though, there is another way to access the object this method belongs to: by using the special value `this`.

```
var hero = {
  name: 'Rafaelo',
  sayName: function() {
    return this.name;
  }
}
>>> hero.sayName();
```

"Rafaelo"

So when you say `this`, you are actually saying "this object" or "the current object".

Constructor Functions

There is another way to create objects: by using constructor functions. Let's see an example:

```
function Hero() {
  this.occupation = 'Ninja';
}
```

In order to create an object using this function, you use the `new` operator, like this:

```
>>> var hero = new Hero();
>>> hero.occupation;
```

"Ninja"

The benefit of using constructor functions is that they accept parameters, which can be used when creating new objects. Let's modify the constructor to accept one parameter and assign it to the name property.

```
function Hero(name) {
  this.name = name;
  this.occupation = 'Ninja';
  this.whoAreYou = function() {
    return "I'm " + this.name + " and I'm a " + this.occupation;
  }
}
```

Now you can create different objects using the same constructor:

```
>>> var h1 = new Hero('Michelangelo');
>>> var h2 = new Hero('Donatello');
>>> h1.whoAreYou();
```

"I'm Michelangelo and I'm a Ninja"

```
>>> h2.whoAreYou();
```

"I'm Donatello and I'm a Ninja"

By convention, you should capitalize the first letter of your constructor functions so that you have a visual clue that this is not a normal function. If you call a function that is designed to be a constructor, but you omit the new operator, this is not an error, but it may not behave as you could expect.

```
>>> var h = Hero('Leonardo');
>>> typeof h
```

"undefined"

What happened here? As there was no new operator, we didn't create a new object. The function was called like any other function, so h contains the value that the function returns. The function does not return anything (there's no return), so it actually returns **undefined**, which gets assigned to h.

In this case, what does this refer to? It refers to the *global object*.

The Global Object

Previously we discussed global variables (and how you should avoid them) and also the fact that JavaScript programs run inside a host environment (the browser for example). Now that you know about objects, it is time for the whole truth: the host environment provides a global object and all global variables are actually properties of the global object.

If your host environment is the web browser, the global object is called `window`.

As an illustration, you can try declaring a global variable, outside of any function, such as:

```
>>> var a = 1;
```

Then you can access this global variable in various ways:

- As a variable `a`
- As a property of the global object, for example `window['a']` or `window.a`

Let's go back to the case where you define a constructor function and call it without the `new` operator. In such cases `this` refers to the global object and all properties set with `this` become properties of `window`.

Declaring a constructor function and calling it without `new`, returns **"undefined"**:

```
>>> function Hero(name) {this.name = name;}
>>> var h = Hero('Leonardo');
>>> typeof h
```

"undefined"

```
>>> typeof h.name
```

h has no properties

Because you had `this` inside `Hero`, a global variable (a property of the global object) called `name` was created.

```
>>> name
```

"Leonardo"

```
>>> window.name
```

"Leonardo"

If you call the same constructor function but this time using `new`, then a new object is returned and `this` refers to it.

```
>>> var h2 = new Hero('Michelangelo');
>>> typeof h2
```

"object"

```
>>> h2.name
```

"Michelangelo"

The global functions you saw in Chapter 3 can also be invoked as methods of the `window` object. So the following two codes are equivalent:

```
>>> parseInt('101 dalmatians')
```

101

```
>>> window.parseInt('101 dalmatians')
```

101

constructor Property

When an object is created, a special property is assigned to it behind the scenes — the `constructor` property. It contains a reference to the constructor function used to create this object.

Continuing from the previous example:

```
>>> h2.constructor
```

Hero(name)

Because the `constructor` property contains a reference to a function, you might as well call this function to produce a new object. The following code is like saying, "I don't care how object h2 was created, but I want another one just like it".

```
>>> var h3 = new h2.constructor('Rafaello');
>>> h3.name;
```

"Rafaello"

If an object was created using the object literal notation, its constructor is the built-in `Object()` constructor function (more about this later in this chapter).

```
>>> var o = {};
>>> o.constructor;
```

Object()

```
>>> typeof o.constructor;
```

"function"

instanceof Operator

Using the `instanceof` operator, you can test if an object was created with a specific constructor function:

```
>>> function Hero(){}
>>> var h = new Hero();
>>> var o = {};
>>> h instanceof Hero;
```

true

```
>>> h instanceof Object;
```

false

```
>>> o instanceof Object;
```

true

Note that you don't put parentheses after the function name (don't use h instanceof Hero()). This is because you're not invoking this function, but just referring to it by name, as for any other variable.

Functions that Return Objects

In addition to using constructor functions and the new operator to create objects, you can also use a normal function and create objects without new. You can have a function that does some preparatory work and has an object as a return value.

For example, here's a simple factory() function that produces objects:

```
function factory(name) {
  return {
    name: name
  };
}
```

Using the factory():

```
>>> var o = factory('one');
>>> o.name
```

"one"

```
>>> o.constructor
```

Object()

In fact, you can also use constructor functions and return objects, different from this. This means you can modify the default behavior of the constructor function. Let's see how.

Here's the normal constructor scenario:

```
>>> function C() {this.a = 1;}
>>> var c = new C();
>>> c.a
```

1

But now look at this scenario:

```
>>> function C2() {this.a = 1; return {b: 2};}
>>> var c2 = new C2();
>>> typeof c2.a
```

"undefined"

```
>>> c2.b
```

2

What happened here? Instead of returning the object `this`, which contains the property `a`, the constructor returned another object that contains the property `b`. This is possible only if the return value is an object. Otherwise, if you try to return anything that is not an object, the constructor will proceed with its usual behavior and return `this`.

Passing Objects

When you copy an object or pass it to a function, you only pass a reference to that object. Consequently, if you make a change to the reference, you are actually modifying the original object.

Here's an example of how you can assign an object to another variable and then make a change to the copy. As a result, the original object is also changed:

```
>>> var original = {howmany: 1};
>>> var copy = original;
>>> copy.howmany
```

1

```
>>> copy.howmany = 100;
```

100

```
>>> original.howmany
```

100

The same thing applies when passing objects to functions:

```
>>> var original = {howmany: 100};
>>> var nullify = function(o) {o.howmany = 0;}
>>> nullify(original);
>>> original.howmany
```

0

Comparing Objects

When you compare objects, you'll get `true` only if you compare two references to the same object. Comparing two distinct objects that happen to have the exact same methods and properties will return `false`.

Let's create two objects that look the same:

```
>>> var fido  = {breed: 'dog'};
>>> var benji = {breed: 'dog'};
```

Comparing them will return `false`:

```
>>> benji === fido
```

false

```
>>> benji == fido
```

false

You can create a new variable `mydog` and assign one of the objects to it, this way `mydog` actually points to the same object.

```
>>> var mydog = benji;
```

In this case `benji` is `mydog` because they are the same object (changing `mydog`'s properties will change `benji`'s). The comparison returns **true**.

```
>>> mydog === benji
```

true

And because `fido` is a different object, it does not compare to `mydog`:

```
>>> mydog === fido
```

false

Objects in the Firebug Console

Before diving into the built-in objects in JavaScript, let's quickly say a few words about working with objects in the Firebug console.

After playing around with the examples in this chapter, you might have already noticed how objects are displayed in the console. If you create an object and type its name, you'll get a string representation of the object including the properties (but only the first few properties if there are too many of them).

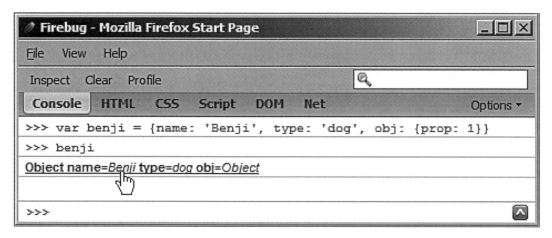

The object is clickable and takes you to the **DOM** tab in Firebug, which lists all of the properties of the object. If a property is also an object, there is a plus (+) sign to expand it. This is handy as it gives you an insight into exactly what this object contains.

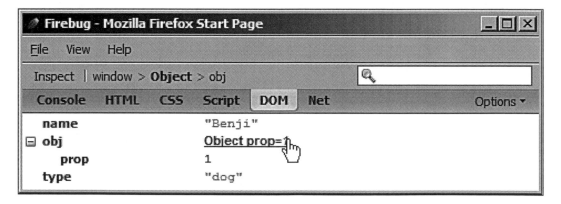

The console also offers you an object called `console` and some methods, such as `console.log()`, `console.error()`, and `console.info()` which you can use to display any value you want in the console.

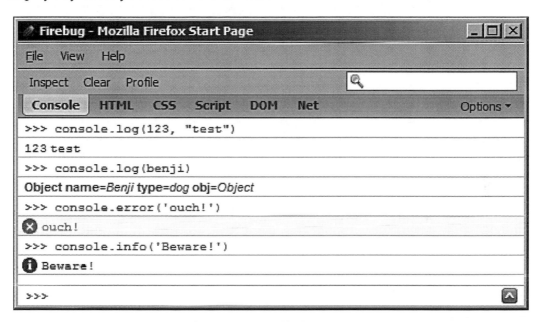

`console.log()` is convenient when you want to quickly test something, as well as in your real scripts when you want to dump some intermediate debuging information. Here's how you can experiment with loops, for example:

```
>>> for(var i = 0; i < 5; i++) { console.log(i); }
0

1

2

3

4
```

Built-in Objects

Earlier in this chapter we came across the `Object()` constructor function. It is returned when you create objects with the object literal notation and access their `constructor` property. `Object()` is one of the built-in constructors; there are others and in the rest of this chapter you'll see all of them.

The built-in objects can be divided into three groups:

- Data wrapper objects—`Object`, `Array`, `Function`, `Boolean`, `Number`, and `String`. These objects correspond to the different data types in JavaScript. Basically, there is a data wrapper object for each different value returned by `typeof` (discussed in Chapter 2) with the exception of "undefined" and "null".
- Utility objects—These are `Math`, `Date`, `RegExp` and can come in very handy.
- Error objects—The generic `Error` object as well as other, more specific objects that can help your program recover its working state when something unexpected happens.

Only a handful of methods of the built-in objects will be discussed in this chapter. For a full reference, see Appendix C.

If you're confused about what is a built-in object and what is a built-in constructor, well, they are the same thing. In a moment, you will see how functions, and therefore constructor functions, are also objects.

Object

`Object` is the parent of all JavaScript objects, which means that every object you create inherits from it. To create a new empty object you can use the literal notation or the `Object()` constructor function. The following two lines are equivalent:

```
>>> var o = {};
>>> var o = new Object();
```

An empty object is not completely useless because it already contains some methods and properties. Let's see a few:

- `o.constructor` property returns the constructor function
- `o.toString()` is a method that returns a string representation of the object
- `o.valueOf()` returns a single-value representation of the object, often this is the object itself

Let's see these methods in action. First, create an object:

```
>>> var o = new Object();
```

Calling `toString()` returns a string representation of the object.

```
>>> o.toString()
```

"[object Object]"

`toString()` will be called internally by JavaScript, when an object is used in a string context. For example `alert()` works only with strings, so if you call the `alert()` function passing an object, the method `toString()` will be called behind the scenes. These two lines will produce the same result:

```
>>> alert(o)
>>> alert(o.toString())
```

Another type of string context is the string concatenation. If you try to concatenate an object with a string, the object's `toString()` will be called first:

```
>>> "An object: " + o
```

"An object: [object Object]"

`valueOf()` is another method that all objects provide. For the simple objects (whose constructor is `Object()`) the `valueOf()` method will return the object itself.

```
>>> o.valueOf() === o
```

true

To summarize:

- You can create objects either with `var o = {};` (object literal notation, the preferred method) or with `var o = new Object();`
- Any object, no matter how complex, inherits from the `Object` object and therefore offers methods such as `toString()` and properties such as `constructor`.

Array

`Array()` is a built-in function that you can use as a constructor to create arrays:

```
>>> var a = new Array();
```

This is equivalent to the array literal notation:

```
>>> var a = [];
```

No matter how the array is created, you can add elements to it as usual:

```
>>> a[0] = 1; a[1] = 2; a;
```

[1, 2]

When using the `Array()` constructor, you can also pass values which will be assigned to the new array's elements.

```
>>> var a = new Array(1,2,3,'four');
>>> a;
```

[1, 2, 3, "four"]

An exception to this is when you pass a single number to the constructor. In this case, the number passed will be considered to be the length of the array.

```
>>> var a2 = new Array(5);
>>> a2;
```

[undefined, undefined, undefined, undefined, undefined]

Because arrays are created with a constructor, does this mean that arrays are in fact objects? Yes, and you can verify this by using the `typeof` operator:

```
>>> typeof a;
```

"object"

Because arrays are objects, this means that they inherit the properties and methods of the parent `Object`.

```
>>> a.toString();
```

"1,2,3,four"

```
>>> a.valueOf()
```

[1, 2, 3, "four"]

```
>>> a.constructor
```

Array()

Arrays are objects, but of a special type because:

- The names of their properties are automatically assigned using numbers starting from 0
- They have a `length` property which contains the number of elements in the array
- They have additional built-in methods in addition to those inherited from the parent object

Let's examine the differences between an array and an object, starting by creating the empty object `o` and the empty array `a`:

```
>>> var a = [], o = {};
```

Array objects have a `length` property automatically defined for them, while normal objects do not:

```
>>> a.length
```

0

```
>>> typeof o.length
```

"undefined"

It's OK to add both numeric and non-numeric properties to both arrays and objects:

```
>>> a[0] = 1; o[0] = 1;
>>> a.prop = 2; o.prop = 2;
```

The `length` property is always up-to-date with the number of numeric properties, ignoring the non-numeric ones.

```
>>> a.length
```

1

The `length` property can also be set by you. Setting it to a greater value than the current number of items in the array creates empty elements (with a value of `undefined`).

```
>>> a.length = 5
```

5

```
>>> a
```

[1, undefined, undefined, undefined, undefined]

Setting the `length` to a lower value removes the trailing elements:

```
>>> a.length = 2;
```

2

```
>>> a
```

[1, undefined]

Interesting Array Methods

In addition to the methods inherited from the parent object, array objects also have some more useful methods, such as `sort()`, `join()`, and `slice()`, among others (see Appendix C for the full list).

Let's take one array and experiment with some of these methods:

```
>>> var a = [3, 5, 1, 7, 'test'];
```

The `push()` method appends a new element at the end of the array. The `pop()` method removes the last element. `a.push('new')` works just like `a[a.length] = 'new'` and `a.pop()` is the same as `a.length--`.

`push()` returns the length of the changed array, `pop()` returns the element that it removed.

```
>>> a.push('new')
```

6

```
>>> a
```

[3, 5, 1, 7, "test", "new"]

```
>>> a.pop()
```

"new"

```
>>> a
```

[3, 5, 1, 7, "test"]

The `sort()` method sorts the array and returns the modified array. In the next example, after the sort, both `a` and `b` contain pointers to the same array.

```
>>> var b = a.sort();
>>> b
```

[1, 3, 5, 7, "test"]

```
>>> a
```

[1, 3, 5, 7, "test"]

`join()` returns a string containing the values of all the elements in the array, concatenated together using the string parameter passed to `join()`

```
>>> a.join(' is not ');
```

"1 is not 3 is not 5 is not 7 is not test"

`slice()` returns a piece of the array without modifying the source array. The first parameter to `slice()` is the start index and the second is the end index (both indices are zero-based).

```
>>> b = a.slice(1, 3);
```
[3, 5]
```
>>> b = a.slice(0, 1);
```
[1]
```
>>> b = a.slice(0, 2);
```
[1, 3]

After all the slicing, the source array is still the same:

```
>>> a
```
[1, 3, 5, 7, "test"]

`splice()` modifies the source array. It removes a slice, returns it, and optionally fills the gap with new elements. The first two parameters define start and end of the slice to be removed; the other parameters pass the new values.

```
>>> b = a.splice(1, 2, 100, 101, 102);
```
[3, 5]
```
>>> a
```
[1, 100, 101, 102, 7, "test"]

Filling the gap with new elements is optional and you can skip it:

```
>>> a.splice(1, 3)
```
[100, 101, 102]
```
>>> a
```
[1, 7, "test"]

Function

You already know that functions are a special data type. But it turns out that there's more to it than that—functions are actually objects. There is a built-in constructor function called `Function()` which allows an alternative (but not recommended) way to create a function.

The following three ways of defining a function are equivalent:

```
>>> function sum(a, b) {return a + b;};
>>> sum(1, 2)

3

>>> var sum = function(a, b) {return a + b;};
>>> sum(1, 2)

3

>>> var sum = new Function('a', 'b', 'return a + b;');
>>> sum(1, 2)

3
```

When using the `Function()` constructor, you pass the parameter names first (as strings) and then the source code for the body of the function (again as a string). The JavaScript engine then needs to evaluate the source code you pass and create the new function for you. This source code evaluation suffers from the same drawbacks as the `eval()` function, so defining functions using the `Function()` constructor should be avoided when possible.

If you use the `Function` constructor to create functions that have lots of parameters, bear in mind that the parameters can be passed as a single comma-delimited list, so, for example, these are the same:

```
>>> var first = new Function('a, b, c, d', 'return arguments;');
>>> first(1,2,3,4);
```

[1, 2, 3, 4]

```
>>> var second = new Function('a, b, c', 'd', 'return arguments;');
>>> second(1,2,3,4);
```

[1, 2, 3, 4]

```
>>> var third = new Function('a', 'b', 'c', 'd',
                              'return arguments;');
>>> third(1,2,3,4);
```

[1, 2, 3, 4]

Best Practice

Do not use the `Function()` constructor. As with `eval()` and `setTimeout()` (discussed further in the book), always try to stay away from cases where you pass JavaScript code as a string.

Properties of the Function Objects

Like any other object, functions have a `constructor` property that contains a reference to the `Function()` constructor function.

```
>>> function myfunc(a){return a;}
>>> myfunc.constructor
```

Function()

Functions also have a `length` property, which contains the number of parameters the function accepts.

```
>>> function myfunc(a, b, c){return true;}
>>> myfunc.length
```

3

There is another interesting property, which doesn't exist in the ECMA standard, but is implemented across the browsers—the `caller` property. This returns a reference to the function that called our function. Let's say there is a function `A()` that gets called from function `B()`. If inside `A()` you put `A.caller`, it will return the function `B()`.

```
>>> function A(){return A.caller;}
>>> function B(){return A();}
>>> B()
```

B()

This could be useful if you want your function to respond differently depending on the function from which it was called. If you call `A()` from the global space (outside of any function), `A.caller` will be `null`.

```
>>> A()
```

null

The most important property of a function is the `prototype` property. We'll discuss this property in detail in the next chapter, but for now let's just say this:

- The `prototype` property of a function contains an object
- It is only useful when you use this function as a constructor
- All objects created with this function keep a reference to the `prototype` property and can use its properties as their own

Let's see a quick example to demonstrate the `prototype` property. Let's start with a simple object that has a property `name` and a method `say()`.

```
var some_obj = {
  name: 'Ninja',
  say: function(){
    return 'I am a ' + this.name;
  }
}
```

If you create a hollow function, you can verify that it automatically has a `prototype` property that contains an empty object.

```
>>> function F(){}
>>> typeof F.prototype
```

"object"

It gets interesting when you modify the `prototype` property. You can replace the default empty object with any other object. Let's assign our `some_obj` to the prototype.

```
>>> F.prototype = some_obj;
```

Now, using the function `F()` as a constructor function, you can create a new object `obj` which will have access to the properties of `F.prototype` as if it were its own.

```
>>> var obj = new F();
>>> obj.name
```

"Ninja"

```
>>> obj.say()
```

"I am a Ninja"

There will be more about the `prototype` property in the next chapter.

Methods of the Function Objects

The function objects, being a descendant of the top parent `Object`, get the default methods, such as `toString()`. When invoked on a function, the `toString()` method returns the source code of the function.

```
>>> function myfunc(a, b, c) {return a + b + c;}
>>> myfunc.toString()
```

"function myfunc(a, b, c) {

   return a + b + c;

}"

If you try to peek into the source code of the built-in functions, you'll get the hardly useful `[native code]` string:

```
>>> eval.toString()
```

"function eval() {

   [native code]

}"

Two useful methods of the function objects are `call()` and `apply()`. They allow your objects to borrow methods from other objects and invoke them as their own. This is an easy and powerful way to reuse code.

Let's say you have a `some_obj` object, which contains the method `say()`

```
var some_obj = {
  name: 'Ninja',
  say: function(who){
    return 'Haya ' + who + ', I am a ' + this.name;
  }
}
```

You can call the `say()` method which internally uses `this.name` to gain access to its own `name` property.

```
>>> some_obj.say('Dude');
```

"Haya Dude, I am a Ninja"

Now let's create a simple object `my_obj`, which only has a `name` property:

```
>>> my_obj = {name: 'Scripting guru'};
```

`my_obj` likes `some_obj`'s `say()` method so much that it wants to invoke it as its own. This is possible using the `call()` method of the `say()` function object:

```
>>> some_obj.say.call(my_obj, 'Dude');
```

"Haya Dude, I am a Scripting guru"

It worked! But what happened here? We invoked the `call()` method of the `say()` function object passing two parameters: the object `my_obj` and the string **'Dude'**. The result is that when `say()` was invoked, the references to `this` value that it contains, pointed to `my_obj`. This way `this.name` didn't return **Ninja**, but **Scripting guru** instead.

If you have more parameters to pass when invoking the `call()` method, you just keep adding them:

```
some_obj.someMethod.call(my_obj, 'a', 'b', 'c');
```

If you don't pass an object as a first parameter to `call()` or pass `null`, the global object will be assumed.

The method `apply()` works the same way as `call()` but with the difference that all parameters you want to pass to the method of the other object are passed as an array. The following two lines are equivalent:

```
some_obj.someMethod.apply(my_obj, ['a', 'b', 'c']);
some_obj.someMethod.call(my_obj, 'a', 'b', 'c');
```

Continuing the example above, you can use:

```
>>> some_obj.say.apply(my_obj, ['Dude']);
```

"Haya Dude, I am a Scripting guru"

The arguments Object Revisited

In the previous chapter, you saw how, from inside a function, you have access to something called `arguments`, which contains the values of all parameters passed to the function:

```
>>> function f() {return arguments;}
>>> f(1,2,3)
```

[1, 2, 3]

`arguments` looks like an array but is actually an array-like object. It resembles an array because it contains indexed elements and a `length` property. However, the similarity ends here, as `arguments` doesn't provide any of the array methods, such as `sort()` or `slice()`.

The `arguments` object has another interesting property — the `callee` property. This contains a reference to the function being called. If you create a function that returns `arguments.callee` and you call this function, it will simply return a reference to itself.

```
>>> function f(){return arguments.callee;}
>>> f()
```

f()

`arguments.callee` allows anonymous functions to call themselves recursively. Here's an example:

```
(
  function(count){
    if (count < 5) {
      alert(count);
      arguments.callee(++count);
    }
  }
) (1)
```

Here you have an anonymous function that receives a `count` parameter, alerts it, and then calls itself with an incremented `count`. The whole function is wrapped in parentheses and followed by another set of parentheses, which invokes the function right away, passing the initial value 1. The result of this code is four alerts showing the numbers **1, 2, 3,** and **4.**

Boolean

Our journey through the built-in objects in JavaScript continues, and the next ones are fairly easy; they merely wrap the primitive data types boolean, number, and string.

You already know a lot about booleans from Chapter 2. Now, let's meet the `Boolean()` constructor:

```
>>> var b = new Boolean();
```

It is important to note that this creates a new object b, and not a primitive boolean value. To get the primitive value, you can call the `valueOf()` method (inherited from `Object`).

```
>>> var b = new Boolean();
>>> typeof b
```

"object"

```
>>> typeof b.valueOf()
```

"boolean"

```
>>> b.valueOf()
```

false

Overall, objects created with the `Boolean()` constructor are not too useful, as they don't provide any methods or properties, other than the inherited ones.

The `Boolean()` function is useful when called as a normal function, without `new`. This converts non-booleans to booleans (which is the same as using a double negation `!!value`).

```
>>> Boolean("test")
```

true

```
>>> Boolean("")
```

false

```
>>> Boolean({})
```

true

Apart from the six falsy values, everything else is truthy in JavaScript, including the empty objects. This also means that all boolean objects created with `new Boolean()` evaluate to **true**, as they are objects.

Let's create two boolean objects, one truthy and one falsy:

```
>>> var b1 = new Boolean(true)
>>> b1.valueOf()
```

true

```
>>> var b2 = new Boolean(false)
>>> b2.valueOf()
```

false

Now let's convert them to primitive boolean values. They both convert to `true` because all objects are truthy.

```
>>> Boolean(b1)
```

true

```
>>> Boolean(b2)
```

true

Number

Similarly to `Boolean()`, the `Number()` function can be used:

- As a normal function in order to try to convert any value to a number. This is similar to the use of `parseInt()` or `parseFloat()`.
- As a constructor function (with `new`) to create objects

```
>>> var n = Number('12.12');
>>> n
```

12.12

```
>>> typeof n
```

"number"

```
>>> var n = new Number('12.12');
>>> typeof n
```

"object"

Because functions are objects, they can have properties. The `Number()` function contains some interesting built-in properties (which you cannot modify):

```
>>> Number.MAX_VALUE
```

1.7976931348623157e+308

```
>>> Number.MIN_VALUE
```

5e-324

```
>>> Number.POSITIVE_INFINITY
```

Infinity

```
>>> Number.NEGATIVE_INFINITY
```

-Infinity

```
>>> Number.NaN
```

NaN

The number objects provide three methods—`toFixed()`, `toPrecision()` and `toExponential()` (see Appendix C for details).

```
>>> var n = new Number(123.456)
>>> n.toFixed(1)
```

"123.5"

Note that you can use these methods without explicitly creating a number object. In such cases, the number object will be created (and destroyed) for you behind the scenes:

```
>>> (12345).toExponential()
```

"1.2345e+4"

As with all objects, number objects also provide the toString() method. It is interesting to note that this method accept an optional radix parameter (10 is the default).

```
>>> var n = new Number(255);
>>> n.toString();
```

"255"

```
>>> n.toString(10);
```

"255"

```
>>> n.toString(16);
```

"ff"

```
>>> (3).toString(2);
```

"11"

```
>>> (3).toString(10);
```

"3"

String

Using the String() constructor function you can create string objects. Objects produced this way provide some useful methods when it comes to text manipulation, but if you don't plan on using these methods, you're probably better off just using primitive strings.

Here's an example that shows the difference between a string object and a primitive string data type.

```
>>> var primitive = 'Hello';
>>> typeof primitive;
```

"string"

```
>>> var obj = new String('world');
>>> typeof obj;
```

"object"

A string object is very similar to an array of characters. The string objects have an indexed property for each character and they also have a `length` property.

```
>>> obj[0]
```

"w"

```
>>> obj[4]
```

"d"

```
>>> obj.length
```

5

To extract the primitive value from the string object, you can use the `valueOf()` or `toString()` methods inherited from `Object`. You'll probably never need to do this, as `toString()` is called behind the scenes if you use an object in a string context.

```
>>> obj.valueOf()
```

"world"

```
>>> obj.toString()
```

"world"

```
>>> obj + ""
```

"world"

Primitive strings are not objects, so they don't have any methods or properties. But JavaScript still offers you the syntax to treat primitive strings as objects.

In the following example, string objects are being created (and then destroyed) behind the scenes every time you access a primitive string as if it was an object:

```
>>> "potato".length
```

6

```
>>> "tomato"[0]
```

"t"

```
>>> "potato"["potato".length - 1]
```

"o"

One final example to illustrate the difference between a string primitive and a string object: let's convert them to boolean. The empty string is a falsy value, but any string object is truthy.

```
>>> Boolean("")
```

false

```
>>> Boolean(new String(""))
```

true

Similarly to `Number()` and `Boolean()`, if you use the `String()` function without `new`, it converts the parameter to a primitive string. This means calling `toString()` method, if the input is an object.

```
>>> String(1)
```

"1"

```
>>> String({p: 1})
```

"[object Object]"

```
>>> String([1,2,3])
```

"1,2,3"

Interesting Methods of the String Objects

Let's experiment with some of the methods you can call for string objects (see Appendix C for the full list).

Start off by creating a string object:

```
>>> var s = new String("Couch potato");
```

`toUpperCase()` and `toLowerCase()` are convenient ways to transform the capitalization of the string:

```
>>> s.toUpperCase()
```

"COUCH POTATO"

```
>>> s.toLowerCase()
```

"couch potato"

`charAt()` tells you the character found at the position you specify, which is the same as using square brackets (a string is an array of characters).

```
>>> s.charAt(0);
```

"C"

```
>>> s[0]
```

"C"

If you pass a non-existing position to `charAt()`, you get an empty string:

```
>>> s.charAt(101)
```

""

`indexOf()` allows you to search within a string. If there is a match, the method returns the position at which the first match is found. The position count starts at 0, so the second character in "Couch" is "o" at position 1.

```
>>> s.indexOf('o')
```

1

You can optionally specify where (at what position) to start the search. The following finds the second "o", because `indexOf()` is instructed to start the search at position 2:

```
>>> s.indexOf('o', 2)
```

7

`lastIndexOf()` starts the search from the end of the string (but the position of the match is still counted from the beginning):

```
>>> s.lastIndexOf('o')
```

11

You can search for strings, not only characters, and the search is case sensitive:

```
>>> s.indexOf('Couch')
```

0

If there is no match, the function returns a position -1:

```
>>> s.indexOf('couch')
```

-1

To perform a case-insensitive search you can transform the string to lowercase first and then search it:

```
>>> s.toLowerCase().indexOf('couch')
```

0

When you get 0, this means that the matching part of the string starts at position 0. This can cause confusion when you check with `if`, because `if` will convert the position 0 to a boolean `false`. So while this is syntactically correct, it is logically wrong:

```
if (s.indexOf('Couch')) {...}
```

The proper way to check if a string contains another string is to compare the result of `indexOf()` to the number -1.

```
if (s.indexOf('Couch') !== -1) {...}
```

`slice()` and `substring()` return a piece of the string when you specify start and end positions:

```
>>> s.slice(1, 5)
```

"ouch"

```
>>> s.substring(1, 5)
```

"ouch"

Note that the second parameter you pass is the end position, not the length of the piece. The difference between these two methods is how they treat negative arguments. `substring()` treats them as zeros, while `slice()` adds them to the length of the string. So if you pass parameters (1, -1) it's the same as `substring(1, 0)` and `slice(1, s.length - 1)`:

```
>>> s.slice(1, -1)
```

"ouch potat"

```
>>> s.substring(1, -1)
```

"C"

The `split()` method creates an array from the string, using a string that you pass as a separator:

```
>>> s.split(" ")
```

["Couch", "potato"]

`split()` is the opposite of `join()` which creates a string from an array:

```
>>> s.split(' ').join(' ');
```

"Couch potato"

`concat()` glues strings together, the way the + operator does for primitive strings:

```
>>> s.concat("es")
```

"Couch potatoes"

Note that while some of the methods discussed above return new primitive strings, none of them modify the source string. After all the methods we called, our initial string is still the same:

```
>>> s.valueOf()
```

"Couch potato"

We looked at `indexOf()` and `lastIndexOf()` to search within strings, but there are more powerful methods (`search()`, `match()`, and `replace()`) which take regular expressions as parameters. You'll see these later, when we get to the `RegExp()` constructor function.

At this point we're done with all of the data wrapper objects, so off we go to the utility objects `Math`, `Date`, and `RegExp`.

Math

`Math` is a little different from the other built-in global objects you saw above. It's not a normal function and therefore cannot be used with `new` to create objects. `Math` is a built-in global object, which provides a number of methods and properties that are useful for mathematical operations.

`Math`'s properties are constants so you can't change their values. Their names are all in upper case to emphasize the difference between them and a normal variable property. Let's see some of these constant properties:

The number π:

```
>>> Math.PI
```

3.141592653589793

Square root of 2:

```
>>> Math.SQRT2
```

1.4142135623730951

Euler's constant e:

```
>>> Math.E
```

2.718281828459045

Natural logarithm of 2:

```
>>> Math.LN2
```

0.6931471805599453

Natural logarithm of 10:

```
>>> Math.LN10
```

2.302585092994046

Now you know how to impress your friends the next time they (for whatever awkward reason) start wondering, "What was the value of *e*? I can't remember." Just type `Math.E` in the console and you have the answer.

Let's take a look at some of the methods the `Math` object provides (the full list is in Appendix C).

Generating random numbers:

```
>>> Math.random()
```

0.3649461670235814

`random()` returns a number between 0 and 1, so if you want a number between, let's say 0 and 100, you can do:

```
>>> 100 * Math.random()
```

For numbers between any two values `min` and `max`, use the formula `((max - min) * Math.random()) + min`. For example, a random number between 2 and 10 would be:

```
>>> 8 * Math.random() + 2
```

9.175650496668485

If you only need an integer, you can use one of rounding methods — `floor()` to round down, `ceil()` to round up or `round()` to round to the nearest. For example to get either 0 or 1:

```
>>> Math.round(Math.random())
```

If you need the lowest or the highest among a set of numbers, you have the methods `min()` and `max()`. So if you have a form on a page that asks for a valid month, you can make sure that you always work with sane data:

```
>>> Math.min(Math.max(1, input), 12)
```

The `Math` object also provides you with the ability to perform mathematical operations for which you don't have a designated operator. This means that you can raise to a power using `pow()`, find the square root using `sqrt()` and perform all the trigonometric operations — `sin()`, `cos()`, `atan()`, and so on.

2 to the power of 8:

```
>>> Math.pow(2, 8)
```

256

Square root of 9:

```
>>> Math.sqrt(9)
```

3

Date

`Date()` is a constructor function that creates date objects. You can create a new object by passing:

- Nothing (defaults to today's date)
- A date-like string
- Separate values for day, month, time, and so on
- A timestamp

An object instantiated with today's date/time:

```
>>> new Date()
```

Tue Jan 08 2008 01:10:42 GMT-0800 (Pacific Standard Time)

(As with all objects, the Firefox console displays the result of the `toString()` method, so this long string "Tue Jan 08...." is what you get when you call `toString()` on a date object.)

Here are some examples of using strings to initialize a date object. It's interesting how many different formats you can use to specify the date.

```
>>> new Date('2009 11 12')
```

Thu Nov 12 2009 00:00:00 GMT-0800 (Pacific Standard Time)

```
>>> new Date('1 1 2012')
```

Sun Jan 01 2012 00:00:00 GMT-0800 (Pacific Standard Time)

```
>>> new Date('1 mar 2012 5:30')
```

Thu Mar 01 2012 05:30:00 GMT-0800 (Pacific Standard Time)

It is good that JavaScript can figure out a date from different strings, but this is not really a reliable way of defining a precise date. The better way is to pass numeric values to the `Date()` constructor representing:

- Year
- Month: 0 (January) to 11 (December)
- Day: 1 to 31
- Hour: 0 to 23
- Minutes: 0 to 59
- Seconds: 0 to 59
- Milliseconds: 0 to 999

Let's see some examples.

Passing all the parameters:

```
>>> new Date(2008, 0, 1, 17, 05, 03, 120)
```

Tue Jan 01 2008 17:05:03 GMT-0800 (Pacific Standard Time)

Passing date and hour:

```
>>> new Date(2008, 0, 1, 17)
```

Tue Jan 01 2008 17:00:00 GMT-0800 (Pacific Standard Time)

Watch out for the fact that the month starts from 0, so 1 is February:

```
>>> new Date(2008, 1, 28)
```

Thu Feb 28 2008 00:00:00 GMT-0800 (Pacific Standard Time)

If you pass a value greater than allowed, your date "overflows" forward. Because there's no February 30 in 2008, this means it has to be March 1st (remember that 2008 was a leap-year).

```
>>> new Date(2008, 1, 29)
```

Fri Feb 29 2008 00:00:00 GMT-0800 (Pacific Standard Time)

```
>>> new Date(2008, 1, 30)
```

Sat Mar 01 2008 00:00:00 GMT-0800 (Pacific Standard Time)

Similarly, Dec 32nd becomes Jan 01st of the next year:

```
>>> new Date(2008, 11, 31)
```

Wed Dec 31 2008 00:00:00 GMT-0800 (Pacific Standard Time)

```
>>> new Date(2008, 11, 32)
```

Thu Jan 01 2009 00:00:00 GMT-0800 (Pacific Standard Time)

Finally, a date object can be initialized with a timestamp (the number of milliseconds since the UNIX epoch, where 0 milliseconds is 1st January 1970).

```
>>> new Date(1199865795109)
```

Wed Jan 09 2008 00:03:15 GMT-0800 (Pacific Standard Time)

If you call Date() without new, you get a string representing the current date, whether or not you pass any parameters. This gives the current time (current when this example was run):

```
>>> Date()
```

"Thu Jan 17 2008 23:11:32 GMT-0800 (Pacific Standard Time)"

```
>>> Date(1, 2, 3, "it doesn't matter");
```

"Thu Jan 17 2008 23:11:35 GMT-0800 (Pacific Standard Time)"

Methods to Work with Date Objects

Once you've created a date object, there are lots of methods you can call on that object. Most of the methods can be divided into `set*()` and `get*()` methods. For example `getMonth()`, `setMonth()`, `getHours()`, `setHours()`, and so on. Let's see some examples.

Creating a date object:

```
>>> var d = new Date();
>>> d.toString();
```

"Wed Jan 09 2008 00:26:39 GMT-0800 (Pacific Standard Time)"

Setting the month to March (months start from 0):

```
>>> d.setMonth(2);
```

1205051199562

```
>>> d.toString();
```

"Sun Mar 09 2008 00:26:39 GMT-0800 (Pacific Standard Time)"

Getting the month:

```
>>> d.getMonth();
```

2

In addition to all the methods of the date instances, there are also two methods that are properties of the `Date()` function/object. These do not need a date instance; they work just like `Math`'s methods. In class-based languages, such methods would be called "static" because they don't require an instance.

`Date.parse()` takes a string and returns a timestamp:

```
>>> Date.parse('Jan 1, 2008')
```

1199174400000

`Date.UTC()` takes all parameters for year, month, day, and so on, and produces a timestamp in Universal time.

```
>>> Date.UTC(2008, 0, 1)
```

1199145600000

Because the `new Date()` constructor can accept timestamps, you can pass the result of `Date.UTC()` to it. Using the following example you can see how `UTC()` works with universal time, while `new Date()` works with local time:

```
>>> new Date(Date.UTC(2008, 0, 1));
```

Mon Dec 31 2007 16:00:00 GMT-0800 (Pacific Standard Time)

```
>>> new Date(2008, 0, 1);
```

Tue Jan 01 2008 00:00:00 GMT-0800 (Pacific Standard Time)

Let's see one final example of working with the `Date` object. I was curious about which day my birthday falls on in 2012:

```
>>> var d = new Date(2012, 5, 20);
>>> d.getDay();
```

3

Starting the count from 0 (Sunday), 3 means Wednesday. Is that so?

```
>>> d.toDateString();
```

"Wed Jun 20 2012"

OK, Wednesday is good but not necessarily the best day for a party. So how about a loop that tells how many times June 20 is a Friday from year 2012 to year 3012. Actually, let's see the distribution of all the days of the week. (After all, with all the medical progress, we're all going to be alive and kicking in 3012.)

First, let's initialize an array with seven elements, one for each day of the week. These will be used as counters. As we loop our way up to 3012, we'll increment the counters.

```
var stats = [0,0,0,0,0,0,0];
```

The loop:

```
for (var i = 2012; i < 3012; i++) {
  stats[new Date(i, 5, 20).getDay()]++;
}
```

And the result:

```
>>> stats;
```

[139, 145, 139, 146, 143, 143, 145]

143 Fridays and 145 Saturdays. Woo-hoo!

RegExp

Regular expressions provide a powerful way to search and manipulate text. If you're familiar with SQL, you can think of regular expressions as being somewhat similar to SQL: you use SQL to find and update data inside a database, and you use regular expressions to find and update data inside a piece of text.

Different languages have different implementations (think "dialects") of the regular expressions syntax. JavaScript uses the Perl 5 syntax.

Instead of saying "regular expression", people often shorten it to "regex" or "regexp".

A regular expression consists of:

- A *pattern* you use to match text
- Zero or more *modifiers* (also called *flags*) that provide more instructions on how the pattern should be applied

The pattern can be as simple as literal text to be matched verbatim, but that is rare and in such cases you're better off using indexOf(). Most of the times, the pattern is more complex and could be difficult to understand. Mastering regular expressions patterns is a large topic, which won't be discussed in details here; instead, you'll see what JavaScript provides in terms of syntax, objects and methods in order to support the use of regular expressions. You can also refer to Appendix D as a reference when writing patterns.

JavaScript provides the RegExp() constructor which allows you to create regular expression objects.

```
>>> var re = new RegExp("j.*t");
```

There is also the more convenient regexp literal:

```
>>> var re = /j.*t/;
```

In the example above, j.*t is the regular expression pattern. It means, "Match any string that starts with j, ends with t and has zero or more characters in between". The asterisk * means "zero or more of the preceding"; the dot (.) means "any character". The pattern needs to be placed in quotation marks when used in a RegExp() constructor.

Properties of the RegExp Objects

The regular expression objects have the following properties:

- `global`: If this property is `false`, which is the default, the search stops when the first match is found. Set this to `true` if you want all matches.
- `ignoreCase`: Case sensitive match or not, defaults to `false`.
- `multiline`: Search matches that may span over more than one line, defaults to `false`.
- `lastIndex`: The position at which to start the search, defaults to 0.
- `source`: Contains the regexp pattern.

None of these properties, except for `lastIndex`, can be changed once the object has created.

The first three parameters represent the regex *modifiers*. If you create a regex object using the constructor, you can pass any combination of the following characters as a second parameter:

- "g" for `global`
- "i" for `ignoreCase`
- "m" for `multiline`

These letters can be in any order. If a letter is passed, the corresponding modifier is set to `true`. In the following example, all modifiers are set to `true`:

```
>>> var re = new RegExp('j.*t', 'gmi');
```

Let's verify:

```
>>> re.global;
```

true

Once set, the modifier cannot be changed:

```
>>> re.global = false;
>>> re.global
```

true

To set any modifiers using the regex literal, you add them after the closing slash.

```
>>> var re = /j.*t/ig;
>>> re.global
```

true

Methods of the RegExp Objects

The regex objects provide two methods you can use to find matches: `test()` and `exec()`. They both accept a string parameter. `test()` returns a boolean (`true` when there's a match, `false` otherwise), while `exec()` returns an array of matched strings. Obviously `exec()` is doing more work, so use `test()` unless you really need to do something with the matches. People often use regular expressions for validation purposes, in this case `test()` would probably be enough.

No match, because of the capital J:

```
>>> /j.*t/.test("Javascript")
```

false

Case insensitive test gives a positive result:

```
>>> /j.*t/i.test("Javascript")
```

true

The same test using `exec()` returns an array and you can access the first element as shown below:

```
>>> /j.*t/i.exec("Javascript")[0]
```

"Javascript"

String Methods that Accept Regular Expressions as Parameters

Previously in this chapter we talked about the `String` object and how you can use the methods `indexOf()` and `lastIndexOf()` to search within text. Using these methods you can only specify literal string patterns to search. A more powerful solution would be to use regular expressions to find text. String objects offer you this ability.

The string objects provide the following methods that accept regular expression objects as parameters:

- `match()` returns an array of matches
- `search()` returns the position of the first match
- `replace()` allows you to substitute matched text with another string
- `split()` also accepts a regexp when splitting a string into array elements

search() and match()

Let's see some examples of using the methods `search()` and `match()`. First, you create a string object.

```
>>> var s = new String('HelloJavaScriptWorld');
```

Using `match()` you get an array containing only the first match:

```
>>> s.match(/a/);
```

["a"]

Using the `g` modifier, you perform a global search, so the result array contains two elements:

```
>>> s.match(/a/g);
```

["a", "a"]

Case insensitive match:

```
>>> s.match(/j.*a/i);
```

["Java"]

The `search()` method gives you the position of the matching string:

```
>>> s.search(/j.*a/i);
```

5

replace()

`replace()` allows you to replace the matched text with some other string. The following example removes all capital letters (it replaces them with blank strings):

```
>>> s.replace(/[A-Z]/g, '');
```

"elloavacriptorld"

If you omit the `g` modifier, you're only going to replace the first match:

```
>>> s.replace(/[A-Z]/, '');
```

"elloJavaScriptWorld"

When a match is found, if you want to include the matched text in the replacement string, you can access it using `$&`. Here's how to add an underscore before the match while keeping the match:

```
>>> s.replace(/[A-Z]/g, "_$&");
```

"_Hello_Java_Script_World"

When the regular expression contains groups (denoted by parentheses), the matches of each group are available as `$1` is the first group, `$2` the second and so on.

```
>>> s.replace(/([A-Z])/g, "_$1");
```

"_Hello_Java_Script_World"

Imagine you have a registration form on your web page that asks for email address, username, and password. The user enters their email, and then your JavaScript kicks in and suggests the username, taking it from the email address:

```
>>> var email = "stoyan@phpied.com";
>>> var username = email.replace(/(.*)@.*/, "$1");
>>> username;
```

"stoyan"

Replace callbacks

When specifying the replacement, you can also pass a function that returns a string. This gives you the ability to implement any special logic you may need before specifying the replacements.

```
>>> function replaceCallback(match){return "_" +
            match.toLowerCase();}
>>> s.replace(/[A-Z]/g, replaceCallback);
```

"_hello_java_script_world"

The callback function will receive a number of parameters (we ignored all but the first one in the example above):

- The first parameter is the match
- The last is the string being searched
- The one before last is the position of the match
- The rest of the parameters contain any strings matched by any groups in your regex pattern

Let's test this. First, let's create a variable to store the whole arguments array passed to the callback function:

```
>>> var glob;
```

Next, we'll define a regular expression that has three groups and matches email addresses in the format something@something.something:

```
>>> var re = /(.*)@(.*)\.(.*)/;
```

Finally, we'll define a callback function that stores the arguments in glob and then returns the replacement:

```
var callback = function(){
  glob = arguments;
  return arguments[1] + ' at ' + arguments[2] + ' dot ' +
         arguments[3];
}
```

We can then call this as follows:

```
>>> "stoyan@phpied.com".replace(re, callback);
```

"stoyan at phpied dot com"

Here's what the callback function received as arguments:

```
>>> glob
```

["stoyan@phpied.com", "stoyan", "phpied", "com", 0, "stoyan@phpied.com"]

split()

You already know about the method split(), which creates an array from an input string and a delimiter string. Let's take a string of comma-separated values and split it:

```
>>> var csv = 'one, two,three ,four';
>>> csv.split(',');
```

["one", " two", "three ", "four"]

Because the input string has some inconsistent spaces before and after the commas, the array result has spaces too. With a regular expression, we can fix this, using \s*, which means "zero or more spaces":

```
>>> csv.split(/\s*,\s*/)
```

["one", "two", "three", "four"]

Passing a String When a regexp is Expected

One last thing to note is that the four methods you just saw (`split()`, `match()`, `search()`, and `replace()`) can also take strings as opposed to regular expressions. In this case the string argument is used to produce a new regex as if it was passed to `new RegExp()`.

Example of passing a string to replace:

```
>>> "test".replace('t', 'r')
```

"rest"

The above is the same as:

```
>>> "test".replace(new RegExp('t'), 'r')
```

"rest"

When you pass a string, you cannot set modifiers as you can with a normal constructor or regex literal.

Error Objects

Errors happen, and it's good to have the mechanisms in place so that your code can realize that there has been an error condition and recover from it in a graceful manner. JavaScript provides the statements `try`, `catch`, and `finally` to help you deal with errors. If an error occurs, an error object is thrown. Error objects are created by using one of these built-in constructors: `EvalError`, `RangeError`, `ReferenceError`, `SyntaxError`, `TypeError`, and `URIError`. All of these constructors inherit from the `Error` object.

Let's just cause an error and see what happens. An example of an error will be trying to call a function that doesn't exist. Type this into the Firebug console:

```
>>> iDontExist();
```

You'll get something like this:

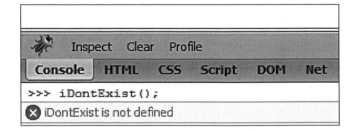

In the bottom right corner, instead of Firebug's usual icon, you'll see:

If you open Firefox's error console (**Tools | Error console**), you'll see:

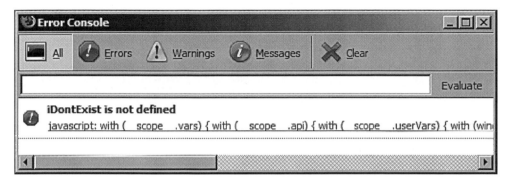

The display of errors can vary greatly between browsers and other host environments. In Internet Explorer you might see something like this in the lower left corner of the window:

If you double-click the message, you can get some more information:

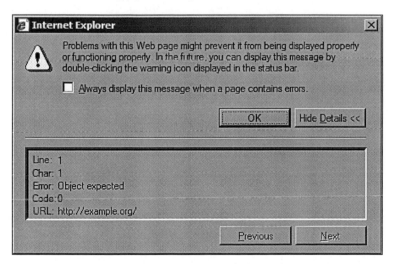

Depending on your browser's configuration, you might not even notice that an error occurred. However, you cannot assume that all of your users have disabled the display of errors and it is your responsibility to ensure an error-free experience for them. The error above propagated to the user because the code didn't try to trap (catch) this error, it didn't expect the error and was unprepared for handling it. Fortunately, it's really easy to trap the error. All you need is the `try` statement, followed by a `catch`.

This code will not cause any of the error displays from the screenshots above

```
try {
  iDontExist();
} catch (e) {
  // do nothing
}
```

Here you have:

- The `try` statement, followed by a block of code
- `catch` statement, followed by a variable name in parentheses and another block of code

There is also an optional `finally` statement, not used in this example, which is executed regardless of whether there was an error or not.

In the example above, the code block that follows the `catch` didn't do anything, but this is the place where you put the code that will recover from the error, or at least give some feedback to the user that you application is aware that there was a special condition.

The variable e in the parentheses after the `catch` statement contains an error object. Like any other object, it contains some useful properties and methods. Unfortunately, different browsers implement these methods and properties differently, but there are two properties that are consistently implemented — e.name and e.message.

Let's try this code now:

```
try {
  iDontExist();
} catch (e) {
  alert(e.name + ': ' + e.message);
} finally {
  alert('Finally!');
}
```

This will present an `alert()` showing e.name and e.message and then another `alert()` saying **Finally!**.

In Firefox, the first alert will say **ReferenceError: iDontExist is not defined**. In Internet Explorer it will be **TypeError: Object expected**. This tells us two things:

- e.name contains the name of the constructor that was used to create the error object.
- Because the error objects are not consistent across host environments (browsers), it would be somewhat tricky to have your code act differently depending on the type of error (the value of e.name).

You can also create error objects yourself using new Error() or any of the other error constructors, and then let the JavaScript engine know that there's an erroneous condition, using the throw statement.

For example, imagine a scenario where you call maybeExists() function and after that make some calculations. You want to trap all errors in a consistent way, no matter whether the error is that maybeExists() doesn't exist or that your calculations found a problem. Consider this code:

```
try {
  var total = maybeExists();
  if (total === 0) {
    throw new Error('Division by zero!');
  } else {
    alert(50 / total);
  }
} catch (e){
  alert(e.name + ': ' + e.message);
} finally {
  alert('Finally!');
}
```

This code will alert() different messages, depending on whether or not maybeExists() is defined and the values it returns:

- If maybeExists() doesn't exist, you get **ReferenceError: maybeExists() is not defined** in Firefox and **TypeError: Object expected** in IE
- If maybeExists() returns 0, you'll get **Error: Division by zero!**
- If maybeExists() returns 2, you'll get an alert that says **25**

In all cases, there will be a second alert that says **Finally!**

Instead of throwing a generic error `throw new Error('Division by zero!')`, you can be more specific if you choose to, for example, by throwing `throw new RangeError('Division by zero!')`. Alternatively, you don't need any constructor; you can simply throw a normal object:

```
throw {
  name: "MyError",
  message: "OMG! Something terrible has happened"
}
```

Summary

In Chapter 2, you saw that there are five primitive data types (number, string, boolean, null, and undefined) and we also said that everything that is not a primitive piece of data is an object. Now you also know that:

- Objects are like arrays but you specify the keys.
- Objects contain properties.
- Some of the properties can be functions (functions are data, `var f = function(){};`). Properties that are functions are also called methods.
- Arrays are actually objects with predefined numeric properties and a `length` property.
- Array objects have a number of useful methods (such as `sort()` or `slice()`).
- Functions are also objects and they have properties (such as `length` and `prototype`) and methods (such as `call()` and `apply()`).

Regarding the five primitive data types, apart from `undefined` (which is essentially nothing) and `null` (which is also an object), the other three have corresponding constructor functions: `Number()`, `String()`, and `Boolean()`. Using these, you can create objects, called wrapper objects, which contain some useful methods for working with primitive data elements.

`Number()`, `String()`, and `Boolean()` can be invoked:

- With the `new` operator—to create new objects
- Without `new`—to convert any value to a corresponding primitive data type

Other built-in constructor functions you're now familiar with include: `Object()`, `Array()`, `Function()`, `Date()`, `RegExp()`, and `Error()`. You are also familiar with `Math`, which is not a constructor.

Now you can see how objects have a central role in the JavaScript programming, as pretty much everything is an object or can be wrapped into an object.

Finally, let's wrap up the literal notations you're now familiar with.

Name	literal	constructor	Example
Object	{}	new Object()	{prop: 1}
Array	[]	new Array()	[1,2,3,'test']
regular expression	/pattern/modifiers	new RegExp('pattern', 'modifiers')	/java.*/img

Exercises

1. Look at this code:

```
function F() {
  function C() {
    return this;
  }
  return C();
}
var o = new F();
```

The value of this refers to the global object or the object o?

2. What's the result of executing this piece of code?

```
function C(){
  this.a = 1;
  return false;
}
console.log(typeof new C());
```

3. What's the result of executing the following piece of code?

```
>>> c = [1, 2, [1, 2]];
>>> c.sort();
>>> c.join('--');
>>> console.log(c);
```

4. Imagine the String() constructor didn't exist. Create a constructor function MyString() that acts like String() as closely as possible. You're not allowed to use any built-in string methods or properties, and remember that String() doesn't exist. You can use this code to test your constructor:

```
>>> var s = new MyString('hello');
>>> s.length;
```

5

```
>>> s[0];
```
"h"
```
>>> s.toString();
```
"hello"
```
>>> s.valueOf();
```
"hello"
```
>>> s.charAt(1);
```
"e"
```
>>> s.charAt('2');
```
"l"
```
>>> s.charAt('e');
```
"h"
```
>>> s.concat(' world!');
```
"hello world!"
```
>>> s.slice(1,3);
```
"el"
```
>>> s.slice(0,-1);
```
"hell"
```
>>> s.split('e');
```
["h", "llo"]
```
>>> s.split('l');
```
["he", "", "o"]

 You can use a for-in to loop through the input string, treating it as an array.

5. Update your MyString() constructor to include a reverse() method.

Try to leverage the fact that arrays have a `reverse()` method.

6. Imagine `Array()` doesn't exist and the array literal notation doesn't exist either. Create a constructor called `MyArray()` that behaves as close to `Array()` as possible. Test with this code:

```
>>> var a = new MyArray(1,2,3,"test");
>>> a.toString();
```

"1,2,3,test"

```
>>> a.length;
```

4

```
>>> a[a.length - 1]
```

"test"

```
>>> a.push('boo');
```

5

```
>>> a.toString();
```

"1,2,3,test,boo"

```
>>> a.pop();
```

[1, 2, 3, "test"]

```
>>> a.toString();
```

"1,2,3,test"

```
>>> a.join(',')
```

"1,2,3,test"

```
>>> a.join(' isn\'t ')
```

"1 isn't 2 isn't 3 isn't test"

If you found this exercise amusing, don't stop with the `join()`; go on with as many methods as possible.

7. Imagine `Math` didn't exist. Create a `MyMath` object that also provides some additional methods:

    *   `MyMath.rand(min, max, inclusive)` — generates a random number between `min` and `max`, inclusive if `inclusive` is `true` (default)

    *   `MyMath.min(array)` — returns the smallest number in a given array

    *   `MyMath.max(array)` — returns the largest number in a given array

5
Prototype

In this chapter you'll learn about the `prototype` property of the function objects. Understanding how the prototype works is an important part of learning the JavaScript language. After all, JavaScript is classified as having a prototype-based object model. There's nothing particularly difficult about the prototype, but it is a new concept and as such may sometimes take some time to sink in. It's one of these things in JavaScript (closures are another) which, once you "get" them, they seem so obvious and make perfect sense. As with the rest of the book, you're strongly encouraged to type in and play around with the examples; this makes it much easier to learn and remember the concepts.

The following topics are discussed in this chapter:

- Every function has a `prototype` property and it contains an object
- Adding properties to the prototype object
- Using the properties added to the prototype
- The difference between own properties and properties of the prototype
- `__proto__`, the secret link every object keeps to its prototype
- Methods such as `isPrototypeOf()`, `hasOwnProperty()`, and `propertyIsEnumerable()`
- How to enhance built-in objects, such as arrays or strings

The prototype Property

The functions in JavaScript are objects and they contain methods and properties. Some of the methods that you are already familiar with are `apply()` and `call()` and some of the properties are `length` and `constructor`. Another property of the function objects is `prototype`.

If you define a simple function `foo()` you can access its properties as you would do with any other object:

```
>>> function foo(a, b){return a * b;}
>>> foo.length
```

2

```
>>> foo.constructor
```

Function()

`prototype` is a property that gets created as soon as you define the function. Its initial value is an empty object.

```
>>> typeof foo.prototype
```

"object"

It's as if you added this property yourself like this:

```
>>> foo.prototype = {}
```

You can augment this empty object with properties and methods. They won't have any effect of the `foo()` function itself; they'll only be used when you use `foo()` as a constructor.

Adding Methods and Properties Using the Prototype

In the previous chapter you learned how to define constructor functions which can be used to create (construct) new objects. The main idea was that inside a function invoked with `new` you have access to the value `this`, which contains the object to be returned by the constructor. Augmenting (adding methods and properties to) `this` object is the way to add functionality to the object being created.

Let's take a look at the constructor function `Gadget()` which uses `this` to add two properties and one method to the objects it creates.

```
function Gadget(name, color) {
  this.name = name;
  this.color = color;
  this.whatAreYou = function(){
    return 'I am a ' + this.color + ' ' + this.name;
  }
}
```

Adding methods and properties to the `prototype` property of the constructor function is another way to add functionality to the objects this constructor produces. Let's add two more properties, `price` and `rating`, and a `getInfo()` method. Since `prototype` contains an object, you can just keep adding to it like this:

```
Gadget.prototype.price = 100;
Gadget.prototype.rating = 3;
Gadget.prototype.getInfo = function() {
  return 'Rating: ' + this.rating + ', price: ' + this.price;
};
```

Instead of adding to the `prototype` object, another way to achieve the above result is to overwrite the prototype completely, replacing it with an object of your choice:

```
Gadget.prototype = {
  price: 100,
  rating: 3,
  getInfo: function() {
    return 'Rating: ' + this.rating + ', price: ' + this.price;
  }
};
```

Using the Prototype's Methods and Properties

All the methods and properties you have added to the prototype are directly available as soon as you create a new object using the constructor. If you create a `newtoy` object using the `Gadget()` constructor, you can access all the methods and properties already defined.

```
>>> var newtoy = new Gadget('webcam', 'black');
>>> newtoy.name;
```

"webcam"

```
>>> newtoy.color;
```

"black"

```
>>> newtoy.whatAreYou();
```

"I am a black webcam"

```
>>> newtoy.price;
```

100

```
>>> newtoy.rating;
```

3

```
>>> newtoy.getInfo();
```

"Rating: 3, price: 100"

It's important to note that the prototype is "live". Objects are passed by reference in JavaScript, and therefore the prototype is not copied with every new object instance. What does this mean in practice? It means that you can modify the prototype at any time and all objects (even those created before the modification) will inherit the changes.

Let's continue the example, adding a new method to the prototype:

```
Gadget.prototype.get = function(what) {
  return this[what];
};
```

Even though newtoy was created *before* the get() method was defined, newtoy will still have access to the new method:

```
>>> newtoy.get('price');
```

100

```
>>> newtoy.get('color');
```

"black"

Own Properties versus prototype Properties

In the example above getInfo() used this internally to address the object. It could've also used Gadget.prototype to achieve the same result:

```
Gadget.prototype.getInfo = function() {
  return 'Rating: ' + Gadget.prototype.rating + ', price: ' + Gadget.
prototype.price;
};
```

What's is the difference? To answer this question, let's examine how the prototype works in more detail.

Let's again take our newtoy object:

```
>>> var newtoy = new Gadget('webcam', 'black');
```

When you try to access a property of `newtoy`, say `newtoy.name` the JavaScript engine will look through all of the properties of the object searching for one called `name` and, if it finds it, will return its value.

```
>>> newtoy.name
```

"webcam"

What if you try to access the `rating` property? The JavaScript engine will examine all of the properties of `newtoy` and will not find the one called `rating`. Then the script engine will identify the prototype of the constructor function used to create this object (same as if you do `newtoy.constructor.prototype`). If the property is found in the prototype, this property is used.

```
>>> newtoy.rating
```

3

This would be the same as if you accessed the prototype directly. Every object has a constructor property, which is a reference to the function that created the object, so in our case:

```
>>> newtoy.constructor
```

Gadget(name, color)

```
>>> newtoy.constructor.prototype.rating
```

3

Now let's take this lookup one step further. Every object has a constructor. The prototype is an object, so it must have a constructor too. Which in turn has a prototype. In other words you can do:

```
>>> newtoy.constructor.prototype.constructor
```

Gadget(name, color)

```
>>> newtoy.constructor.prototype.constructor.prototype
```

Object price=100 rating=3

This might go on for a while, depending on how long the prototype chain is, but you eventually end up with the built-in `Object()` object, which is the highest-level parent. In practice, this means that if you try `newtoy.toString()` and `newtoy` doesn't have an own `toString()` method and its prototype doesn't either, in the end you'll get the Object's `toString()`

```
>>> newtoy.toString()
```

"[object Object]"

Overwriting Prototype's Property with Own Property

As the above discussion demonstrates, if one of your objects doesn't have a certain property of its own, it can use one (if exists) somewhere up the prototype chain. What if the object does have its own property and the prototype also has one with the same name? The own property takes precedence over the prototype's.

Let's have a scenario where a property name exists both as an own property and as a property of the prototype object:

```
function Gadget(name) {
  this.name = name;
}
Gadget.prototype.name = 'foo';
```

"foo"

Creating a new object and accessing its `name` property gives you the object's own `name` property.

```
>>> var toy = new Gadget('camera');
>>> toy.name;
```

"camera"

If you delete this property, the prototype's property with the same name "shines through":

```
>>> delete toy.name;
```

true

```
>>> toy.name;
```

"foo"

Of course, you can always re-create the object's own property:

```
>>> toy.name = 'camera';
>>> toy.name;
```

"camera"

Enumerating Properties

If you want to list all properties of an object, you can use a `for-in` loop. In Chapter 2, you saw how you could loop through all the elements of an array:

```
var a = [1, 2, 3];
for (var i in a) {
  console.log(a[i]);
}
```

Arrays are objects, so you can expect that the `for-in` loop works for objects too:

```
var o = {p1: 1, p2: 2};
for (var i in o) {
  console.log(i + '=' + o[i]);
}
```

This produces:

p1=1

p2=2

There are some details to be aware of:

- Not all properties show up in a `for-in` loop. For example, the `length` (for arrays) and `constructor` properties will not show up. The properties that do show up are called *enumerable*. You can check which ones are enumerable with the help of the `propertyIsEnumerable()` method that every object provides.
- Prototypes that come through the prototype chain will also show up, provided they are enumerable. You can check if a property is an own property versus prototype's using the `hasOwnProperty()` method.
- `propertyIsEnumerable()` will return `false` for all of the prototype's properties, even those that are enumerable and will show up in the `for-in` loop.

Let's see these methods in action. Take this simplified version of `Gadget()`:

```
function Gadget(name, color) {
  this.name = name;
  this.color = color;
  this.someMethod = function(){return 1;}
}
Gadget.prototype.price = 100;
Gadget.prototype.rating = 3;
```

Creating a new object:

```
var newtoy = new Gadget('webcam', 'black');
```

Now if you loop using a for-in, you see of the object's all properties, including those that come from the prototype:

```
for (var prop in newtoy) {
  console.log(prop + ' = ' + newtoy[prop]);
}
```

The result also contains the object's methods (as methods are just properties that happen to be functions):

name = webcam

color = black

someMethod = function () { return 1; }

price = 100

rating = 3

If you want to distinguish between the object's own properties versus the prototype's properties, use hasOwnProperty(). Try first:

```
>>> newtoy.hasOwnProperty('name')
```

true

```
>>> newtoy.hasOwnProperty('price')
```

false

Let's loop again, but showing only own properties:

```
for (var prop in newtoy) {
  if (newtoy.hasOwnProperty(prop)) {
    console.log(prop + '=' + newtoy[prop]);
  }
}
```

The result:

name=webcam

color=black

someMethod=function () { return 1; }

Now let's try `propertyIsEnumerable()`. This method returns `true` for own properties that are not built-in:

```
>>> newtoy.propertyIsEnumerable('name')
```

true

Most built-in properties and methods are not enumerable:

```
>>> newtoy.propertyIsEnumerable('constructor')
```

false

Any properties coming down the prototype chain are not enumerable:

```
>>> newtoy.propertyIsEnumerable('price')
```

false

Note, however, that such properties are enumerable if you reach the object contained in the prototype and invoke its `propertyIsEnumerable()`.

```
>>> newtoy.constructor.prototype.propertyIsEnumerable('price')
```

true

isPrototypeOf()

Every object also gets the `isPrototypeOf()` method. This method tells you whether that specific object is used as a prototype of another object.

Let's take a simple object `monkey`.

```
var monkey = {
  hair: true,
  feeds: 'bananas',
  breathes: 'air'
};
```

Now let's create a `Human()` constructor function and set its `prototype` property to point to `monkey`.

```
function Human(name) {
  this.name = name;
}
Human.prototype = monkey;
```

Now if you create a new `Human` object called `george` and ask: "Is `monkey` `george`'s prototype?", you'll get `true`.

```
>>> var george = new Human('George');
>>> monkey.isPrototypeOf(george)
```

true

The Secret __proto__ Link

As you know already, the prototype property will be consulted when you try to access a property that does not exist in the current object.

Let's again have an object called `monkey` and use it as a prototype when creating objects with the `Human()` constructor.

```
var monkey = {
  feeds: 'bananas',
  breathes: 'air'
};
function Human() {}
Human.prototype = monkey;
```

Now let's create a `developer` object and give it some properties:

```
var developer = new Human();
developer.feeds = 'pizza';
developer.hacks = 'JavaScript';
```

Now let's consult some of the properties. `hacks` is a property of the `developer` object.

```
>>> developer.hacks
```

"JavaScript"

`feeds` could also be found in the object.

```
>>> developer.feeds
```

"pizza"

`breathes` doesn't exist as a property of the `developer` object, so the prototype is looked up, as if there is a secret link pointing to the prototype object.

```
>>> developer.breathes
```

"air"

Can you get from the developer object to the prototype object? Well, you could, using `constructor` as the middleman, so having something like `developer.constructor.prototype` should point to `monkey`. The problem is that this is not very reliable, because `constructor` is more for informational purposes and can easily be overwritten at any time. You can overwrite it with something that's not even an object and this will not affect the normal functioning of the prototype chain.

Let's set the constructor property to some string:

```
>>> developer.constructor = 'junk'
```

"junk"

It seems like the `prototype` is now all messed up:

```
>>> typeof developer.constructor.prototype
```

"undefined"

...but it isn't, because the `developer` still `breathes` **"air"**:

```
>>> developer.breathes
```

"air"

This shows that the secret link to the prototype still exists. The secret link is exposed in Firefox as the __proto__ property (the word "proto" with two underscores before and two after).

```
>>> developer.__proto__
```

Object feeds=bananas breathes=air

You can use this secret property for learning purposes but it's not a good idea to use it in your real scripts, because it does not exist in Internet Explorer, so your scripts won't be portable. For example, let's say you have created a number of objects with `monkey` as a prototype and now you want to change something in all objects. You can change `monkey` and all instances will inherit the change:

```
>>> monkey.test = 1
```

1

```
>>> developer.test
```

1

__proto__ is not the same as prototype. __proto__ is a property of the instances, whereas prototype is a property of the constructor functions.

```
>>> typeof developer.__proto__
```

"object"

```
>>> typeof developer.prototype
```

"undefined"

Once again, you should use __proto__ only for learning or debugging purposes.

Augmenting Built-in Objects

The built-in objects such as the constructor functions Array, String, and even Object, and Function can be augmented through their prototypes, which means that you can, for example, add new methods to the Array prototype and in this way make them available to all arrays. Let's do this.

In PHP there is a function called in_array() that tells you if a value exists in an array. In JavaScript there is no inArray() method, so let's implement it and add it to Array.prototype.

```
Array.prototype.inArray = function(needle) {
  for (var i = 0, len = this.length; i < len; i++) {
    if (this[i] === needle) {
      return true;
    }
  }
  return false;
}
```

Now all arrays will have the new method. Let's test:

```
>>> var a = ['red', 'green', 'blue'];
>>> a.inArray('red');
```

true

```
>>> a.inArray('yellow');
```

false

That was nice and easy! Let's do it again. Imagine your application often needs to reverse strings and you feel there should be a built-in `reverse()` method for string objects. After all, arrays have `reverse()`. You can easily add this `reverse()` method to the String prototype, borrowing `Array.prototype.reverse()` (there was a similar exercise at the end of Chapter 4).

```
String.prototype.reverse = function() {
    return Array.prototype.reverse.apply(this.split('')).join('');
}
```

This code uses `split()` to create an array from a string, then calls the `reverse()` method on this array, which produces a reversed array. The result array is turned back into a string using `join()`. Let's test the new method:

```
>>> "Stoyan".reverse();
```

"nayotS"

Augmenting Built-in Objects—Discussion

Augmenting built-in objects through the prototype is a very powerful technique and you can use it to shape JavaScript any way you like. Because of its power, you should always thoroughly consider your options before using this approach.

Take the popular JavaScript library called Prototype. Its creator liked this approach so much that he even named the library after it. Using this library, you can work with JavaScript using methods very similar to the Ruby language.

YUI (Yahoo! User Interface) library is another popular JavaScript library. Its creators are on the exact opposite side of the spectrum: they won't modify the built-in objects in any way. The reason is that once you know JavaScript, you're expecting it to work the same way, no matter which library you're using. Modifying core objects could only confuse the user of the library and create unexpected errors.

The fact is that JavaScript changes and browsers come up with new versions that support more features. What you consider a missing feature today and decide to augment a prototype for, might be a built-in method tomorrow. In this case, your method is no longer needed. However, what if you have already written a lot of code that uses the method and your method is slightly different from the new built-in implementation?

The very least you can do is check if the method exists before implementing it. Our last example should read something like:

```
if (!String.prototype.reverse) {
  String.prototype.reverse = function() {
    return Array.prototype.reverse.apply(this.split('')).join('');
  }
}
```

> **Best Practice**
>
> If you decide to augment the prototype of built-in objects with a new property, do check for existence of the new property first.

Some Prototype gotchas

Here are two interesting behaviors to consider when dealing with prototypes:

- The prototype chain is live with the exception of when you completely replace the prototype object
- `prototype.constructor` is not reliable

Creating a simple constructor function and two objects:

```
>>> function Dog(){this.tail = true;}
>>> var benji = new Dog();
>>> var rusty = new Dog();
```

Even after you create the objects, you can still add properties to the prototype and the objects will have access to the new properties. Let's throw in the method `say()`:

```
>>> Dog.prototype.say = function(){return 'Woof!';}
```

Both objects have access to the new method:

```
>>> benji.say();
```

"Woof!"

```
>>> rusty.say();
```

"Woof!"

Up to this point if you consult your objects, asking which constructor function was used to create them, they'll report it correctly.

```
>>> benji.constructor;
```

Dog()

```
>>> rusty.constructor;
```

Dog()

It is interesting to note that if you ask what is the constructor of the prototype object, you'll also get Dog(), which is not quite correct. The prototype is just a normal object created with Object(). It doesn't have any of the properties of an object constructed with Dog().

```
>>> benji.constructor.prototype.constructor
```

Dog()

```
>>> typeof benji.constructor.prototype.tail
```

"undefined"

Now let's completely overwrite the prototype object with a brand new object:

```
>>> Dog.prototype = {paws: 4, hair: true};
```

It turns out that our old objects do not get access to the new prototype's properties; they still keep the secret link pointing to the old prototype object:

```
>>> typeof benji.paws
```

"undefined"

```
>>> benji.say()
```

"Woof!"

```
>>> typeof benji.__proto__.say
```

"function"

```
>>> typeof benji.__proto__.paws
```

"undefined"

Any new objects you create from now on will use the updated prototype:

```
>>> var lucy = new Dog();
>>> lucy.say()
```

TypeError: lucy.say is not a function

```
>>> lucy.paws
```

4

The secret __proto__ link points to the new prototype object:

```
>>> typeof lucy.__proto__.say
```

"undefined"

```
>>> typeof lucy.__proto__.paws
```

"number"

Now the constructor property of the new objects no longer reports correctly. It should point to Dog(), but instead it points to Object().

```
>>> lucy.constructor
```

Object()

```
>>> benji.constructor
```

Dog()

The most confusing part is when you look up the prototype of the constructor:

```
>>> typeof lucy.constructor.prototype.paws
```

"undefined"

```
>>> typeof benji.constructor.prototype.paws
```

"number"

The following would have fixed all of the unexpected behavior described above:

```
>>> Dog.prototype = {paws: 4, hair: true};
>>> Dog.prototype.constructor = Dog;
```

[**Best Practice**
When you overwrite the prototype, it is a good idea to reset the
constructor property.]

Summary

Let's summarize the most important topics you have learned in this chapter.

- All functions have a property called `prototype`. Initially it contains an empty object.
- You can add properties and methods to the prototype object. You can even replace it completely with an object of your choice.
- When you create objects using a function as a constructor (with `new`), the objects will have a secret link pointing to their prototype, and can access the prototype's properties as their own.
- Own properties take precedence over prototype's properties with the same name.
- Use the `hasOwnProperty()` method to differentiate between own properties and prototype properties.
- There is a prototype chain: if your object `foo` doesn't have a property `bar`, when you do `foo.bar`, JavaScript will look for a `bar` property of the prototype. If none is found, it will keep searching in the prototype's prototype, then the prototype of the prototype's prototype and keep going all the way up to the highest-level parent `Object`.
- You can augment built-in constructor functions and all objects will see your additions. Assign a function to `Array.prototype.flip` and all arrays will immediately get a `flip()` method, `[1,2,3].flip()`. Do check if the method/property you want to add already exists, so you can future-proof your scripts.

Exercises

1. Create an object called `shape` that has a `type` property and a `getType()` method.
2. Define a `Triangle()` constructor function whose prototype is `shape`. Objects created with `Triangle()` should have three own properties—a, b, c representing the sides of a triangle.
3. Add a new method to the prototype called `getPerimeter()`.

4. Test your implementation with this code:

```
>>> var t = new Triangle(1, 2, 3);
>>> t.constructor
```

Triangle(a, b, c)

```
>>> shape.isPrototypeOf(t)
```

true

```
>>> t.getPerimeter()
```

6

```
>>> t.getType()
```

"triangle"

5. Loop over t showing only own properties and methods (none of the prototype's).

6. Make this code work:

```
>>> [1,2,3,4,5,6,7,8,9].shuffle()
```

[2, 4, 1, 8, 9, 6, 5, 3, 7]

6
Inheritance

If you go back to Chapter 1 and review the section that listed the different aspects of object-oriented programming, you will see that you already know how most of them apply to JavaScript. You know what objects, methods, and properties are. You know that there are no classes in JavaScript, although you can fake them with constructor functions. Encapsulation? Yes, the objects encapsulate both the data and the means (methods) to do something with the data. Aggregation? Sure, an object can contain other objects. Actually, this is almost always the case as methods are functions, and functions are also objects. Now let's focus on the inheritance part. This is one of the most interesting features, as it allows you to reuse existing code, thus promoting laziness, which is probably what brought us to computer programming in the first place.

JavaScript is a dynamic language and there is usually more than one way to achieve any given task. Inheritance is not an exception to this and in this chapter, you'll see some common patterns for implementing inheritance, starting with the way specified in the ECMAScript standard. Having a good understanding of these patterns will help you pick the right one, or the right mix, depending on your project and your style.

You'll see the name of Douglas Crockford mentioned a few times in this chapter; it's hard to talk about JavaScript and inheritance without quoting his work. In addition to the videos, mentioned in Chapter 1 (`http://developer.yahoo.com/yui/theater/`), you can also read the articles on his website at `http://crockford.com/javascript`.

Prototype Chaining

Let's start with the default way of implementing inheritance—inheritance chaining through the prototype.

As you already know, every function has a `prototype` property, which contains an object. When this function is invoked using the `new` operator, an object is created and this object has a secret link to the prototype object. The secret link (called __proto__ in some environments) allows methods and properties of the prototype object to be used as if they belong to the newly-created object.

The prototype object is just a regular object and therefore it also contains a link to its prototype. And so a chain is created, called a prototype chain.

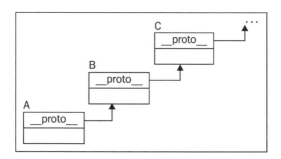

In this illustration, an object **A** contains a number of properties. One of the properties is the hidden __proto__ property, which points to another object, **B**. **B**'s __proto__ property points to **C**. This chain ends with the `Object` object, which is the highest-level parent, and every object inherits from it.

This is all good to know, but how does it help us? The practical side is that when object **A** lacks a property but **B** has it, **A** can still access this property as its own. The same applies if **B** also doesn't have the required property, but **C** does. This is how inheritance takes place: an object can access any property found somewhere up the inheritance chain.

Throughout the rest of this chapter, you'll see different examples that use the following hierarchy: a generic *Shape* parent is inherited by *2D* shape, which in turn is inherited by any number of specific two-dimensional shapes such as *Triangle*, *Rectangle*, and so on.

Prototype Chaining Example

Prototype chaining is the default way to implement inheritance, and is described in the ECMAScript standard. In order to implement our hierarchy, let's define three constructor functions.

```
function Shape(){
  this.name = 'shape';
  this.toString = function() {return this.name;};
}
```

```
function TwoDShape(){
  this.name = '2D shape';
}

function Triangle(side, height) {
  this.name = 'Triangle';
  this.side = side;
  this.height = height;
  this.getArea = function(){return this.side * this.height / 2;};
}
```

The code that performs the inheritance magic is as follows:

```
TwoDShape.prototype = new Shape();
Triangle.prototype = new TwoDShape();
```

What is happening here? You take the object contained in the prototype property of TwoDShape and instead of augmenting it with individual properties, you completely overwrite it with another object, created by invoking the Shape() constructor with new. The same for Triangle: its prototype is replaced with an object created by new TwoDShape(). The important thing to note, especially if you are already familiar with a language such as Java, C++, or PHP, is that JavaScript works with objects, not classes. You need to create an instance using the new Shape() constructor and after that you can inherit its properties; you don't inherit from Shape() directly. Additionally, after inheriting, you can modify Shape(), overwrite it or even delete it, and this will have no effect on TwoDShape, because all you needed was one instance to inherit from.

As you know from the previous chapter, when you completely overwrite the prototype (as opposed to just augmenting it), this has some negative side effects on the constructor property. Therefore, it's a good idea to reset the constructor after inheriting:

```
TwoDShape.prototype.constructor = TwoDShape;
Triangle.prototype.constructor = Triangle;
```

Now let's test what we have so far. Creating a Triangle object and calling its own getArea() method works as expected:

```
>>> var my = new Triangle(5, 10);
>>> my.getArea();
```

25

Although the my object doesn't have its own toString() method, it inherited one and can call it. Note how the inherited method toString() binds the this object to my.

```
>>> my.toString()
```

"Triangle"

It's interesting to note what the JavaScript engine does when you call my.toString():

- It loops through all of the properties of my and doesn't find a method called toString().
- It looks at the object that my.__proto__ points to; this object is the instance new TwoDShape() created during the inheritance process.
- Now the JavaScript engine loops through the instance of TwoDShape and doesn't find a toString() method. It then checks the __proto__ of that object. This time __proto__ points to the instance created by new Shape().
- The instance of new Shape() is examined and toString() is finally found!
- This method is invoked in the context of my, meaning that this points to my.

If you ask my, "who's your constructor?" it will report it correctly because of the constructor property reset that we did after inheriting:

```
>>> my.constructor
```

Triangle(side, height)

Using the instanceof operator you can validate that my is an instance of all three constructors.

```
>>> my instanceof Shape
```

true

```
>>> my instanceof TwoDShape
```

true

```
>>> my instanceof Triangle
```

true

```
>>> my instanceof Array
```

false

The same happens when you call the `isPropertyOf()` method of the constructors passing my:

```
>>> Shape.prototype.isPrototypeOf(my)
```

true

```
>>> TwoDShape.prototype.isPrototypeOf(my)
```

true

```
>>> Triangle.prototype.isPrototypeOf(my)
```

true

```
>>> String.prototype.isPrototypeOf(my)
```

false

You can also create objects using the other two constructors. Objects created with new `TwoDShape()` also get the method `toString()`, inherited from `Shape()`

```
>>> var td = new TwoDShape();
>>> td.constructor
```

TwoDShape()

```
>>> td.toString()
```

"2D shape"

```
>>> var s = new Shape();
>>> s.constructor
```

Shape()

Moving Shared Properties to the Prototype

When you create objects using a constructor function, own properties are added using `this`. This could be inefficient in cases where properties don't change across instances. In the example above, `Shape()` was defined like so:

```
function Shape(){
    this.name = 'shape';
}
```

This means that every time you create a new object using new `Shape()` a new `name` property will be created and stored somewhere in memory. The other option is to have the `name` property added to the prototype and shared among all the instances:

```
function Shape(){}
Shape.prototype.name = 'shape';
```

Now every time you create an object using `new Shape()`, this object will not have its own property `name`, but will use the one added to the prototype. This is more efficient, but you should only use it for properties that don't change from one instance to another. Methods are ideal for this type of sharing.

Let's improve on the example above by adding all methods and suitable properties to the `prototype`. In the case of `Shape()` and `TwoDShape()` everything is meant to be shared:

```
function Shape(){}
// augment prototype
Shape.prototype.name = 'shape';
Shape.prototype.toString = function() {return this.name;};
function TwoDShape(){}
// take care of inheritance
TwoDShape.prototype = new Shape();
TwoDShape.prototype.constructor = TwoDShape;
// augment prototype
TwoDShape.prototype.name = '2D shape';
```

As you can see you have to take care of inheritance first before augmenting the prototype, otherwise anything you add to `TwoDShape.prototype` will be wiped out when you inherit.

The `Triangle` constructor is a little different, because every object it creates is a new triangle, which may have different dimensions. So it's good to keep `side` and `height` as its own properties and share the rest. The method `getArea()`, for example, is the same regardless of the actual dimensions of each triangle. Again, you do the inheritance bit first and then augment the prototype.

```
function Triangle(side, height) {
  this.side = side;
  this.height = height;
}
// take care of inheritance
Triangle.prototype = new TwoDShape();
Triangle.prototype.constructor = Triangle;
// augment prototype
Triangle.prototype.name = 'Triangle';
Triangle.prototype.getArea = function(){return this.side * this.height
/ 2;};
```

All the test code from above will work in exactly the same way, for example:

```
>>> var my = new Triangle(5, 10);
>>> my.getArea()
```

25

```
>>> my.toString()
```

"Triangle"

There is only a slight behind-the-scenes difference when calling `my.toString()`. The difference is that there is one more lookup to be done before the method is found in the `Shape.prototype`, as opposed to in the `new Shape()` instance like it was in the previous example.

You can also play with `hasOwnProperty()` to see the difference between the own property versus a property coming down the prototype chain.

```
>>> my.hasOwnProperty('side')
```

true

```
>>> my.hasOwnProperty('name')
```

false

The calls to `isPrototypeOf()` and the `instanceof` operator from the previous example will work in exactly the same way, like:

```
>>> TwoDShape.prototype.isPrototypeOf(my)
```

true

```
>>> my instanceof Shape
```

true

Inheriting the Prototype Only

As explained above, for reasons of efficiency you should consider adding the reusable properties and methods to the prototype. If you do so, then it's probably a good idea to inherit only the prototype, because all the reusable code is there. This means that inheriting the object contained in `Shape.prototype` is better than inheriting the object created with `new Shape()`. After all, `new Shape()` will only give you own shape properties which are not meant to be reused (otherwise they would be in the prototype). You gain a little more efficiency by:

- Not creating a new object for the sake of inheritance alone, and
- Having less lookups during runtime when it comes to searching for `toString()` for example.

Here's the updated code; the changes are highlighted:

```
function Shape(){}
// augment prototype
Shape.prototype.name = 'shape';
Shape.prototype.toString = function() {return this.name;};

function TwoDShape(){}
// take care of inheritance
TwoDShape.prototype = Shape.prototype;
TwoDShape.prototype.constructor = TwoDShape;
// augment prototype
TwoDShape.prototype.name = '2D shape';

function Triangle(side, height) {
  this.side = side;
  this.height = height;
}

// take care of inheritance
Triangle.prototype = TwoDShape.prototype;
Triangle.prototype.constructor = Triangle;
// augment prototype
Triangle.prototype.name = 'Triangle';
Triangle.prototype.getArea = function(){return this.side * this.height
/ 2;}
```

The test code will give the same result:

```
>>> var my = new Triangle(5, 10);
>>> my.getArea()
```

25

```
>>> my.toString()
```

"Triangle"

What's the difference in the lookups when calling `my.toString()`? First, as usual, the JavaScript engine looks for a method `toString()` of the `my` object itself. The engine doesn't find such a method, so it inspects the prototype. The prototype turns out to be pointing to the same object that `TwoDShape`'s prototype points to and also the same object that `Shape.prototype` points to. Remember that objects are not copied by value, but only by reference. So the lookup is only a two-step process as opposed to four (in the previous example) or three (in the first example).

Simply copying the prototype is more efficient but it has a side effect: because all of the children and parents point to the same object, when a child modifies the prototype, the parents get the changes, and so do the siblings.

Look at this line:

```
Triangle.prototype.name = 'Triangle';
```

It changes the `name` property, so it effectively changes `Shape.prototype.name` too. If you create an instance using `new Shape()`, its `name` property will say **"Triangle"**:

```
>>> var s = new Shape()
>>> s.name
```

"Triangle"

A Temporary Constructor—new F()

A solution to the problem outlined above, where all prototypes point to the same object and the parents get children's properties, is to use an intermediary to break the chain. The intermediary is in the form of a temporary constructor function. Creating an empty function F() and setting its prototype to the prototype of the parent constructor, allows you to call `new F()` and create objects that have no properties of their own, but inherit everything from the parent's `prototype`.

Let's take a look at the modified code:

```
function Shape(){}
// augment prototype
Shape.prototype.name = 'shape';
Shape.prototype.toString = function() {return this.name;};

function TwoDShape(){}
// take care of inheritance
var F = function(){};
F.prototype = Shape.prototype;
TwoDShape.prototype = new F();
TwoDShape.prototype.constructor = TwoDShape;
// augment prototype
TwoDShape.prototype.name = '2D shape';

function Triangle(side, height) {
  this.side = side;
  this.height = height;
}
```

```
// take care of inheritance
var F = function(){};
F.prototype = TwoDShape.prototype;
Triangle.prototype = new F();
Triangle.prototype.constructor = Triangle;
// augment prototype
Triangle.prototype.name = 'Triangle';
Triangle.prototype.getArea = function(){return this.side * this.height
/ 2;};
```

Creating my triangle and testing the methods:

```
>>> var my = new Triangle(5, 10);
>>> my.getArea()
```

25

```
>>> my.toString()
```

"Triangle"

Using this approach, we keep the prototype chain in place and the parents' properties are not overwritten by the children:

```
>> my.__proto__.__proto__.__proto__.constructor
```

Shape()

```
>>> var s = new Shape();
>>> s.name
```

"shape"

At the same time, this approach supports the idea that only properties and methods added to the prototype should be inherited, and own properties should not be inherited. The rationale behind this is are that own properties are likely to be too specific to be reusable.

Uber—Access to the Parent from a Child Object

Classical OO languages usually have a special syntax that gives you access to the parent class, also referred to as superclass. This could be convenient when a child wants to have a method that does everything the parent's method does plus something in addition. In such cases, the child calls the parent's method with the same name and works with the result.

In JavaScript, there is no such special syntax, but it's easy to achieve the same functionality. Let's rewrite the last example and, while taking care of inheritance, also create an uber property that points to the parent's prototype object.

```
function Shape(){}
// augment prototype
Shape.prototype.name = 'shape';
Shape.prototype.toString = function(){
  var result = [];
  if (this.constructor.uber) {
    result[result.length] = this.constructor.uber.toString();
  }
  result[result.length] = this.name;
  return result.join(', ');
};

function TwoDShape(){}
// take care of inheritance
var F = function(){};
F.prototype = Shape.prototype;
TwoDShape.prototype = new F();
TwoDShape.prototype.constructor = TwoDShape;
TwoDShape.uber = Shape.prototype;
// augment prototype
TwoDShape.prototype.name = '2D shape';

function Triangle(side, height) {
  this.side = side;
  this.height = height;
}

// take care of inheritance
var F = function(){};
F.prototype = TwoDShape.prototype;
Triangle.prototype = new F();
Triangle.prototype.constructor = Triangle;
Triangle.uber = TwoDShape.prototype;
// augment prototype
Triangle.prototype.name = 'Triangle';
Triangle.prototype.getArea = function(){return this.side * this.height
/ 2;}
```

The new things here are:

- The way the uber property is set to point to the parent's prototype
- The updated toString()

Previously, toString() only returned this.name. Now, in addition to that, there is a check to see whether this.constructor.uber exists and, if it does, call its toString() first. this.constructor is the function itself, and this.constructor. uber points to the parent's prototype. The result is that when you call toString() for a Triangle instance, all toString() methods up the prototype chain are called:

```
>>> var my = new Triangle(5, 10);
>>> my.toString()
```

"shape, 2D shape, Triangle"

The name of the property uber could've been "superclass" but this would suggest that JavaScript has classes. Ideally it could've been "super" (as in Java), but "super" is a reserved word in JavaScript. The German word "über" suggested by Douglass Crockford, means more or less the same as "super" and, you have to admit, it sounds *uber-cool*.

Isolating the Inheritance Part into a Function

Let's move the code that takes care of all of the inheritance details into a reusable extend() function:

```
function extend(Child, Parent) {
  var F = function(){};
  F.prototype = Parent.prototype;
  Child.prototype = new F();
  Child.prototype.constructor = Child;
  Child.uber = Parent.prototype;
}
```

Using this function (or your own custom version of it) will help you keep your code clean with regard to the repetitive inheritance-related tasks. This way you can inherit by simply using:

```
extend(TwoDShape, Shape);
```

and

```
extend(Triangle, TwoDShape);
```

This approach is the way the YUI (Yahoo! User Interface) library implements inheritance through its extend() method. For example, if you use YUI and you want your Triangle to inherit from Shape, you use:

```
YAHOO.lang.extend(Triangle, Shape)
```

Copying Properties

Now let's try a slightly different approach. Since inheritance is about reusing code, you can simply copy properties from the parent to the child. Keeping the same interface as the extend() function above, you can create a function extend2() which takes two constructor functions and copies all of the properties from the parent's prototype to the child's prototype. This will include methods, as methods are just properties that happen to be functions.

```
function extend2(Child, Parent) {
  var p = Parent.prototype;
  var c = Child.prototype;
  for (var i in p) {
    c[i] = p[i];
  }
  c.uber = p;
}
```

As you can see, a simple loop through the properties is all it takes. As with the previous example, you can set an uber property if you want to have easy access to parent's methods from the child. Unlike the previous example though, it is not necessary to reset the Child.prototype.constructor because here the child prototype is augmented, not overwritten completely, so the constructor property will point to the correct value.

This method may be a little inefficient compared to the previous method because properties of the child prototype are being duplicated instead of simply being looked up via the prototype chain during execution. Bear in mind that this is only true for properties containing primitive types. All objects (including functions and arrays) are *not* duplicated, because these are passed by reference only.

Let's see an example of using two constructor functions, Shape() and TwoDShape(). Shape()'s prototype object contains a primitive property, name, and a non-primitive one—the method toString():

```
var Shape = function(){};
var TwoDShape = function(){};
Shape.prototype.name = 'shape';
Shape.prototype.toString = function(){return this.name;};
```

If you inherit with extend(), neither the instances of TwoDShape() nor its prototype will get a name property, but they will have access to the one they inherit.

```
>>> extend(TwoDShape, Shape);
>>> var td = new TwoDShape();
>>> td.name
```

"shape"

```
>>> TwoDShape.prototype.name
```

"shape"

```
>>> td.__proto__.name
```

"shape"

```
>>> td.hasOwnProperty('name')
```

false

```
>>> td.__proto__.hasOwnProperty('name')
```

false

If you inherit with extend2(), the prototype of TwoDShape() will get its own copy of the name property. It will also get its own copy of toString(), but this a reference copy, so the function will not be recreated a second time.

```
>>> extend2(TwoDShape, Shape);
>>> var td = new TwoDShape();
>>> td.__proto__.hasOwnProperty('name')
```

true

```
>>> td.__proto__.hasOwnProperty('toString')
```

true

```
>>> td.__proto__.toString === Shape.prototype.toString
```

true

As you can see, the two toString() methods are actually the same function object. This is good because it means that no unnecessary duplicates of the methods are created.

So we can say that extend2() is less efficient than extend() because it recreates the properties of the prototype. Nevertheless, this is not so bad because only the primitive data types are duplicated. Furthermore, it can actually be a benefit during the prototype chain lookups as there will be fewer chain links to follow before finding the property.

Heads-up When Copying by Reference

The fact that objects (including functions and arrays) are copied by reference could sometimes lead to results you don't expect.

Let's create two constructor functions and add some properties to the prototype of the first one:

```
>>> var A = function(){}, B = function(){};
>>> A.prototype.stuff = [1,2,3];
```

[1, 2, 3]

```
>>> A.prototype.name = 'a';
```

"a"

Now let's have B inherit from A (either extend() or extend2() will do):

```
>>> extend2(B, A);
```

Using extend2(), B's prototype inherited A.prototype's properties as own properties.

```
>>> B.prototype.hasOwnProperty('name')
```

true

```
>>> B.prototype.hasOwnProperty('stuff')
```

true

The name property is primitive so a new copy of it is created. The property stuff is an array object so it is copied by reference:

```
>>> B.prototype.stuff
```

[1, 2, 3]

```
>>> B.prototype.stuff === A.prototype.stuff
```

true

Changing B's copy of name doesn't affect A:

```
>>> B.prototype.name += 'b'
```

"ab"

```
>>> A.prototype.name
```

"a"

Changing B's stuff property, however, affects A, because both prototypes point to the same array.

```
>>> B.prototype.stuff.push(4,5,6);
```

6

```
>>> A.prototype.stuff
```

[1, 2, 3, 4, 5, 6]

It's a different story when you completely overwrite B's copy of stuff with another object (as opposed to modifying the existing one). In this case A's stuff keeps pointing to the old object, while B's points to a new one.

```
>>> B.prototype.stuff = ['a', 'b', 'c'];
```

["a", "b", "c"]

```
>>> A.prototype.stuff
```

[1, 2, 3, 4, 5, 6]

Think of an object as something that is created and stored in a physical location in memory. Variables and properties just point to this location, so when you assign a brand new object to B.prototype.stuff you basically say, "Hey, forget about this old object, move your pointer to this new one instead".

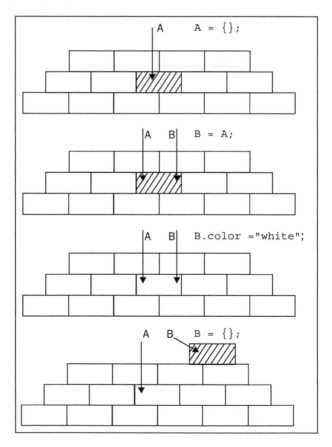

Objects Inherit from Objects

All of the examples so far in this chapter assume that you create your objects with constructor functions and you want objects created with one constructor to inherit properties that come from another constructor. However, you can also create objects without the help of a constructor function, just by using the object literal and this is, in fact, less typing. So how about inheriting those?

In Java or PHP, you define classes and have them inherit from other classes. Hence the name, classical, because the OO functionality comes from the use of classes. In JavaScript, there are no classes so programmers that come from a classical background resort to constructor functions because it's the closest to what they are used to. In addition, JavaScript provides the new operator, which can further suggest that JavaScript is like Java. The truth is that, in the end, it all comes back to objects. The first example in this chapter used this syntax:

```
Child.prototype = new Parent();
```

Here the Child constructor (or class, if you will) inherits from Parent. But this is done through creating an object using new Parent() and inheriting from it. That's why this is also referred to as a pseudo-classical inheritance pattern, because it looks like classical inheritance, although it isn't (because there are no classes involved).

So why not get rid of the middle-man (the constructor/class) and just have objects inherit from objects? In extend2() the properties of the parent prototype object were copied as properties of the child prototype object. The two prototypes are in essence just objects. Forgetting about prototypes and constructor functions, you can simply take an object and copy all of its properties into another object.

Objects can start as a blank canvas by using var o = {}; and get properties later. Instead of doing this, you can start by copying all of the properties of an existing object. Here's a function that does exactly that: it takes an object and returns a new copy of it.

```
function extendCopy(p) {
  var c = {};
  for (var i in p) {
    c[i] = p[i];
  }
  c.uber = p;
  return c;
}
```

Simply copying all of the properties is a very simple pattern, but it is widely used. The code behind Firebug has an extend() function that works this way. Also, some popular JavaScript libraries like jQuery and Prototype followed this basic pattern in earlier versions.

Let's see this function in action. You start by having a base object:

```
var shape = {
  name: 'shape',
  toString: function() {return this.name;}
}
```

In order to create a new object that builds upon the old one, you can call the function `extendCopy()` which returns a new object. Then you can augment the new object with additional functionality.

```
var twoDee = extendCopy(shape);
twoDee.name = '2D shape';
twoDee.toString = function(){return this.uber.toString() + ', ' +
this.name;};
```

A triangle object that inherits the 2D shape object:

```
var triangle = extendCopy(twoDee);
triangle.name = 'Triangle';
triangle.getArea = function(){return this.side * this.height / 2;}
```

Using the triangle:

```
>>> triangle.side = 5; triangle.height = 10; triangle.getArea();
```

25

```
>>> triangle.toString();
```

"shape, 2D shape, Triangle"

A possible drawback of this method is the somewhat verbose way of initializing the new triangle object, where you manually set values for `side` and `height`, as opposed to passing them as values to a constructor. But this is easily resolved by having a function, for example called `init()` (or `__construct()` if you come from PHP5) that acts as constructor and accepts initialization parameters.

Deep Copy

The function `extendCopy()`, discussed above, creates what is called a *shallow copy* of an object. The opposite of a shallow copy would be, naturally, a *deep copy*. As discussed above (in the section "Heads-up When Copying by Reference", when you copy objects you only copy pointers to the location in memory where the object is stored. This is what happens in a shallow copy. If you modify an object in the copy, you also modify the original. The deep copy avoids this problem.

The deep copy is implemented the same way as the shallow copy: you loop through the properties and copy them one by one. Only when you encounter a property that points to an object, do you call the deep copy function again:

```
function deepCopy(p, c) {
  var c = c || {};
  for (var i in p) {
    if (typeof p[i] === 'object') {
      c[i] = (p[i].constructor === Array) ? [] : {};
      deepCopy(p[i], c[i]);
    } else {
      c[i] = p[i];
    }
  }
  return c;
}
```

Let's create an object that has arrays and a sub-object as properties.

```
var parent = {
  numbers: [1, 2, 3],
  letters: ['a', 'b', 'c'],
  obj: {
    prop: 1
  },
  bool: true
};
```

Let's test this by creating a deep copy and a shallow copy. Unlike the shallow copy, when you update the numbers property of a deep copy, the original is not affected.

```
>>> var mydeep = deepCopy(parent);
>>> var myshallow = extendCopy(parent);
>>> mydeep.numbers.push(4,5,6);
```

6

```
>>> mydeep.numbers
```

[1, 2, 3, 4, 5, 6]

```
>>> parent.numbers
```

[1, 2, 3]

```
>>> myshallow.numbers.push(10)
```

4

```
>>> myshallow.numbers
```

[1, 2, 3, 10]

```
>>> parent.numbers[1, 2, 3, 10]

>>> mydeep.numbers
```

[1, 2, 3, 4, 5, 6]

The idea of the deep copy inheritance is implemented in more recent versions
of jQuery.

object()

Based on the idea that objects inherit from objects, Douglas Crockford suggests the
use of an object() function that accepts an object and returns a new one that has the
parent as a prototype.

```
function object(o) {
    function F() {}
    F.prototype = o;
    return new F();
}
```

If you need access to an uber property, you can modify the object() function
like so:

```
function object(o) {
    var n;
    function F() {}
    F.prototype = o;
    n = new F();
    n.uber = o;
    return n;
}
```

Using this function will be the same as the extendCopy(): you basically take an
object such as twoDee, create a new object from it and then proceed to augmenting
the new object.

```
var triangle = object(twoDee);
triangle.name = 'Triangle';
triangle.getArea = function(){return this.side * this.height / 2;};
```

The new triangle still behaves the same way:

```
>>> triangle.toString()
```

"shape, 2D shape, Triangle"

This pattern is also referred to as prototypal inheritance, because you use a parent
object as the prototype of a child object.

Using a Mix of Prototypal Inheritance and Copying Properties

When you use inheritance, you will most likely want to take some existing functionality and then build upon it. This means creating a new object by inheriting from an existing object and then adding some additional methods and properties. You can do this with one function call, using a combination of the last two approaches just discussed.

You can:

- Use prototypal inheritance to clone an existing object
- Copy all of the properties of another object

```
function objectPlus(o, stuff) {
  var n;
  function F() {}
  F.prototype = o;
  n = new F();
  n.uber = o;

  for (var i in stuff) {
    n[i] = stuff[i];
  }
  return n;
}
```

This function takes an object o to inherit from and another object stuff that has the additional methods and properties that are to be copied. Let's see this in action.

Start with the base shape object:

```
var shape = {
  name: 'shape',
  toString: function() {return this.name;}
};
```

Create a 2D object by inheriting shape and adding more properties. The additional properties are simply created in an anonymous object literal.

```
var twoDee = objectPlus(shape, {
  name: '2D shape',
  toString: function(){return this.uber.toString() + ', ' + this.name}
});
```

Now let's create a `triangle` object that inherits from 2D and adds some more properties.

```
var triangle = objectPlus(twoDee, {
  name: 'Triangle',
  getArea: function(){return this.side * this.height / 2;},
  side: 0,
  height: 0
});
```

Testing how it all works by creating a concrete triangle `my` with defined `side` and `height`:

```
>>> var my = objectPlus(triangle, {side: 4, height: 4});
>>> my.getArea()
```

8

```
>>> my.toString()
```

"shape, 2D shape, Triangle, Triangle"

The difference here, when executing `toString()`, is that the **Triangle** name is repeated twice. That's because our concrete instance was created by inheriting `triangle`, so there was one more level of inheritance. You could give the new instance a name:

```
>>> var my = objectPlus(triangle, {side: 4, height: 4,
                                     name: 'My 4x4'});
>>> my.toString()
```

"shape, 2D shape, Triangle, My 4x4"

Multiple Inheritance

Multiple inheritance is where a child inherits from more than one parent. Some OO languages support multiple inheritance, and some don't. You can argue both ways: that multiple inheritance is convenient, or that it's unnecessary, complicates application design, and it's better to use an inheritance chain instead. In any event, it's easy to implement multiple inheritance in dynamic languages such as JavaScript, although the language doesn't have a specific syntax for it. Leaving the discussion of multiple inheritance's pros and cons to the long, cold winter nights, let's see how you can do it in practice.

The implementation can be pretty simple. Just take the idea of inheritance by copying properties, and expand it so that it takes an unlimited number of input objects to inherit from.

Let's create a `multi()` function that accepts any number of input objects. You can wrap the loop that copies properties in another loop that goes through all the objects passed as `arguments` to the function.

```
function multi() {
  var n = {}, stuff, j = 0, len = arguments.length;
  for (j - 0; j < len; j++) {
    stuff = arguments[j];
    for (var i in stuff) {
      n[i] = stuff[i];
    }
  }
  return n;
}
```

Let's test this by creating three objects: `shape`, `twoDee` and a third, unnamed object. Creating a `triangle` object will mean calling `multi()` and passing all three objects.

```
var shape = {
  name: 'shape',
  toString: function() {return this.name;}
};

var twoDee = {
  name: '2D shape',
  dimensions: 2
};

var triangle = multi(shape, twoDee, {
  name: 'Triangle',
  getArea: function(){return this.side * this.height / 2;},
  side: 5,
  height: 10
});
```

Will it work? Let's see:

```
>>> triangle.getArea()
```

25

```
>>> triangle.dimensions
```

2

```
>>> triangle.toString()
```

"Triangle"

Bear in mind that `multi()` loops through the input objects in the order they appear and if it happens that two of them have the same property, the one passed later will take precedence.

Mixins

You might come across the term mixin, which is quite popular in some languages such as Ruby. You can think of a mixin as an object that provides some useful functionality but is not meant to be inherited and extended by sub-objects. The approach to multiple inheritance outlined above can be considered an implementation of the mixins idea. When you create a new object you can pick and choose any other objects to mix into your new object. By passing them all to `multi()` you get all their functionality without making them part of the inheritance tree.

Parasitic Inheritance

If you like the fact that you can have all kinds of different ways to implement inheritance in JavaScript, and you're hungry for more, here's another one. This pattern, courtesy of Douglas Crockford, is called parasitic inheritance. It basically means that you can have a function that creates objects by taking all of the functionality of another object, augmenting it and returning it, "pretending that it has done all the work".

Here's an ordinary object, defined with an object literal, and unaware of the fact that it is soon going to fall victim to parasitism:

```
var twoD = {
  name: '2D shape',
  dimensions: 2
};
```

A function that creates triangle objects could:

- Clone the `twoD` object into an object called `that`. This can be done in any way you saw above, for example using the `object()` function or copying all the properties.
- Augment `that` with more properties.
- Return `that`.

```
function triangle(s, h) {
  var that = object(twoD);
  that.name ='Triangle';
  that.getArea = function(){return this.side * this.height / 2;};
  that.side = s;
  that.height = h;
  return that;
}
```

Because `triangle()` is a normal function, not a constructor, it doesn't require the `new` operator. But because it returns an object, calling it with `new` by mistake will work in exactly the same way.

```
>>> var t = triangle(5, 10);
>>> t.dimensions
```

2

```
>>> var t2 = new triangle(5,5);
>>> t2.getArea();
```

12.5

Note that `that` is just a name; it doesn't have a special meaning, the way `this` does.

Borrowing a Constructor

One more way of implementing inheritance (the last one in the chapter, I promise) has to do again with constructor functions, and not the objects directly. In this pattern the constructor of the child calls the constructor of the parent using either of the `call()` or `apply()` methods. This can be called stealing a constructor, or borrowing a constructor if you want to be more subtle about it.

`call()` and `apply()` were discussed in Chapter 4, but here's a refresher: they allow you to call a function and pass an object that the function should bind to its `this` value. So for inheritance purposes, the child constructor calls the parent's constructor and binds child's newly-created `this` object as the parent's `this`.

Let's have this parent constructor `Shape()`:

```
function Shape(id) {
  this.id = id;
}
Shape.prototype.name = 'shape';
Shape.prototype.toString = function(){return this.name;};
```

Now let's define `Triangle()` which uses `apply()` to call the `Shape()` constructor, passing `this` (an instance created with `new Triangle()`) and any additional arguments.

```
function Triangle() {
    Shape.apply(this, arguments);
}
Triangle.prototype.name = 'Triangle';
```

Note that both `Triangle()` and `Shape()` add some extra properties to their prototypes.

Now let's test this by creating a new triangle object:

```
>>> var t = new Triangle(101);
>>> t.name
```

"Triangle"

The new triangle object inherits the `id` property from the parent, but it doesn't inherit anything added to the parent's prototype:

```
>>> t.id
```

101

```
>>> t.toString();
```

"[object Object]"

The triangle failed to get `Shape`'s prototype properties because we never created a new `Shape()` instance, so the prototype was never used. This is easy to do, as you saw at the very beginning of this chapter. You can redefine `Triangle` like this:

```
function Triangle() {
    Shape.apply(this, arguments);
}
Triangle.prototype = new Shape();
Triangle.prototype.name = 'Triangle';
```

In this inheritance pattern, the parent's own properties are recreated as the child's own properties (as opposed to children's *prototype* properties as was the case in the prototype-chaining pattern). That's also the main benefit of borrowing constructors: if a child inherits an array or other object, it's a completely new value (not a reference) and modifying it won't affect the parent.

The drawback is that the parent's constructor gets called twice: once with `apply()` to inherit own properties and once with `new` to inherit the prototype. In fact the own properties of the parent will be inherited twice. Let's take this simplified scenario:

```
function Shape(id) {
  this.id = id;
}
function Triangle() {
    Shape.apply(this, arguments);
}
Triangle.prototype = new Shape(101);
```

Creating a new instance:

```
>>> var t = new Triangle(202);
>>> t.id
```

202

There's an own property id, but there's also one that comes down the prototype chain, ready to shine through:

```
>>> t.__proto__.id
```

101

```
>>> delete t.id
```

true

```
>>> t.id
```

101

Borrow a Constructor and Copy its Prototype

The problem of the double work performed by calling the constructor twice can easily be corrected. You can call apply() on the parent constructor to get all own properties and then copy the prototype's properties using a simple iteration (or extend2() as discussed previously).

```
function Shape(id) {
  this.id = id;
}
Shape.prototype.name = 'shape';
Shape.prototype.toString = function(){return this.name;};

function Triangle() {
    Shape.apply(this, arguments);
}
extend2(Triangle, Shape);
Triangle.prototype.name = 'Triangle';
```

Testing:

```
>>> var t = new Triangle(101);
>>> t.toString();

"Triangle"
>>> t.id
```

101

No double inheritance:

```
>>> typeof t.__proto__.id
```

"undefined"

extend2() also gives access to uber if needed:

```
>>> t.uber.name
```

"shape"

Summary

In this chapter you learned quite a few ways (patterns) for implementing inheritance. The different types can roughly be divided into:

- Patterns that work with constructors
- Patterns that work with objects

You can also classify the patterns based on whether they:

- Use the prototype
- Copy properties
- Do both (copy properties of the prototype)

Method	Name	Example	Classification	Notes
1	Prototype chaining (pseudo-classical)	`Child.prototype = new Parent();`	Works with constructors Uses the prototype chain	The default mechanism described in the ECMA standard. Tip: move all properties/methods that are meant to be reused to the prototype, and add the non-reusable as own properties
2	Inherit only the prototype	`Child.prototype = Parent.prototype;`	Works with constructors Copies the prototype (no prototype chain, all share the same prototype object)	More efficient since no new instances are created just for the sake of inheritance. Prototype chain lookup during runtime is fast, since there's no chain. Drawback: children can modify parents' functionality
3	Temporary constructor	```function extend(Child, Parent) { var F = function(){}; F.prototype = Parent.prototype; Child.prototype = new F(); Child.prototype.constructor = Child; Child.uber = Parent.prototype; }```	Works with constructors Uses the prototype chain	Unlike #1, it only inherits properties of the prototype. Own properties (created with `this` inside the constructor) are not inherited. Used in YUI and Ext.js libraries Provides convenient access to the parent (through `uber`)

Method	Name	Example	Classification	Notes
4	Copying the prototype properties	```function extend2(Child, Parent) { var p = Parent. prototype; var c = Child. prototype; for (var i in p) { c[i] = p[i]; } c.uber = p; }```	Works with constructors Copies properties Uses the prototype chain	All properties of the parent prototype become properties of the child prototype No need to create a new object only for inheritance Shorter prototype chains
5	Copy all properties (shallow copy)	```function extendCopy(p) { var c = {}; for (var i in p) { c[i] = p[i]; } c.uber = p; return c; }```	Works with objects Copies properties	Very simple Used in Firebug, earlier jQuery and Prototype.js versions Also known as *shallow copy* Doesn't use prototypes
6	Deep copy	same as above, but recurse into objects	Works with objects Copies properties	Same as #5, but copies the objects by value Used in more recent versions of jQuery
7	Prototypal inheritance	```function object(o){ function F() {} F.prototype = o; return new F(); }```	Works with objects Uses the prototype chain	No pseudo-classes; objects inherit from objects Leverages the benefits of the prototype

Method	Name	Example	Classification	Notes
8	Extend and augment	```function objectPlus(o, stuff) { var n; function F() {} F.prototype = o; n = new F(); n.uber = o; for (var i in stuff) { n[i] = stuff[i]; } return n; }```	Works with objects Uses the prototype chain Copies properties	Mix of prototypal inheritance (#7) and copying properties (#5) One function call to inherit and extend at the same time
9	Multiple inheritance	```function multi() { var n = {}, stuff, j = 0, len = arguments.length; for (j = 0; j < len; j++) { stuff = arguments[j]; for (var i in stuff) { n[i] = stuff[i]; } } return n; }```	Works with objects Copies properties	A mixin-style implementation Copies all the properties of all the parent objects in the order of appearance
10	Parasitic inheritance	```function parasite(victim) { var that = object(victim); that.more = 1; return that; }```	Works with objects Uses the prototype chain	Constructor-like function, creates objects Copies an object; augments and returns the copy

Method	Name	Example	Classification	Notes

11	Borrowing constructors	`function Child() {`
		`  Parent.`
		`apply(this,`
		`arguments);`
		`}`
			Works with constructors	Inherits only own properties
				
				Can be combined with #1 to inherit prototype too
				
				Easy way to deal with the issues when a child inherits a property that is an object (and therefore passed by reference)

12	Borrow a constructor and copy the prototype	`function Child() {`
		`  Parent.`
		`apply(this,`
		`arguments);`
		`}`
		`extend2(Child,`
		`Parent);`
			Works with constructors
			
			Uses the prototype chain
			
			Copies properties
				Combination of #11 and #4
				
				Allows you to inherit both own properties and prototype properties without calling the parent constructor twice

Given so many options, you are probably wondering which is the right one? That depends on your style and preferences, your project, task, and team. Are you more comfortable thinking in terms of classes? Then pick one of the methods that work with constructors. Are you going to need just one or a few instances of your "class"? Then choose an object-based pattern.

Are these the only ways of implementing inheritance? No. You can chose a pattern from the table above or you can mix them, or you can think of your own. The important thing is to understand and be comfortable with objects, prototypes, and constructors; the rest is easy.

Case Study: Drawing Shapes

Let's finish off this chapter with a more practical example of using inheritance. The task is to be able to calculate the area and the perimeter of different shapes, as well as to draw them, while reusing as much code as possible.

Analysis

Let's have one `Shape` constructor that contains all of the common parts. From there, we can have `Triangle`, `Rectangle` and `Square` constructors, all inheriting from `Shape`. A square is really a rectangle with same-length sides, so let's reuse `Rectangle` when building the `Square`.

In order to define a shape, we'll use points with x and y coordinates. A generic shape can have any number of points. A triangle is defined with three points, a rectangle (to keep it simpler) — with one point and the lengths of the sides. The perimeter of any shape is the sum of its sides' lengths. The area is shape-specific and will be implemented by each shape.

The common functionality in Shape would be:

- A draw() method that can draw any shape given the points
- A getParameter() method
- A property that contains an array of points
- Other methods and properties as needed

For the drawing part we'll use a <canvas> tag. It's not supported in IE, but hey, this is just an exercise.

Let's have two other helper constructors — Point and Line. Point will help when defining shapes; Line will ease some calculations, as it can give the length of the line connecting any two given points.

You can play with a working example here: http://www.phpied.com/files/canvas/. Just open the Firebug console and start creating new shapes as you'll see in a moment.

Implementation

Let's start by adding a canvas tag to a blank HTML page:

```
<canvas height="600" width="800" id="canvas" />
```

Then, inside <script> tags, we'll put the JavaScript code:

```
<script type="text/javascript">
  // ... code goes here
</script>
```

Now let's take a look at what's in the JavaScript part.

First, the helper Point constructor. It just can't get any more trivial than this:

```
function Point(x, y) {
  this.x = x;
  this.y = y;
}
```

Bear in mind that the coordinates of the points on the canvas start from x=0, y=0, which is the top left. The bottom right will be x = 800, y = 600.

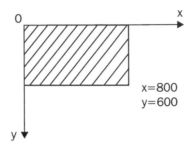

Next, the `Line` constructor. It takes two points and calculates the length of the line between them, using the Pythagorean Theorem $a^2 + b^2 = c^2$ (imagine a right -angled triangle where the hypotenuse connects the two given points).

```
function Line(p1, p2) {
   this.p1 = p1;
   this.p2 = p2;
   this.length = Math.sqrt(Math.pow(p1.x - p2.x, 2) + Math.pow(p1.y -
p2.y, 2));
}
```

Next comes the `Shape` constructor. The shapes will have their points (and the lines that connect them) as own properties. The constructor also invokes an initialization method, `init()`, that will be defined in the prototype.

```
function Shape() {
   this.points = [];
   this.lines  = [];
   this.init();
}
```

Now the big part: the methods of `Shape.prototype`. Let's define all of these methods using the object literal notation. Refer to the comments for guidelines as to what each method does.

```
Shape.prototype = {
   // reset pointer to constructor
   constructor: Shape,
   // initialization, sets this.context to point
   // to the context of the canvas object
   init: function() {
     if (typeof this.context === 'undefined') {
       var canvas = document.getElementById('canvas');
       Shape.prototype.context = canvas.getContext('2d');
```

```javascript
    }
  },
  // method that draws a shape by looping through this.points
  draw: function() {
    var ctx = this.context;
    ctx.strokeStyle = this.getColor();
    ctx.beginPath();
    ctx.moveTo(this.points[0].x, this.points[0].y);
    for(var i = 1; i < this.points.length; i++) {
      ctx.lineTo(this.points[i].x, this.points[i].y);
    }
    ctx.closePath();
    ctx.stroke();
  },
  // method that generates a random color
  getColor: function() {
    var rgb = [];
    for (var i = 0; i < 3; i++) {
      rgb[i] = Math.round(255 * Math.random());
    }
    return 'rgb(' + rgb.join(',') + ')';
  },
  // method that loops through the points array,
  // creates Line instances and adds them to this.lines
  getLines: function() {
    if (this.lines.length > 0) {
      return this.lines;
    }
    var lines = [];
    for(var i = 0; i < this.points.length; i++) {
      lines[i] = new Line(this.points[i], (this.points[i+1]) ?
                          this.points[i+1] : this.points[0]);
    }
    this.lines = lines;
    return lines;
  },
  // shell method, to be implemented by children
  getArea: function(){},
  // sums the lengths of all lines
  getPerimeter: function(){
    var lines = this.getLines();
    var perim = 0;
    for (var i = 0; i < lines.length; i++) {
      perim += lines[i].length;
    }
    return perim;
  }
}
```

Now the children constructor functions. Triangle first:

```
function Triangle(a, b, c){
  this.points = [a, b, c];
  this.getArea = function(){
    var p = this.getPerimeter();
    var s = p / 2;
    return Math.sqrt(
      s
      * (s - this.lines[0].length)
      * (s - this.lines[1].length)
      * (s - this.lines[2].length)
    );
  };
}
```

The `Triangle` constructor takes three point objects and assigns them to `this.points` (its own collection of points). Then it implements the `getArea()` method, using Heron's formula:

```
Area = s(s-a)(s-b)(s-c)
```
`s` is the semi-perimeter (perimeter divided by two).

Next comes the `Rectangle` constructor. It receives one point (the upper-left point) and the lengths of the two sides. Then it populates its `points` array starting from that one point.

```
function Rectangle(p, side_a, side_b){
  this.points = [
    p,
    new Point(p.x + side_a, p.y),          // top right
    new Point(p.x + side_a, p.y + side_b), // bottom right
    new Point(p.x, p.y + side_b)           // bottom left
  ];
  this.getArea = function() {return side_a * side_b;};
}
```

The last child constructor is `Square`. A square is a special case of a rectangle, so it makes sense to reuse `Rectangle`. The easiest thing to do here is to borrow the constructor.

```
function Square(p, side){
  Rectangle.call(this, p, side, side);
}
```

Now that we have all constructors, let's take care of inheritance. Any pseudo-classical pattern (one that works with constructors as opposed to objects) will do. Let's try using a modified and simplified version of the prototype-chaining pattern (the first method described in this chapter). This pattern calls for creating a new instance of the parent and setting it as the child's prototype. In this case, it's not necessary to have a new instance for each child—they can all share it.

```
(function () {
  var s = new Shape();
  Triangle.prototype = s;
  Rectangle.prototype = s;
  Square.prototype = s;
})()
```

Testing

Let's test this by drawing some shapes. First, let's define three points for a triangle:

```
>>> var p1 = new Point(100, 100);
>>> var p2 = new Point(300, 100);
>>> var p3 - new Point(200, 0);
```

Now you can create a triangle by passing the three points to the `Triangle` constructor:

```
>>> var t = new Triangle(p1, p2, p3);
```

You can call the methods to draw the triangle on the canvas and get its area and perimeter:

```
>>> t.draw();
>>> t.getPerimeter()
```

482.842712474619

```
>>> t.getArea()
```

10000.000000000002

Now let's play with a rectangle instance:

```
>>> var r = new Rectangle(new Point(200, 200), 50, 100);
>>> r.draw();
>>> r.getArea()
```

5000

```
>>> r.getPerimeter()
```

300

And finally, a square:

```
>>> var s = new Square(new Point(130, 130), 50);
>>> s.draw();
>>> s.getArea()
```

2500

```
>>> s.getPerimeter()
```

200

It's fun to draw these shapes. You can also be as lazy as the following example, which draws another square, reusing a triangle's point:

```
>>> new Square(p1, 200).draw()
```

The result of the tests will be something like this:

Exercises

Use the canvas example to practice. Try out different things, for example:

1. Draw some triangles, squares, and rectangles.

2. Add constructors for more shapes, such as Trapezoid, Rhombus, Kite, Diamond, and Pentagon. If you want to learn more about the canvas tag, create a Circle constructor too. It will need to overwrite the draw() method of the parent.

3. Can you think of another way to approach the problem and use some other type of inheritance?

4. Pick one of the methods that uses uber as a way for a child to access its parent. Add functionality where the parents can keep track of who their children are. Perhaps by using a property that contains a children array?

7
The Browser Environment

You know that JavaScript programs don't run on their own; they need a host environment. Pretty much everything discussed so far in this book was related to core ECMAScript/JavaScript and can be used in many different host environments. Now let's shift our focus to the browser, as this is the most popular and natural host environment for JavaScript programs. In this chapter, you will learn about:

- The BOM (Browser Object Model)
- The DOM (Document Object Model)
- Listening to browser events
- The XMLHttpRequest object

Including JavaScript in an HTML Page

In order to include JavaScript in an HTML page, you need to use the `<script>` tag:

```
<!DOCTYPE html PUBLIC "-//W3C//DTD XHTML 1.0 Strict//EN"
  "http://www.w3.org/TR/xhtml1/DTD/xhtml1-strict.dtd">
<html>
  <head>
    <title>JS test</title>
    <script type="text/javascript" src="somefile.js"></script>
  </head>
  <body>
    <script type="text/javascript">
      var a = 1;
      a++;
    </script>
  </body>
</html>
```

In this example, the first `<script>` tag includes an external file, `somefile.js`, which contains JavaScript code. The second `<script>` tag includes the JavaScript code directly in the HTML code of the page. In both cases, the `<script>` tag takes a `type` attribute, which is required in XHTML 1.0, although the code will work even without it. The browser executes the JavaScript in the sequence it finds it in the page. This means that if you define a variable in `somefile.js`, it will also exist in the second `<script>` block.

BOM and DOM—An Overview

The JavaScript code in a page has access to a number of objects. These objects can be divided into:

- Objects that have to do with the currently loaded page (the page is also called the document), and
- Objects that deal with things outside the page (the browser window and the desktop screen)

The first collection of objects makes up the Document Object Model (DOM) and the second the Browser Object Model (BOM).

The DOM is a standard, governed by the World Wide Web Consortium (W3C) and has different versions, called *levels*, such as DOM Level 1, DOM Level 2, and — the last one so far — DOM Level 3. Modern browsers have different degrees of compliance with the standard, but in general, they almost all completely implement DOM Level 1. The DOM was standardized post-factum, after the browser vendors had each implemented their own ways to access the document. The legacy part (from before the W3C took over) is still around and is referred to as DOM 0, although no real DOM Level 0 standard exists. Some parts of DOM 0 have become de-facto standards as all major browsers support them. Some of these were added to the DOM Level 1 standard. The rest of DOM 0 that didn't find its way to DOM 1 is too browser-specific and won't be discussed here.

BOM is not a part of any standard. Similar to DOM 0, it has a subset of objects that is supported by all major browsers, and another subset that is browser-specific.

This chapter will discuss only cross-browser subsets of BOM and DOM Level 1 (unless noted otherwise in the text). Even these "safe" subsets constitute a large topic, and a full reference is beyond the scope of this book. You can also consult:

- The Mozilla DOM reference for Firefox information (`http://developer.mozilla.org/en/docs/Gecko_DOM_Reference`)
- Microsoft's documentation for Internet Explorer (`http://msdn2.microsoft.com/en-us/library/ms533050(vs.85).aspx`)
- W3C' DOM specs (`http://www.w3.org/DOM/DOMTR`)

BOM

The BOM (Browser Object Model) is a collection of objects that give you access to the browser and the computer screen. These objects are accessible through the global objects `window` and `window.screen`.

The window Object Revisited

As you know already, in JavaScript there's a global object provided by every host environment. In the browser environment, this is the `window` object. All *global variables* become *properties* of the `window` object.

```
>>> window.somevar = 1;
```
1
```
>>> somevar
```
1

Also, all of the core JavaScript functions (discussed in Chapter 2) are *methods* of the `window` object.

```
>>> parseInt('123a456')
```
123
```
>>> window.parseInt('123a456')
```
123

In addition to being the global object, the `window` object also serves a second purpose and that is to provide data about the browser environment. There's a `window` object for every frame, iframe, popup, or browser tab.

Let's see some of the browser-related properties of the `window` object. Again, these can vary from one browser to another, so we'll only bother with those properties that are implemented consistently and reliably across all modern browsers.

window.navigator

The `navigator` is an object that has some information about the browser and its capabilities. One property is `navigator.userAgent`, which is a long string of browser identification. In Firefox, you'll get something like this:

```
>>> window.navigator.userAgent
```

"Mozilla/5.0 (Windows; U; Windows NT 5.1; en-US; rv:1.8.1.12) Gecko/20080201 Firefox/2.0.0.12"

The `userAgent` string in Microsoft Internet Explorer would be something like:

Mozilla/4.0 (compatible; MSIE 7.0; Windows NT 5.1; .NET CLR 1.1.4322; .NET CLR 2.0.50727; .NET CLR 3.0.04506.30)

Because the browsers have different capabilities, developers have been using the `userAgent` string to identify the browser and provide different versions of the code. For example, this code searches for the presence of the string `MSIE` to identify Internet Explorer:

```
if (navigator.userAgent.indexOf('MSIE') !== -1) {
  // this is IE
} else {
  // not IE
}
```

It is better not to rely on the user agent string, but to use *feature sniffing* (also called *capabilities detection*) instead. The reason for this is that it's hard to keep track of all browsers and their different versions. It's much easier to simply check if the feature you intend to use is indeed available in the user's browser. For example:

```
if (typeof window.addEventListener === 'function') {
  // feature is supported, let's use it
} else {
  // hmm, this feature is not supported, will have to
  // think of another way
}
```

Another reason to avoid user agent sniffing is that some browsers allow users to modify the string and pretend they are using a different browser.

Firebug as a Cheat Sheet

The Firebug console offers a lazy way to inspect what's in an object, and this includes all the BOM and DOM properties. Therefore, you can type:

```
>>> navigator
```

Then click the result. Alternatively, you can type:

```
>>> console.dir(navigator)
```

The result is a list of properties and their values.

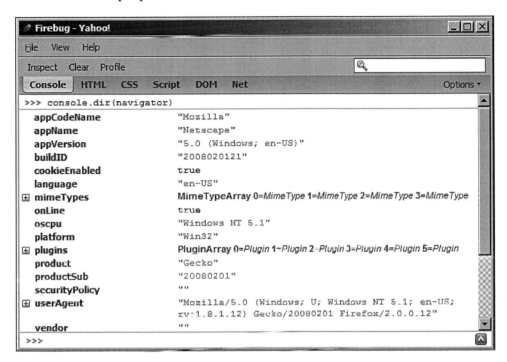

window.location

The `location` property points to an object that contains information about the URL of the currently loaded page. For example, `location.href`, is the full URL and `location.hostname` is only the domain. With a simple loop, you can see the full list of properties of the `location` object.

Imagine you're on a page with a URL like this:

```
http://search.phpied.com:8080/search?p=javascript#results
    >>> for(var i in location) {console.log(i + ' = "' + location[i] +
                              '"')}
```

href = "http://search.phpied.com:8080/search?p=javascript#results"

hash = "#results"

host = "search.phpied.com:8080"

hostname = "search.phpied.com"

> **pathname = "/search"**
>
> **port = "8080"**
>
> **protocol = "http:"**
>
> **search = "?p=javascript"**

There are also three methods that `location` provides — `reload()`, `assign()`, and `replace()`.

It's interesting to note how many different ways exist for you to navigate to another page. Here's a partial list:

```
>>> window.location.href = 'http://www.packtpub.com'
>>> location.href = 'http://www.packtpub.com'
>>> location = 'http://www.packtpub.com'
>>> location.assign('http://www.packtpub.com')
```

`replace()` is almost the same as `assign()`. The difference is that it doesn't create an entry in the browser's history list:

```
>>> location.replace('http://www.yahoo.com')
```

To reload a page you can use:

```
>>> location.reload()
```

Alternatively, you can use `location.href` to point it to itself, like so:

```
>>> window.location.href = window.location.href
```

Or simply:

```
>>> location = location
```

window.history

`window.history` allows limited access to the previously-visited pages in the same browser session. For example, you can see how many pages the user has visited before coming to your page:

```
>>> window.history.length
```

5

You cannot see the actual URLs though. For privacy reasons this doesn't work:

```
>>> window.history[0]
```

You can, however, navigate back and forth through the user's session as if the user had clicked the Back/Forward browser buttons:

```
>>> history.forward()
>>> history.back()
```

You can also skip pages back and forth with `history.go()`. This is same as calling `history.back()`:

```
>>> history.go(-1);
```

Two pages back:

```
>>> history.go(-2);
```

Reload the current page:

```
>>> history.go(0);
```

window.frames

`window.frames` is a collection of all of the frames in the current page. Note that it doesn't distinguish between frames and iframes. Regardless of whether there are frames on the page or not, `window.frames` always exists and points to `window`.

```
>>> window.frames === window
```

true

In order to tell if there are any frames on the page, you can check the `length` property:

```
>>> frames.length
```

1

Each frame contains another page which has its own global `window` object. Imagine you have a page with one iframe.

```
<iframe name="myframe" src="about:blank" />
```

To get access to the iframe's `window`, you can do any of these:

```
>>> window.frames[0]
>>> window.frames[0].window
>>> frames[0].window
>>> frames[0]
```

From the parent page, you can access properties of the child frame so, for example, you can reload the frame like this:

```
>>> frames[0].window.location.reload()
```

From inside the child you can access the parent:

```
>>> frames[0].parent === window
```

true

Using a property called `top`, you can access the topmost page (the one that contains all the other frames) from within any frame:

```
>>> window.frames[0].window.top === window
```

true

```
>>> window.frames[0].window.top === window.top
```

true

```
>>> window.frames[0].window.top === top
```

true

In addition, `self` is the same as `window`.

```
>>> self === window
```

true

```
>>> frames[0].self == frames[0].window
```

true

If a frame has a `name` attribute, you can also access the frame by name, not only by index.

```
>>> window.frames['myframe'] === window.frames[0]
```

true

window.screen

`screen` provides information about the desktop outside the browser. The `screen.colorDepth` property contains the color bit-depth (the color quality) of the monitor. This could be useful for statistical purposes.

```
>>> window.screen.colorDepth
```

32

You can also check the available screen real estate (the resolution):

```
>>> screen.width
```

1440

```
>>> screen.availWidth
```

1440

```
>>> screen.height
```

900

```
>>> screen.availHeight
```

847

The difference between `height` and `availHeight` is that the `height` is the total resolution, while `availHeight` subtracts any operating system menus such as the Windows task bar. The same is the case for `width` and `availWidth`.

window.open()/close()

Having explored some of the most common cross-browser properties of the `window` object, let's move to some of the methods. One such method is `open()`, which allows you to open up new browser windows (popups). Various browser policies and user settings may prevent you from opening a popup (due to abuse of the technique for marketing purposes), but generally you should be able to open a new window if it was initiated by the user. Otherwise, if you try to open a popup as the page loads, it will most likely be blocked, because the user didn't initiate it explicitly.

`window.open()` accepts the following parameters:

- URL to load in the new window
- Name of the new window, which can be used as the value of a form's `target` attribute
- Comma-separated list of features, such as:
    - `resizable` — should the user be able to resize the new window
    - `width, height` of the popup
    - `status` — should the status bar be visible
    - and so on

`window.open()` returns a reference to the `window` object of the newly created browser instance. Here's an example:

```
var win = window.open('http://www.packtpub.com', 'packt',
                      'width=300,height=300,resizable=yes');
```

`win` points to the `window` object of the popup. You can check if `win` has a falsy value, which means that the popup was blocked.

`win.close()` closes the new window.

It's best to stay away from opening new windows for accessibility and usability reasons. If you don't like sites to pop-up windows to you, why would do it to your users? There may be legitimate purposes, such as providing help information while filling out a form, but often the same can be achieved with alternative solutions, such as using a floating `<div>` inside the page.

window.moveTo(), window.resizeTo()

Continuing with the shady practices from the past, here are more methods to irritate your users, provided their browser and personal settings allow you to.

- `window.moveTo(100, 100)` will move the browser window to screen location $x = 100$ and $y = 100$ (counted from the top left corner).

- `window.moveBy(10, -10)` will move the window 10 pixels to the right and 10 pixels up from its current location.

- `window.resizeTo(x, y)` and `window.resizeBy(x, y)` accept the same parameters as the move methods but they resize the window as opposed to moving it.

Again, try to solve the problem you're facing without resorting to these methods.

window.alert(), window.prompt(), window.confirm()

In Chapter 2 we came across the function `alert()`. Now you know that global functions are methods of the global object so `alert('Watch out!')` and `window.alert('Watch out!')` are exactly the same.

`alert()` is not an ECMAScript function, but a BOM method. In addition to it, two other BOM methods allow you to interact with the user through system messages:

- `confirm()` gives the user two options—**OK** and **Cancel**, and
- `prompt()` collects textual input

See how this works:

```
>>> var answer = confirm('Are you cool?');
                        console.log(answer);
```

It presents you with a window similar to the following (the exact look depends on the browser and the operating system):

You'll notice that:

- Nothing gets written to the Firebug console until you close this message, this means that any JavaScript code execution freezes, waiting for the user's answer.
- Clicking **OK** returns **true**, clicking **Cancel** or closing the message using the **X** icon (or the *ESC* key) returns **false**.

This is handy for confirming user actions, such as:

```
if (confirm('Are you sure you want to delete this item?')) {
  // delete
} else {
  // abort
}
```

Make sure you provide an alternative way to confirm user actions for people who have disabled JavaScript (or for search engine spiders).

`window.prompt()` presents the user with a dialog to enter text.

```
>>> var answer = prompt('And your name was?'); console.log(answer);
```

This results in the following dialog box (on Windows/Firefox):

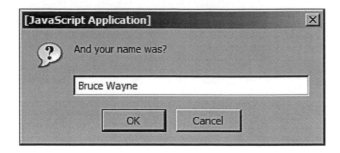

The value of answer will be:

- **null** if you click **Cancel** or the **X** icon, or press *ESC*
- "" (empty string) if you click **OK** or press *Enter* without typing anything
- A text string if you type something and then click **OK** (or press *Enter*)

The function also takes a string as a second parameter and displays it as a default value pre-filled into the input field.

window.setTimeout(), window.setInterval()

setTimeout() and setInterval() allow for scheduling the execution of a piece of code. setTimeout() executes the given code once after a specified number of milliseconds. setInterval() executes it repeatedly after a specified number of milliseconds has passed.

This will show an alert after 2 seconds (2000 milliseconds):

```
>>> function boo(){alert('Boo!');}
>>> setTimeout(boo, 2000);
```

4

As you can see the function returned the integer **4**, this is the ID of the timeout. You can use this ID to cancel the timeout using clearTimeout(). In the following example, if you're quick enough, and clear the timeout before two seconds have passed, the alert will never be shown.

```
>>> var id = setTimeout(boo, 2000);
>>> clearTimeout(id);
```

Let's change boo() to something less intrusive:

```
>>> function boo() {console.log('boo')};
```

Now, using `setInterval()` you can schedule `boo()` to execute every two seconds, until you cancel the scheduled execution with `clearInterval()`.

```
>>> var id = setInterval(boo, 2000);
```

boo

boo

boo

boo

boo

boo

```
>>> clearInterval(id)
```

Note that both functions accept a pointer to a callback function as a first parameter. They can also accept a string which will be evaluated with `eval()` but, as you know, `eval()` is evil, so it should be avoided. And what if you want to pass arguments to the function? In such cases, you can just wrap the function call inside another function.

The code below is valid, but not recommended:

```
var id = setInterval("alert('boo, boo')", 2000);
```

This alternative is preferred:

```
var id = setInterval(
  function(){
    alert('boo, boo')
  }, 2000
);
```

window.document

`window.document` is a BOM object that refers to the currently loaded document (page). Its methods and properties fall into the DOM category of objects. Take a deep breath (and maybe look at the BOM exercises at the end of the chapter) and let's dive into the DOM.

DOM

The DOM (Document Object Model) is a way to represent an XML or an HTML document as a tree of nodes. Using DOM methods and properties, you can access any element on the page, modify or remove elements, or add new ones. The DOM is a language-independent API (Application Programming Interface) and can be implemented not only in JavaScript, but also in any other language. For example, you can generate pages on the server-side with PHP's DOM implementation (http://php.net/dom).

Take a look at this example HTML page:

```
<!DOCTYPE html PUBLIC "-//W3C//DTD XHTML 1.0 Strict//EN"
    "http://www.w3.org/TR/xhtml1/DTD/xhtml1-strict.dtd">
<html>
  <head>
    <title>My page</title>
  </head>
  <body>
    <p class="opener">first paragraph</p>
    <p><em>second</em> paragraph</p>
    <p id="closer">final</p>
    <!-- and that's about it -->
  </body>
</html>
```

Taking the second paragraph (`<p><em>second</em> paragraph</p>`), you see that it's a p tag, and it's contained in the body tag. You can say that body is the parent of p and p is the child. The first and the third paragraphs would be children of the body too, and they're also siblings of the second paragraph. The em tag is a child of the second p, so p is its parent. The parent-child relationships can be represented graphically in an ancestry tree, called the *DOM tree*.

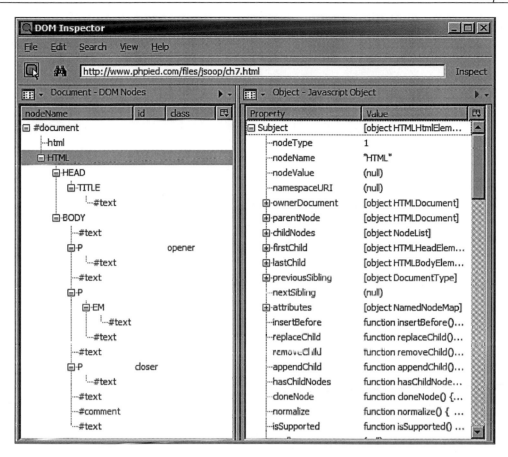

You can see how all of the tags are shown as expandable *nodes* on the tree. The words **#text** scattered around the tree also represent nodes but a different type — *text nodes*. For example the **#text** inside the **EM** is the word "second". Whitespace is also considered a text node, that's why, for example, there is a **#text** between **BODY** and the first **P** although there's no actual text in the code there, just spaces. Comments inside the HTML code are also nodes in the tree; the `<!--` and `that's about it -->` comment in the HTML source is the node **#comment** on the tree.

The screenshot above is taken from the **DOM Inspector** feature of Firefox. This feature doesn't get installed by default, so, if you are running Firefox 2, you may need to reinstall Firefox on top of your existing installation (you won't lose any preferences or extensions) and when prompted for the type of installation, choose **Custom** instead of **Standard** and then make sure you select the **DOM Inspector** checkbox. If you are running Firefox 3, you can get the DOM Inspector as an add-on from `https://addons.mozilla.org/en-us/firefox/addon/6622`.

Once installed, the DOM Inspector is reachable via **Tools | DOM Inspector**.

In the **DOM Inspector,** you have the DOM tree on the left and then information about the selected node on the right. The screenshot above shows the **Javascript Object** panel for the selected HTML node. The **Javascript Object** is not the default view, but you can bring it up by clicking the small "Views" icon as shown in the following screenshot.

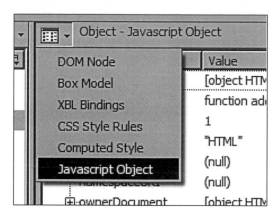

Every node in the DOM tree is an object and the **Javascript Object** view of the **DOM Inspector** lists all of the properties and methods of these objects. You can also see the constructor function that was used behind the scenes to create each of these objects. Although this is not very useful for day-to-day tasks, it may be interesting to know that, for example, `window.document` is created by the `HTMLDocument()` costructor; the object that represents the `head` tag is created by `HTMLHeadElement()` and so on. You cannot create objects using these constructors directly, though.

Core DOM and HTML DOM

One last diversion before moving on to examples that are more practical. As you now know, the DOM represents both XML documents and HTML documents. In fact, HTML documents are XML documents, but a little more specific. Therefore, as part of DOM Level 1, there is a *Core DOM* specification that is applicable to all XML documents, and there is also an *HTML DOM* specification which extends and builds upon the core DOM. Of course, the HTML DOM doesn't apply to all XML documents, but only to HTML documents. Let's see some example of Core DOM and HTML DOM constructors.

Constructor	Inherits from	Core or HTML	Comment
`Node`		Core	Any node on the tree.
`Document`	`Node`	Core	The `document` object; the main entry point to any XML document.
`HTMLDocument`	`Document`	HTML	This is `window.document` or simply `document`, the HTML-specific version of the previous object, which you'll use extensively.
`Element`	`Node`	Core	Every tag in the source is represented by an element. That's why you say "the P element" meaning "the `<p></p>` tag".
`HTMLElement`	`Element`	HTML	General-purpose constructor; all constructors for HTML elements inherit from it.
`HTMLBodyElement`	`HTMLElement`	HTML	Element representing the `<body>` tag.
`HTMLLinkElement`	`HTMLElement`	HTML	An A element (an `<a href="..." ></a>` tag).
	`HTMLElement`	HTML	All the rest of the HTML elements...
`CharacterData`	`Node`	Core	General-purpose constructor for dealing with texts.
`Text`	`CharacterData`	Core	Text node inside a tag. In `<em>second</em>` you have the element node EM and the text node with value "second".
`Comment`	`CharacterData`	Core	`<!-- any comment -->`
`Attr`	`Node`	Core	Represents an attribute of a tag, In `<p id="closer">` the id attribute is a DOM object created by the `Attr()` constructor.
`NodeList`		Core	A list of nodes; an array-like object that has a `length` property.
`NamedNodeMap`		Core	Same as above but the nodes can be accessed by name, not only by numeric index.
`HTMLCollection`		HTML	Similar to above but specific for HTML.

These are by no means all of the Core DOM and HTML DOM objects. For the full list consult `http://www.w3.org/TR/DOM-Level-1/`.

Now that this bit of DOM theory is behind us let's focus on the practical side of things. In the following sections, you'll learn how to:

- Access DOM nodes
- Modify nodes
- Create new nodes
- Remove nodes

Accessing DOM Nodes

Before you can validate a form on a page, or swap an image, you need to get access to the element you want to inspect or modify. Luckily, there are many ways to get to any element, either by navigating around traversing the DOM tree or by using a shortcut.

It's best if you start experimenting with all of the new objects and methods. The examples you'll see use the same simple document that you saw at the beginning of the DOM section, and which you can access at `http://www.phpied.com/files/jsoop/ch7.html`. Open the Firebug console, and let's get started.

The document Node

`document` gives you access to the current document. To explore this object, you can once again use Firebug as a cheat sheet. Type `document` and click on the result.

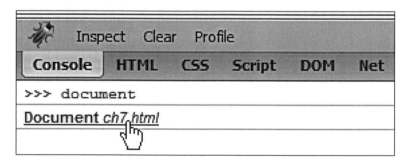

This takes you to the **DOM** tab where you can browse all of the properties and methods of the `document` object.

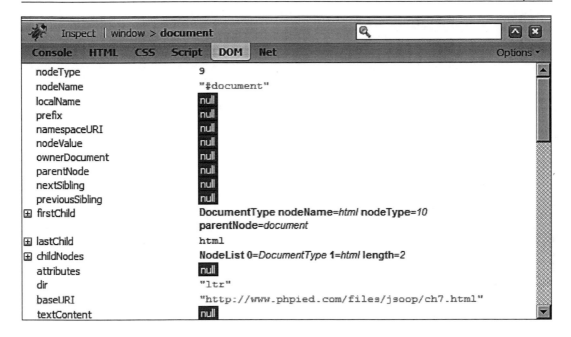

All nodes (this also includes the document node, text nodes, element nodes, and attribute nodes) have `nodeType`, `nodeName`, and `nodeValue` properties.

```
>>> document.nodeType
```

9

There are 12 node types, represented by integers. As you can see, the document node type is **9**. The most useful are 1 (element), 2 (attribute), and 3 (text).

Nodes also have names. For HTML tags the node name is the tag name (`tagName` property). For text nodes, it is **#text**, and for document nodes:

```
>>> document.nodeName
```

"#document"

Nodes can also have node values, for example for text nodes; the value is the actual text. The document node doesn't have a value:

```
>>> document.nodeValue
```

null

documentElement

Now let's move around the tree. XML documents always have one root node that wraps the rest of the document. For HTML documents, the root is the `<html>` tag. To access the root, you use the `documentElement` property of the `document` object.

```
>>> document.documentElement
```

<html>

`nodeType` is 1 (an element node):

```
>>> document.documentElement.nodeType
```

1

For element nodes, both `nodeName` and `tagName` properties contain the name of the tag.

```
>>> document.documentElement.nodeName
```

"HTML"

```
>>> document.documentElement.tagName
```

"HTML"

Child Nodes

In order to tell if a node has any children you use `hasChildNodes()`:

```
>>> document.documentElement.hasChildNodes()
```

true

The HTML element has two children—the `head` and the `body` elements. You can access them using the `childNodes` array-like collection.

```
>>> document.documentElement.childNodes.length
```

2

```
>>> document.documentElement.childNodes[0]
```

<head>

```
>>> document.documentElement.childNodes[1]
```

<body>

Any child has access to its parent through the `parentNode` property:

```
>>> document.documentElement.childNodes[1].parentNode
```

<html>

Let's assign a reference to `body` to a variable:

```
>>> var bd = document.documentElement.childNodes[1];
```

How many children does the `body` element have?

```
>>> bd.childNodes.length
```

9

As a refresher, here again is the body of the document we're looking at:

```
<body>
  <p class="opener">first paragraph</p>
  <p><em>second</em> paragraph</p>
  <p id="closer">final</p>
  <!-- and that's about it -->
</body>
```

How come `body` has 9 children? Well, 3 paragraphs plus one comment makes 4 nodes. The white space between these 4 nodes makes 3 more text nodes. This makes a total of 7 so far. The white space between `body` and the first `p` is the eighth node. The white space between the comment and the closing `</body>` is another text node. This makes a total of 9 child nodes.

Attributes

Because the first child of the body is a white space, the second child (index 1) is the first paragraph:

```
>>> bd.childNodes[1]
```

<p class="opener">

You can check whether an element has attributes using `hasAttributes()`:

```
>>> bd.childNodes[1].hasAttributes()
```

true

How many attributes? In this example, one, the `class` attribute.

```
>>> bd.childNodes[1].attributes.length
```

1

You can access the attributes by index and by name. You can also get the value using the `getAttribute()` method

```
>>> bd.childNodes[1].attributes[0].nodeName
```

"class"

```
>>> bd.childNodes[1].attributes[0].nodeValue
```

"opener"

```
>>> bd.childNodes[1].attributes['class'].nodeValue
```

"opener"

```
>>> bd.childNodes[1].getAttribute('class')
```

"opener"

Accessing the Content Inside a Tag

Let's take a look at the first paragraph:

```
>>> bd.childNodes[1].nodeName
```

"P"

You can get the text contained in the paragraph by using the `textContent` property. `textContent` doesn't exist in IE, but another property called `innerText` does and it returns the same value.

```
>>> bg.childNodes[1].textContent
```

"first paragraph"

There is also the `innerHTML` property. It's not part of the DOM standard, but exists in all major browsers. It returns any HTML code contained in the node. You can see how this is a little inconsistent, as DOM treats the document as a tree of nodes, not as a string of tags. But `innerHTML` is so convenient to use that you'll see it everywhere.

```
>>> bd.childNodes[1].innerHTML
```

"first paragraph"

The first paragraph only has text, so `innerHTML` is the same as `textContent` (or `innerText` in IE). However, the second paragraph does contain an `em` node, so you can see the difference:

```
>>> bd.childNodes[3].innerHTML
```

"<em>second</em> paragraph"

```
>>> bd.childNodes[3].textContent
```

"second paragraph"

Another way to get the text contained in the first paragraph is by using the `nodeValue` of the text node contain inside the `p` node:

```
>>> bd.childNodes[1].childNodes.length
```

1

```
>>> bd.childNodes[1].childNodes[0].nodeName
```

"#text"

```
>>> bd.childNodes[1].childNodes[0].nodeValue
```

"first paragraph"

DOM Access Shortcuts

By using `childNodes`, `parentNode`, `nodeName`, `nodeValue`, and `attributes`, you can navigate up and down the tree and pretty much do anything with the document. But the fact that white space is a text node makes this a slightly fragile way of working with the DOM. If the page changes slightly, your script may no longer work correctly. Also, if you want to get to a node deeper in the tree, it might take a bit of code before you get there. That's why you have the shortcut methods — `getElementsByTagName()`, `getElementsByName()`, and `getElcmentById()`.

`getElementsByTagName()` takes a tag name (the name of an element node) and returns an HTML collection (array-like object) of nodes with the matching tag name:

```
>>> document.getElementsByTagName('p').length
```

3

You can access an item in the list, by using the brackets notation, or the method `item()`, and passing the index (0 for the first element). Using `item()` is discouraged, as array brackets are more consistent and also shorter to type.

```
>>> document.getElementsByTagName('p')[0]
```

<p class="opener">

```
>>> document.getElementsByTagName('p').item(0)
```

<p class="opener">

Getting the contents of the first p:

```
>>> document.getElementsByTagName('p')[0].innerHTML
```

"first paragraph"

Accessing the last p:

```
>>> document.getElementsByTagName('p')[2]
```

<p id="closer">

In order to access element's attributes, you can use the `attributes` collection, or `getAttribute()` as shown above. But a shorter way is to use the attribute name as a property of the element you're working with. So to get the value of the `id` attribute, you just use `id` as a property:

```
>>> document.getElementsByTagName('p')[2].id
```

"closer"

Getting the `class` attribute of the first paragraph won't work though. It's an exception, because it just happens so that "class" is a reserved word in ECMAScript. You can use `className` instead:

```
>>> document.getElementsByTagName('p')[0].className
```

"opener"

Using `getElementsByTagName()` you can get all of the elements on the page:

```
>>> document.getElementsByTagName('*').length
```

9

In earlier versions of IE, `'*'` is not acceptable as a tag name. In order to get all elements you can use IE's proprietary `document.all` collection, although selecting every element is rarely useful. In any case, starting with IE version 7, `document.getElementsByTagName('*')` is supported, but it will return all of the nodes, not only the element nodes.

The other shortcut mentioned above is `getElementById()`. This is probably the most common way of accessing an element. You just assign IDs to the elements you plan to play with and they'll be easy to access later on:

```
>>> document.getElementById('closer')
```

<p id="closer">

Siblings, Body, First, and Last Child

`nextSibling` and `previousSibling` are two other convenient properties to navigate the DOM tree, once you have a reference to one element:

```
>>> var para = document.getElementById('closer')
>>> para.nextSibling
```

"\n "

```
>>> para.previousSibling
```

"\n "

```
>>> para.previousSibling.previousSibling
```

 <p>

```
>>> para.previousSibling.previousSibling.previousSibling
```

"\n "

```
>>> para.previousSibling.previousSibling.nextSibling.nextSibling
```

<p id="closer">

The `body` element is used so often that it has its own shortcut:

```
>>> document.body
```

<body>

```
>>> document.body.nextSibling
```

null

```
>>> document.body.previousSibling
```

<head>

`firstChild` and `lastChild` could also be useful. `firstChild` is the same as `childNodes[0]` and `lastChild` is the same as `childNodes[childNodes.length - 1]`.

```
>>> document.body.firstChild
```

"\n "

```
>>> document.body.lastChild
```

"\n "

```
>>> document.body.lastChild.previousSibling
```

Comment length=21 nodeName=#comment

```
>>> document.body.lastChild.previousSibling.nodeValue
```

" and that's about it "

The following illustration shows the family relationships between the body and three paragraphs in it. For simplicity, all the whitespace text nodes are removed from the diagram.

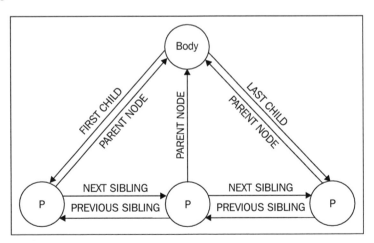

Walk the DOM

To wrap up, here's a function that takes any node and walks through the DOM tree recursively, starting from the given node.

```
function walkDOM(n) {
  do {
    console.log(n);
    if (n.hasChildNodes()) {
      walkDOM(n.firstChild)
    }
  } while (n = n.nextSibling)
}
```

You can test the function as follows:

```
>>> walkDOM(document.documentElement)
>>> walkDOM(document.body)
```

Modifying DOM Nodes

Now that you know a whole lot of methods for accessing any node of the DOM tree and its properties, let's see how you can modify these nodes.

Let's assign a pointer to the last paragraph to the variable my.

```
>>> var my = document.getElementById('closer');
```

Now changing the text of the paragraph can be as easy as changing the innerHTML value:

```
>>> my.innerHTML = 'final!!!';
```

"final!!!"

Because innerHTML accepts a string of HTML source code, you can also create a new em node in the DOM tree:

```
>>> my.innerHTML = '<em>my</em> final';
```

"<em>my</em> final"

The new em node becomes a part of the tree:

```
>>> my.firstChild
```

<em>

```
>>> my.firstChild.firstChild
```

"my"

Another way to change text is to get the actual text node and change its `nodeValue`:

```
>>> my.firstChild.firstChild.nodeValue = 'your';
```

"your"

Modifying Styles

Often you don't change the content of a node but its presentation. The elements have a `style` property, which in turn has a property mapped to each CSS property. For example, changing the style of the paragraph to add a red border:

```
>>> my.style.border = "1px solid red";
```

"1px solid red"

CSS properties often have dashes but dashes are not acceptable in JavaScript names. In such cases, you skip the dash and uppercase the next letter. So `padding-top` becomes `paddingTop`, `margin-left` becomes `marginLeft`, and so on.

```
>>> my.style.fontWeight = 'bold';
```

"bold"

You can also modify attributes regardless of whether they were initially set or not:

```
>>> my.align = "right";
```

"right"

```
>>> my.name
>>> my.name = 'myname';
```

"myname"

```
>>> my.id
```

"closer"

```
>>> my.id = 'further'
```

"further"

Let's see how the tag looks like after all of these modifications:

```
>>> my
```

<p id="further" align="right" style="border: 1px solid red; font-weight: bold;">

Fun with Forms

As mentioned earlier, JavaScript is great for client-side input validation and can save a few round-trips to the server. Let's practice form manipulations and play a little bit with a form located on a popular page—`google.com`.

Selecting all of the input fields:

```
>>> var inputs = document.getElementsByTagName('input');
>>> inputs.length;
```

4

Printing out `inputs[0]`, `inputs[1]`, and so on, you can see that the first input is a hidden field, the second is the search query, the third is the **Google Search** button and the fourth—the **I'm Feeling Lucky** button.

Accessing the search box:

```
>>> inputs[1].name;
```

"q"

Changing the search query, by setting the text contained in the `value` attribute:

```
>>> inputs[1].value = 'my query';
```

"my query"

Now let's have some fun. Changing the word **Lucky** with **Tricky** in the button:

```
>>> inputs[3].value = inputs[3].value.replace(/Lu/, 'Tri');
```

"I'm Feeling Tricky"

Now let's implement the tricky part and make that button show and hide for one second. We can do this with a simple function. Let's call it `toggle()`. Every time you call the function, it checks the value of the CSS property `visibility` and sets it to "visible" if it's "hidden" and vice versa.

```
function toggle(){
  var st = document.getElementsByTagName('input')[3].style;
  st.visibility = (st.visibility === 'hidden') ? 'visible': 'hidden';
}
```

Instead of calling the function manually, let's set an interval and call it every second.

```
>>> var myint = setInterval(toggle, 1000);
```

The result? The button starts blinking (making it trickier to click). When you're tired of chasing it, just remove the timeout interval.

```
>>> clearInterval(myint)
```

Creating New Nodes

In order to create new nodes, you can use the methods `createElement()` and `createTextNode()`. Once you have the new nodes, you add them to the DOM tree with `appendChild()`.

Creating a new `p` element and setting its `innerHTML`:

```
>>> var myp = document.createElement('p');
>>> myp.innerHTML = 'yet another';
```

"yet another"

The new element automatically gets all the default properties, such as `style`, which you can modify:

```
>>> myp.style
```

CSSStyleDeclaration length=0

```
>>> myp.style.border = '2px dotted blue'
```

"2px dotted blue"

Using `appendChild()` you can add the new node to the DOM tree. Calling this method on the `document.body` node means creating one more child node right after the last child:

```
>>> document.body.appendChild(myp)
```

<p style="border: 2px dotted blue;">

Here's an illustration of how the page looked like before and after the new node was appended:

```
first paragraph            first paragraph

second paragraph           second paragraph

final                      final

                           yet another
```

DOM-only Method

Using `innerHTML` was a way to get things done a little more quickly; the pure DOM way would've been:

1. Create a new text node containing the "yet another" text
2. Create new paragraph node
3. Append the text node as a child to the paragraph
4. Append the paragraph as a child to the body

This way you can create any number of text nodes and elements and nest them however you like. Let's say you want to add the following HTML to the end of the body:

```
<p>one more paragraph<strong>bold</strong></p>
```

Presenting this as a hierarchy would be something like:

```
P element
    text node with value "one more paragraph"
    STRONG element
        text node with value "bold"
```

Let's see the code that accomplishes this:

```
// create P
var myp = document.createElement('p');
// create text node and append to P
var myt = document.createTextNode('one more paragraph')
myp.appendChild(myt);
// create STRONG and append another text node to it
var str = document.createElement('strong');
str.appendChild(document.createTextNode('bold'));
// append STRONG to P
myp.appendChild(str);
// append P to BODY
document.body.appendChild(myp);
```

cloneNode()

Another way to create nodes is by copying (or cloning) existing ones. The method `cloneNode()` does this and accepts a boolean parameter (`true` = deep copy with all the children, `false` = shallow copy, only this node). Let's test the method.

Getting a reference to the element you want to clone:

```
>>> var el = document.getElementsByTagName('p')[1];
```

Now `el` refers to the second paragraph on the page that looks like this:

```
<p><em>second</em> paragraph</p>
```

Let's create a shallow clone of `el` and append it to the body:

```
>>> document.body.appendChild(el.cloneNode(false))
```

You won't see a difference on the page, because the shallow copy only copied the P node, without any children. This means that the text inside the paragraph (which is a text node child) was not cloned. The line above would be equivalent to:

```
>>> document.body.appendChild(document.createElement('p'));
```

Now if you create a deep copy, the whole DOM subtree starting from P will be copied, and this includes text nodes and the EM element.

```
>>> document.body.appendChild(el.cloneNode(true))
```

You can also copy only the EM if you want:

```
>>> document.body.appendChild(el.firstChild.cloneNode(true))
```

<em>

Or only the text node with value "second":

```
>>> document.body.appendChild(el.firstChild.
                               firstChild.cloneNode(false))
```

"second"

insertBefore()

Using `appendChild()`, you can only add new children at the end of the selected element. For more control over the exact location, there is `insertBefore()`. This is the same as `appendChild()`, but accepts an extra parameter, specifying before which element to insert the new node. For example, the following code will insert a text node at the end of the `body`:

```
>>> document.body.appendChild(document.createTextNode('boo!'));
```

And this will create the same text node and add it as the first child of the `body`:

```
document.body.insertBefore(
   document.createTextNode('boo!'),
   document.body.firstChild
);
```

Removing Nodes

To remove nodes from the DOM tree, you can use the method `removeChild()`. Again, let's work with this BODY:

```
<body>
  <p class="opener">first paragraph</p>
  <p><em>second</em> paragraph</p>
  <p id="closer">final</p>
  <!-- and that's about it -->
</body>
```

Here's how you can remove the second paragraph:

```
>>> var myp = document.getElementsByTagName('p')[1];
>>> var removed = document.body.removeChild(myp);
```

The method returns the removed node if you want to use it later. You can still use all the DOM methods although the element is no longer in the tree:

```
>>> removed
```

<p>

```
>>> removed.firstChild
```

<em>

There's also the `replaceChild()` method that removes a node and puts another one in its place. Now after removing the node shown above, the tree looks like:

```
<body>
  <p class="opener">first paragraph</p>
  <p id="closer">final</p>
  <!-- and that's about it -->
</body>
```

Now the second paragraph is the one with the ID "closer":

```
>>> var p = document.getElementsByTagName('p')[1];
>>> p
```

<p id="closer">

Let's replace this paragraph with the one we have in the `removed` variable:

```
>>> var replaced = document.body.replaceChild(removed, p);
```

Just like `removeChild()`, `replaceChild()` returns a reference to the node that is now out of the tree:

```
>>> replaced
```

<p id="closer">

Now the body looks like:

```
<body>
  <p class="opener">first paragraph</p>
  <p><em>second</em> paragraph</p>
  <!-- and that's about it -->
</body>
```

A quick way to wipe out all of the content of a subtree is to set the `innerHTML` to a blank string. This will remove all of the children of the BODY:

```
>>> document.body.innerHTML = '';
```

""

Testing:

```
>>> document.body.firstChild
```

null

Removing with `innerHTML` is easy but the DOM-only way would be to go over all of the child nodes and remove each one individually. Here's a little function that removes all nodes from a given start node:

```
function removeAll(n) {
  while (n.firstChild) {
    n.removeChild(n.firstChild);
  }
}
```

If you want to delete all BODY children and leave the page with an empty `<body></body>`:

```
>>> removeAll(document.body);
```

HTML-Only DOM Objects

As you know already, the Document Object Model applies to both XML and HTML documents. What you've learned above about traversing the tree and then adding, removing, or modifying nodes applies to any XML document. There are, however, some HTML-only objects and properties.

`document.body` is one such HTML-only object. It's so common to have a`<body>` tag in HTML documents and it's accessed so often, that it is justifiable in having an object that is much friendlier than the equivalent `document.getElementsByTagName('body')[0]`.

`document.body` is one example of an object that was actually inherited from the pre-historic DOM Level 0 and moved to the HTML extension of the DOM specification. There are other objects like `document.body`. For some of them there is no Core DOM equivalent; for others there is an equivalent, but the DOM0 original was ported anyway for simplicity and legacy purposes. Let's see some of those objects.

Primitive Ways to Access the Document

Unlike the DOM, which gives you access to any element (and even comments and white-space), initially JavaScript had only a limited access to the elements of an HTML document. This was done mainly through a number of collections:

- `document.images` - this is a collection of all of the images on the page. This is the same as the Core DOM equivalent `document.getElementsByTagName('img')`

- `document.applets`—this is the same as `document.getElementsByTagName('applets')`

- `document.links`

- `document.anchors`

- `document.forms`

`document.links` contains a list of all `<a href="...">` `</a>` tags on the page, meaning the A tags that have an `href` attribute. `document.anchors` contains all links with a `name` attribute (`<a name="...">` `</a>`).

One of the most widely used collections is `document.forms`, which contains a list of `<form>` tags. This will give you access to the first form on the page:

```
>>> document.forms[0]
```

This would be the same as:

```
>>> document.getElementsByTagName('forms')[0]
```

The forms collection contains input fields and buttons, accessible through the `elements` property. Here's how to access the first input of the first form on the page:

```
>>> document.forms[0].elements[0]
```

Once you have access to an element, you can access the attributes of the tag as object properties. Imagine the first field of the first form is this:

```
<input name="search" id="search" type="text" size="50"
       maxlength="255" value="Enter email..." />
```

You can change the text in the field (the value of the `value` attribute) by using something like:

```
>>> document.forms[0].elements[0].value = 'me@example.org'
```

"me@example.org"

If you want to disable the field dynamically:

```
>>> document.forms[0].elements[0].disabled = true;
```

When forms or form elements have a `name` attribute, you can access them by name too:

```
>>> document.forms[0].elements['search']; // array notation
>>> document.forms[0].elements.search;    // object property
```

document.write()

The method `document.write()` allows you to insert HTML into the page while the page is being loaded. You can have something like this:

```
<p>It is now <script>document.write("<em>" + new Date()
                                    + "</em>");</script></p>
```

This will be the same as if you had the date directly in source of the HTML document:

```
<p>It is now <em>Sat Feb 23 2008 17:48:04 GMT-0800
  (Pacific Standard Time)</em></p>
```

There's also the `document.writeln()` which is the same as `document.write()`, but it adds a new line "\n" at the end, so these would be equivalent:

```
>>> document.write('boo!\n');
>>> document.writeln('boo!');
```

Note that you can only use `document.write()` while the page is being loaded, if you try it after page load, it will replace the content of the whole page.

It's rare that you would need `document.write()`, and if you think you do, try an alternative approach. The ways to modify the content of the page provided by DOM Level 1 are preferred and are much more flexible.

Cookies, Title, Referrer, Domain

The four additional properties of `document` you'll see in this section are also ported from DOM Level 0 to the HTML extension of DOM Level 1. Unlike the previous ones, for these properties there are no Core DOM equivalents.

`document.cookie` is a property that contains a string. This string is the content of the cookies exchanged between the server and the client. When the server sends a page to the browser, it may include the `Set-Cookie` HTTP header. When the client sends a request to the server, it sends the cookie information back with the `Cookie` header. Using `document.cookie` you can alter the cookies the browser sends to the server. Visiting `cnn.com` for example and typing `document.cookie` in the console gives you something like:

```
>>> document.cookie
```

**"CNNid=Ga50a0c6f-14404-1198821758-6; SelectedEdition=www; s_sess=
%20s_dslv%...**

`document.title` allows you to change the title of the page displayed in the browser window. For example on `cnn.com`, you can do:

```
>>> document.title = 'My title'
```

"My title"

The result will be something like:

Note that this doesn't change the value of the `<title>` tag, but only the display in the browser window, so it is not equivalent to `document.getElementsByTagName('title')[0]`.

`document.referrer` tells you the URL of the previously-visited page. This is the same value the browser sends in the `Referer` HTTP header when requesting the page. (Note that `Referer` is misspelled in the HTTP headers, but is correct in JavaScript's `document.referrer`). If you've visited the CNN page by searching Yahoo! first, you can see something like:

```
>>> document.referrer
```

"http://search.yahoo.com/search?p=cnn&ei=UTF-8&fr=moz2"

`document.domain` gives you access to the domain name of the currently-loaded page. This is useful when you need to perform so-called *domain relaxation*. Imagine your page is `www.yahoo.com` and you have a frame or iframe hosted on `music.yahoo.com`. These are two separate domains so the browser's security restrictions won't allow the page to communicate with the iframe. To resolve this you can set `document.domain` on both pages to `yahoo.com` and they'll be able to "talk" to each other.

Note that you can only set the domain to a less-specific one; for example, you can change `www.yahoo.com` to `yahoo.com`, but you cannot change `yahoo.com` to `www.yahoo.com` or any other non-yahoo domain.

```
>>> document.domain
```

"www.yahoo.com"

```
>>> document.domain = 'yahoo.com'
```

"yahoo.com"

```
>>> document.domain = 'www.yahoo.com'
```

Illegal document.domain value" code: "1009

```
>>> document.domain = 'www.example.org'
```

Illegal document.domain value" code: "1009

Previously in this chapter, you saw the `window.location` object. Well, the same functionality is also available as `document.location`:

```
>>> window.location === document.location
```

true

Events

Imagine you are listening to a radio program and they announce, "Big event! Huge! Aliens have landed on Earth!" You might think "Yeah, whatever", some other listeners might think "They come in peace" and some "We're all gonna die!". Similarly, the browser broadcasts *events* and your code could be notified should it decide to "tune in" and *listen* to the events as they happen. Some example events include:

- The user clicks a button
- The user types a character in a form field
- The page finishes loading

You can *attach* a JavaScript function (called an *event listener* or *event handler*) to a specific event and the browser will execute your function as soon the event occurs. Let's see how this is done.

Inline HTML Attributes

Adding specific attributes to a tag is the laziest way, for example:

```
<div onclick="alert('Ouch!')">click</div>
```

In this case when the user clicks on the `<div>`, the *click* event *fires* and the string of JavaScript code contained in the `onclick` attribute is executed. There's no explicit function that listens to the click event, but behind the scenes a function is still created and it contains the code you specified as a value of the `onclick` attribute.

Element Properties

Another way to have some code executed when a click event fires is to assign a function to the `onclick` property of a DOM node element. For example:

```
<div id="my-div">click</div>
<script type="text/javascript">
  var myelement = document.getElementById('my-div');
  myelement.onclick = function() {
    alert('Ouch!');
    alert('And double ouch!');
  }
</script>
```

This way is actually better because it helps you keep your <div> clean of any JavaScript code. Always keep in mind that HTML is for content, JavaScript for behavior and CSS for formatting, and you should keep these three separate as much as possible.

This method has the drawback that you can attach only one function to the event, as if the radio program has only one listener. It's true that you can have a lot happening inside the same function, but this is not always convenient, as if all the radio listeners are in the same room.

DOM Event Listeners

The best way to work with browser events is to use the event listener approach outlined in DOM Level 2, where you can have many functions listening to an event. When the event fires, all functions are executed. All of the listeners don't need to know about each other and can work independently. They can tune in and out at any time without affecting the other listeners.

Let's use the same simple markup from the previous section (available for you to play with at `http://www.phpied.com/files/jsoop/ch7.html`). We had this piece of markup:

```
<p id="closer">final</p>
```

Your JavaScript code can assign listeners to the click event using the
`addEventListener()` method:

```
>>> var mypara = document.getElementById('my-div');
>>> mypara.addEventListener('click', function()
                            {alert('Boo!')}, false);
>>> mypara.addEventListener('click', console.log, false);
```

As you can see, `addEventListeners()` is a method called on the node object and
accepts the type of event as its first parameter and a function pointer as its second.
You can use anonymous functions such as `function(){alert('Boo!')}` or existing
functions such as `console.log`. The listener functions you specify will be called
when the event happens, and a parameter will be passed to them. This parameter is
an *event* object. If you run the code above and click the last paragraph, you can see
event objects being logged to the Firebug console.

---

first paragraph

second paragraph

final

🦟   Inspect   Clear   Profile

Console   HTML   CSS   Script   DOM   Net

```
>>> var mypara = document.getElementById('closer');
>>> mypara.addEventListener('click', function(){alert('Boo!')}, false);
>>> mypara.addEventListener('click', console.log, false);
click clientX=15 clientY=96
```

Clicking on an event object allows you to see its properties.

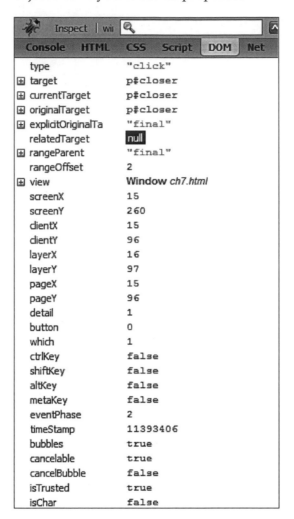

Capturing and Bubbling

In the calls to `addEventListener()` above there was a third parameter, `false`. Let's see what this is for.

Say you have a link inside an unordered list, like so:

```
<body>
  <ul>
    <li><a href="http://phpied.com">my blog</a></li>
  </ul>
</body>
```

When you click the link, you're actually also clicking the list item `<li>`, the list `<ul>`, the `<body>` and eventually the document as a whole. A click on a link can also be seen as click on the document, because of *event propagation*. The process of propagating an event can be implemented in two ways:

- Event capturing — the click happens on the document first, then it propagates to the body, the list, the list item, and finally to the link.

- Event bubbling — the click happens on the link and then bubbles up to the document.

DOM Level 2 Events specification suggests that the events propagate in three phases: capturing, at target, and bubbling. This means that the event propagates from the document to the link (target) and then back up to the document. The event objects have an `eventPhase` property, which reflects the current phase.

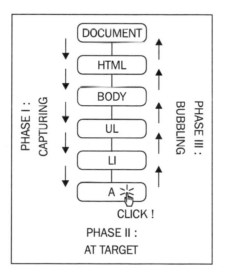

Historically, IE and Netscape (working on their own and without a standard to follow) implemented the exact opposites. IE implemented only bubbling, Netscape only capturing. After the DOM specification, Firefox, Opera, and Safari implemented the three phases, but IE kept only the bubbling.

What are the practical implications related to the event propagation?

- The third parameter to `addEventListener()` specifies whether or not capturing should be used. In order to have your code more portable across browsers, it is better to always set this parameter to `false` and code using bubbling only.

- You can stop the propagation of the event, in your listeners, so that it stops bubbling up and never reaches the document. To do this you can call the `stopPropagation()` method of the event object (there is an example in the next section).

- You can also use *event delegation*. If you have ten buttons inside a `<div>`, you can always attach ten event listeners, one for each button. But a smarter thing to do is to attach only one listener to the wrapping `<div>` and when the event happens, check which button was the target of the click.

To be completely fair, there is a way to use event capturing in IE (using `setCapture()` and `releaseCapture()` methods) but only for mouse events. Capturing any other events (keystroke events for example) is not supported.

Stop Propagation

Let's see an example of how you can stop the event from bubbling up. Going back to the test document, we had:

```
<p id="closer">final</p>
```

Let's define a function that will handle clicks on the paragraph:

```
>>> function paraHandler(){alert('clicked paragraph');}
```

Now let's attach this function as a listener to the click event:

```
>>> var para = document.getElementById('closer');
>>> para.addEventListener('click', paraHandler, false);
```

Let's also attach listeners to the click event on the body, the document, and the browser window:

```
>>> document.body.addEventListener('click', function(){alert
                            ('clicked body')}, false);
>>> document.addEventListener('click', function(){alert
                        ('clicked doc')}, false);
>>> window.addEventListener('click', function(){alert
                        ('clicked window')}, false);
```

Note that the DOM specifications don't say anything about events on the window. And why would they, as DOM deals with the document and not the browser. IE doesn't propagate click events to the window, but Firefox does.

Now, if you click on the paragraph, you'll see four alerts saying:

- **clicked paragraph**
- **clicked body**
- **clicked doc**
- **clicked window**

This illustrates how the same single click event propagates (bubbles up) from the target all the way up to the window.

The opposite of `addEventLister()` is `removeEventListener()` and it accepts exactly the same parameters. Let's remove the listener attached to the paragraph.

```
>>> para.removeEventListener('click', paraHandler, false);
```

If you try now, you'll see alerts only for the click event on the body, document, and window, but not on the paragraph.

Now let's stop the propagation of the event. The function you add as a listener receives the event object as a parameter and you can call the `stopPropagation()` method of that event object:

```
function paraHandler(e){
  alert('clicked paragraph');
  e.stopPropagation();
}
```

Adding the modified listener:

```
>>> para.addEventListener('click', paraHandler, false);
```

Now if you click the paragraph you'll see only one alert, because the event won't bubble up to the body, the document, or the window.

Note that you cannot remove listeners that use anonymous functions. If you remove a listener, you have to pass a pointer to the same function you previously attached. But two anonymous functions are still two separate function objects somewhere in memory, even if they have the exact same bodies. Doing this will not work:

```
document.body.removeEventListener('click',
    function(){
        alert('clicked body')
    },
false); //  does NOT remove the handler
```

Prevent Default Behavior

Some browser events have a pre-defined behavior. For example, clicking a link loads another page. You can attach listeners to clicks on a link and you can also disable the default behavior. In order to do so, you can call the method `preventDefault()` on the event object.

Let's see how you can annoy your visitors by asking **Are you sure you want to follow this link?** every time they click a link. If the user clicks *Cancel* (causing `confirm()` to return `false`), the `preventDefault()` method is called:

```
// all links
var all_links = document.getElementsByTagName('a');
for (var i = 0; i < all_links.length; i++) { // loop all links
  all_links[i].addEventListener(
    'click', // event type
    function(e){ // handler
      if (!confirm('Are you sure you want to follow this link?')){
        e.preventDefault();
      }
    },
    false); // don't use capturing
}
```

Note that not all events allow you to prevent the default behavior. Most do, but if you want to be sure, you can check the `cancellable` property of the event object.

Cross-Browser Event Listeners

As you already know, most modern browsers almost fully implement the DOM Level 1 specification. However, the events were not standardized until DOM 2. As a result, there are quite a few differences in how IE implements this functionality compared to Firefox, Opera, and Safari.

Check out an example that causes the `nodeName` of a clicked element (the *target* element) to be written to the console:

```
document.addEventListener('click', function(e){
  console.log(e.target.nodeName);
}, false);
```

Now let's take a look at how IE is different:

- In IE there's no `addEventListener()` method, although since IE version 5 there is an equivalent `attachEvent()`. For earlier versions, your only choice is accessing the property (such as `onclick`) directly.
- `click` event becomes `onclick` when using `attachEvent()`.

- If you listen to events the old-fashioned way (for example, by setting a function value to the onclick property), when the callback function is invoked, it doesn't get an event object passed as a parameter. But regardless of how you attach the listener, in IE there is always a global object window. event that points to the event.

- In IE the event object doesn't get a target attribute telling you the element on which the event fired, but it does have an equivalent property called srcElement.

- As mentioned before, event capturing doesn't apply to all events, so only bubbling should be used.

- There's no stopPropagation() method, but you can set the IE-only cancelBubble property to true.

- There's no preventDefault() method, but you can set the IE-only returnValue property to false.

- In order to stop listening to an event, instead of removeEventListener() in IE you'll need detachEvent().

So here's the revised version of the code above that will work cross-browser:

```
function callback(evt) {
  // prep work
  evt = evt || window.event;
  var target = (typeof evt.target !== 'undefined') ? evt.target : evt.
srcElement;
  // actual callback work
  console.log(target.nodeName);
}
//  start listening for click events
if (document.addEventListener){ // FF
  document.addEventListener('click', callback, false);
} else if (document.attachEvent){ // IE
  document.attachEvent('onclick', callback);
} else {
  document.onclick = callback;
}
```

Types of Events

Now you know how to handle cross-browser events. But all of the examples above used only click events. What other events are happening out there? As you can probably guess, different browsers provide different events. There is a subset of cross-browser events and some browser-specific ones. For a full list of events, you should consult the browser's documentation, but here's a selection of cross-browser events:

- Mouse events
  - ° mouseup, mousedown, click (the sequence is mousedown-up-click), dblclick
  - ° mouseover (mouse is over an element), mouseout (mouse was over an element but left it), mousemove

- Keyboard events
  - ° keydown, keypress, keyup (occur in this sequence)

- Loading/window events
  - ° load (an image or a page and all of its components are done loading), unload (user leaves the page), beforeunload (the script can provide the user with an option to stop the unload)
  - ° abort (user stops loading the page in Firefox or an image in IE), error (a JavaScript error in Firefox and IE, also when an image cannot be loaded in IE)
  - ° resize (browser window is resized), scroll (the page is scrolled), contextmenu (the right-click menu appears)

- Form events
  - ° focus (enter a form field), blur (leave form field)
  - ° change (leave a field after the value has changed), select (select text in a text field)
  - ° reset, submit

This concludes the discussion of events. Refer to the exercise section at the end of this chapter for a little challenge of creating your own event utility to handle cross-browser events.

XMLHttpRequest

`XMLHttpRequest()` is an object (a constructor function) that allows you to send HTTP requests from JavaScript. Historically, XMLHttpRequest (or XHR for short) was introduced in IE and was initially implemented as an ActiveX object. Starting with IE7 it is a a native browser object, the same way as it is in Firefox, Safari, and Opera. The common implementation of this object across browsers gave birth to the so-called AJAX applications, where it is no longer necessary to refresh the whole page every time you need new content. With JavaScript, you can make an HTTP request to the server, get the response and update only a part of the page. In this way you can build much more responsive, desktop-like web pages.

AJAX stands for Asynchronous JavaScript and XML.

- *Asynchronous* because after sending an HTTP request your code doesn't need to wait for the response, but it can do other stuff and be notified (through an event) when the response arrives.
- *JavaScript* — well, it's pretty obvious, we create XHR objects with JavaScript.
- *XML* because initially developers were making HTTP requests for XML documents and were using the data contained in them to update the page. This is no longer a common practice, though, as you can request data in plain text, in the much more convenient JSON format, or simply as HTML ready to be inserted into the page.

There are effectively two steps to using the XMLHttpRequest:

- Send the request — this includes creating an XMLHttpRequest object and attaching an event listener
- Process the response — your event listener gets notified that the response has arrived and your code gets busy doing something useful with the response

Send the Request

In order to create an object you simply use this (we'll deal with browser inconsistencies in a bit):

```
var xhr = new XMLHttpRequest();
```

The next thing is to attach an event listener to the `readystatechange` event fired by the object:

```
xhr.onreadystatechange = myCallback;
```

Then you need to call the `open()` method, as follows:

```
xhr.open('GET', 'somefile.txt', true);
```

The first parameter specifies the type of HTTP request (GET, POST, HEAD, and so on). GET and POST are the most common. Use GET when you don't need to send much data with the request, otherwise use POST. The second parameter is the URL you are requesting. In this example, it's the text file `somefile.txt` located in the same directory as the page. The last parameter is a boolean specifying whether the request is asynchronous (`true`) or not (`false`).

The last step is to actually fire off the request.

```
xhr.send('');
```

The method `send()` accepts any data you want to send with the request. For GET requests, this is an empty string, because the data is in the URL. For POST request, it's a query string in the form `key=value&key2=value2`.

At this point, the request is sent and your code (and the user) can move on to other tasks. The callback function `myCallback` will be invoked when the response comes back from the server.

Process the Response

We've attached a listener to the `readystatechange` event. What is the ready state and how does it change?

There is a property of the XHR object called `readyState`. Every time it changes, the `readystatechange` event fires. The possible values of the `readyState` property are as follows:

- 0—uninitialized
- 1—loading
- 2—loaded
- 3—interactive
- 4—complete

When `readyState` gets the value of **4**, it means the response is back and ready to be processed. In `myCallback`, after you make sure `readyState` is **4**, the other thing to check is the status code of the HTTP request. You might have requested a non-existing URL for example and get a **404 (File not found)** status code. The interesting code is the **200 (OK)** code, so `myCallback` should check for this value. The status code is available in the `status` property of the XHR object.

Once xhr.readyState is **4** and xhr.status is **200**, you can access the contents of the requested URL, using the xhr.responseText property. Let's see how myCallback could be implemented to simply alert() the contents of the requested URL.

```
function myCallback() {
  if (xhr.readyState < 4) {
    return; // not ready yet
  }
  if (xhr.status !== 200) {
    alert('Error!'); // the HTTP status code is not OK
    return;
  }
  // all is fine, do the work
  alert(xhr.responseText);
}
```

Once you've received the new content you requested, you can add it to the page, or use it for some calculations, or for any other purpose you find suitable.

Overall, this two-step process (send request, process response) is the core of the whole XHR/AJAX functionality. Now that you know the basics, you can move on to building the next Gmail or the next Yahoo! Maps. Oh yes, let's have a look at one minor browser inconsistency.

Creating XMLHttpRequest Objects in IE prior to version 7

In Internet Explorer prior to version 7, the XMLHttpRequest object was an ActiveX object, so creating an XHR instance is a little different. It goes like:

```
var xhr = new ActiveXObject('MSXML2.XMLHTTP.3.0');
```

MSXML2.XMLHTTP.3.0 is the identifier of the object you want to create. There are several versions of the XMLHttpRequest object and if your page visitor doesn't have the latest one installed, you can try two older ones, before you give up.

For a fully-cross-browser solution, you should first test to see if the user's browser supports XMLHttpRequest as a native object, and if not, try the IE way. Therefore, the whole process of creating an XHR instance could be like this:

```
var ids = ['MSXML2.XMLHTTP.3.0',
           'MSXML2.XMLHTTP',
           'Microsoft.XMLHTTP'];

var xhr;
if (typeof window.XMLHttpRequest === 'function') {
  xhr = new XMLHttpRequest();
} else {
  for (var i = 0; i < ids.length; i++) {
    try {
      xhr = new ActiveXObject(ids[i]);
      break;
    } catch (e){}
  }
}
```

What is this doing? The array `ids` contains a list of ActiveX program IDs to try. The variable `xhr` will point to the new XHR object. The code first checks to see if `windows.XMLHttpRequest` is a valid function. If it is, this means that the browser supports `XMLHttpRequest()` natively (so the browser is one of Firefox, Safari, Opera, or IE7 (or greater)). If it is not, the code will loop through `ids` trying to create an object. `catch(e)` quietly catches failures and the loop continues. As soon as an `xhr` object is created, we `break` out of the loop.

As you can see, this is quite a bit of code so it's best to abstract it into a function. Actually, one of the exercises at the end of the chapter prompts you to create your own AJAX utility.

A is for Asynchronous

Now you know how to create an XHR object, give it a URL and handle the response to the request. What happens when you send two requests asynchronously? What if the response to the second request comes before the first?

In the example above, the XHR object was global and `myCallback` was relying on the presence of this global object in order to access its `readyState`, `status` and `responseText` properties. Another way, which will prevent you from relying on global variables, is to wrap the callback in a closure. Let's see how:

```
var xhr = new XMLHttpRequest();
xhr.onreadystatechange = (function(myxhr){
  return function(){myCallback(myxhr);}
```

```
})(xhr);
xhr.open('GET', 'somefile.txt', true);
xhr.send('');
```

In this case `myCallback()` will receive the XHR object as a parameter and is not going to look for it in the global space. This also means that at the time the response is received, the original `xhr` might have been reused for a second request or even destroyed. The closure will keep pointing to the original object.

X is for XML

Although these days JSON (discussed in the next chapter) is preferred over XML as a data transfer format, XML is still an option. In addition to the `responseText` property, the XHR objects also have another property called `responseXML`. If you send an HTTP request for an XML document, `responseXML` will point to an XML DOM document object. To work with this document, you can use all of the core DOM methods discussed previously in this chapter, such as `getElementsByTagName()`, `getElementById()`, and so on.

An Example

Let's wrap up the different XHR topics with an example. You can visit the page located at `http://www.phpied.com/files/jsoop/xhr.html` to work on the example yourself.

The main page, `xhr.html`, is a simple static page that contains nothing but three `<div>`s.

```
<div id="text">Text will be here</div>
<div id="html">HTML will be here</div>
<div id="xml">XML will be here</div>
```

Using the Firebug console, you can write code that will request three files and load their respective contents into each `<div>`.

The three files to load will be:

- `content.txt` —a simple text file containing the text "I am a text file"
- `content.html` —a file containing some HTML code:
  "I am formatted HTML"

- content.xml — an XML file, containing:

```
<?xml version="1.0" ?>
<root>
    I'm XML data.
</root>
```

All of the files are stored in the same directory as xhr.html. Note that for security reasons you can only use XMLHttpRequest to request files that are on the same domain.

First, let's create a function to abstract the request/response part:

```
function request(url, callback) {
  var xhr = new XMLHttpRequest();
  xhr.onreadystatechange = (function(myxhr){
    return function(){
      callback(myxhr);
    }
  })(xhr);
  xhr.open('GET', url, true);
  xhr.send('');
}
```

This function accepts a URL to request and a callback function to call once the response arrives. We can call the function three times, once for each file, like this:

```
request(
  'http://www.phpied.com/files/jsoop/content.txt',
  function(o){
    document.getElementById('text').innerHTML = o.responseText;
  }
);
request(
  'http://www.phpied.com/files/jsoop/content.html',
  function(o){
    document.getElementById('html').innerHTML = o.responseText;
  }
);
request(
  'http://www.phpied.com/files/jsoop/content.xml',
  function(o){
    document.getElementById('xml').innerHTML =
      o.responseXML.getElementsByTagName('root')[0]
                        .firstChild.nodeValue;
  }
);
```

The callback functions are defined inline. The first two are pretty much identical.
They just replace the HTML of the corresponding <div> with the contents of
the requested file. The third one is a little different, as it deals with the XML
document. First, we access the XML DOM object as o.responseXML. Then, using
getElementsByTagName(), we get a list of all <root> tags (there is only one). The
firstChild of the <root> is a text node and using nodeValue we get the text
contained in it ("I'm XML data"). Then we again replace the HTML of the <div
id="xml"> with the new content. The result is shown in on the following illustration:

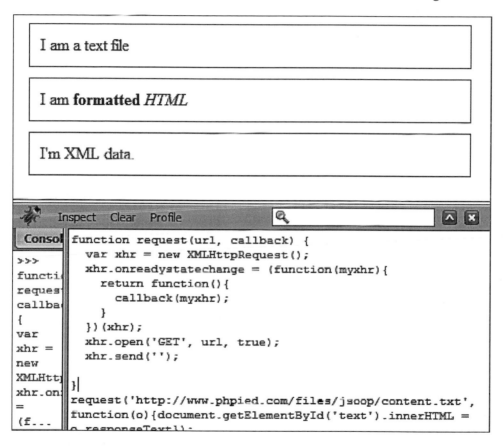

When working with the XML document, you can also use o.responseXML.
documentElement to get to the <root> element, instead of o.responseXML.getElem
entsByTagName('root')[0]. Remember that documentElement gives you the root
node of an XML document. The root in HTML documents is always the <html> tag.

Summary

We have covered quite a bit in this chapter. You have learned some cross-browser *BOM (Browser Object Model)* objects:

- Properties of the global `window` object such as `navigator`, `location`, `history`, `frames`, `screen`
- Methods such as `setInterval()` and `setTimeout()`; `alert()`, `confirm()`, and `prompt()`; `moveTo/By()` and `resizeTo/By()`

Then you learned about the *DOM (Document Object Model)* as a way to represent an HTML (or XML) document as a tree structure where each tag or text is a node on the tree. You learned how to:

- Access nodes:
  - Using parent/child relationship properties parentNode, `childNodes`, `firstChild`, `lastChild`, `nextSibling`, `previousSibling`
  - Using `getElementsById()`, `getElementsByTagName()`, `getElementsByName()`
- Modify nodes:
  - Using `innerHTML` or `innerText/textContent`
  - Using `nodeValue` or `setAttribute()` or just using attributes as object properties
- Remove nodes with `removeChild()` or `replaceChild()`
- And add new ones with `appendChild()`, `cloneNode()`, `insertBefore()`

We also looked at some DOM0 (pre-standardization) properties, ported to DOM Level 1:

- Collections: `document.forms`, `images`, `links`, `anchors`, `applets`. Using these is discouraged, as DOM1 has the much more flexible method `getElementsByTagName()`.
- `document.body` which is convenient way to access the `<body>`.
- `document.title`, `cookie`, `referrer`, `domain`.

Next, you learned about how the browser broadcasts *events* that you can listen to. It's not straightforward to do this in a cross-browser manner, but it is possible. Events bubble up, so you know can use event delegation to listen to events more globally. You can also stop the propagation of events and interfere with the default browser behavior.

Finally, you learned about the XMLHttpRequest object that allows you to build responsive web pages that:

- Make HTTP requests to the server to get pieces of data, and
- Process the response to update portions of the page

Exercises

In the previous chapters, the solutions to the exercises could pretty much be found in the text of the chapter. This time, some of the exercises might require you to do some more reading (or experimentation) outside this book.

1. BOM

   As a BOM exercise, try coding something wrong, obtrusive, user-unfriendly, and, all in all, very Web 1.0: the shaking browser window. Try implementing code that moves the window around as if there's an earthquake. All you'll need is one of the move*() functions, one or more calls to setInterval() and maybe one to setTimeout() to stop the whole thing. Or how about opening a 200x200 popup and then resizing it slowly and gradually to 400x400? Or here's an easier one: print the current date/time in the status bar (window.status) and update it every second, like a clock. Note that for these exercises, you need to allow some features in your browser that are typically disabled by default, since people got fed up with such "effects" that only worsen the user experience (in Firefox go to **Tools | Options | Content | Enable JavaScript | Advanced**).

2. DOM

   2.1. Implement walkDOM() differently. Also make it accept a callback function instead of hardcoding console.log()

   2.2. Removing content with innerHTML is easy (document.body.innerHTML = ' '), but not always best. The thing is that if there are any event listeners, attached to the removed elements, they won't be removed in IE, causing the browser to leak memory, because it stores references to something that doesn't exist. Implement a general-purpose function that deletes DOM nodes, but removes any event listeners first. You can loop through the attributes of a node and check if the value is a function. If it is, it's most likely an attribute like onclick. You need to set it to null before removing the element from the tree.

2.3. Create a function called `include()` that includes external scripts on demand. This means create a new `<script>` tag dynamically and set its `src` attribute. Test by using:

```
>>> include('somescript.js');
```

2.4. Using your function from 2.3., consume a Yahoo! search service with JavaScript. The documentation is here: `http://developer.yahoo.com/search/web/V1/webSearch.html`. When constructing the URL to request, you need to set `output=json` and `callback=console.log`. This way the result of the service call (a JavaScript object) will be printed in the console. Replace `console.log` with a function of your choice to create something more interesting.

3. Events

3.1. Create an event utility (object) called `myevent` which has the following methods working cross-browser:

- `addListener(element, event_name, callback)` — where `element` could also be an array of elements

- `removeListener(element, event_name, callback)`

- `getEvent(event)` — just to check for a `window.event` for older versions of IE

- `getTarget(event)`

- `stopPropagation(event)`

- `preventDefault(event)`

Usage example:

```
function myCallback(e) {
  e = myevent.getEvent(e);
  alert(myevent.getTarget(e).href);
  myevent.stopPropagation(e);
  myevent.preventDefault(e);
}
myevent.addListener(document.links, 'click', myCallback);
```

The result of the example code should be that all of the links in the document lead nowhere but only alert the `href` attribute.

3.2. Create an absolutely positioned `<div>`, say at x=100px, y=100px. Write the code to be able to move the div around the page using the arrow keys or the keys *J* (left), *K* (right), *M* (down), *I* (up). Reuse your own event utility from 3.1.

4. XMLHttpRequest

4.1. Create your own XHR utility (object) called `ajax`. Example use:

```
function myCallback(xhr) {
    alert(xhr.responseText);
}
ajax.request('somefile.txt', 'get', myCallback);
ajax.request('script.php', 'post', myCallback,
             'first=John&last=Smith');
```

4.2. AJAXify the Google search. Using Firebug, you can "plug" JavaScript as if it's part of the page. This will allow you to request pages on `google.com` using XHR. So visit `google.com` and write the code that will allow you to not load a second page when you do a search, but to load the results underneath the search form without a page refresh. Reuse your own event utility (from Exercise 3.1.) and your own AJAX utility (from 4.1.). Follow these steps:

- Attach an event listener to the submit event of the form and prevent the default behavior so that the form is not submitted;

- Create an XHR object and request the page at URL `http://www.google.com/search?q=`**myquery** where **myquery** is whatever you typed in the search field;

- In the callback of the XHR, append a new `<div>` with `id="content"` to the `<body>` and set its `innerHTML` to the `responseText` of the XHR.

This way you should be able to type in the search field, Press *Enter* and get the search results without loading a new page. You should be able to repeat this as many times as you want with the difference that you create the content div only once and then just update its HTML.

8
Coding and Design Patterns

Now that you know about the object-oriented features of JavaScript, such as prototypes and inheritance, and you have seen some practical examples of using the browser objects, let's move forward, or rather, move a level up. Let us have a look at some common patterns of JavaScript utilization. First, let's define what a pattern is. In short, a pattern is a good solution to a common problem.

Sometimes when you are facing a new programming problem, you might recognize right away that you've previously solved another, suspiciously similar problem. In such cases, it is worth isolating this class of problems and searching for a common solution. A pattern is a proven and reusable solution (or an approach to a solution) to a class of problems. Sometimes a pattern is nothing more than an idea or a name, but sometimes just using a name helps you think more clearly about a problem. Also, when working with other developers in a team, it's much easier to communicate when everybody uses the same terminology when discussing a problem or a solution.

Sometimes there might be cases when your problem is rather unique and doesn't fit into a known pattern. Blindly applying a pattern just for the sake of using a pattern is not a good idea. It's actually better to not use a pattern (if you can't come up with a new one) than to try and change your problem so that it fits an existing solution.

This chapter talks about two types of patterns:

- Coding patterns — these are mostly JavaScript-specific best practices
- Design patterns — these are language-independent patterns, popularized by the "Gang of Four" book

Coding Patterns

This first part of the chapter discusses some patterns that reflect JavaScript's unique features. Some patterns aim to help you with organizing your code (such as namespace patterns), others are related to improving performance (such as lazy definitions and init-time branching), and some make up for missing features such as privately scoped properties. The patterns discussed in this section include:

- Separating behavior
- Namespaces
- Init-time branching
- Lazy definition
- Configuration objects
- Private variables and methods
- Privileged methods
- Private functions as public methods
- Self-executable functions
- Chaining
- JSON

Separating Behavior

As discussed previously, the three building blocks of a web page are:

- Content (HTML)
- Presentation (CSS)
- Behavior (JavaScript)

Content

HTML is the content of the web page; the actual text. The content should be marked up using the smallest amount of HTML tags that sufficiently describe the semantic meaning of that content. For example, if you're working on a navigation menu it's probably a good idea to use `<ul>` and `<li>` as a navigation menu is basically a list of links.

Your content (HTML) should be free from any formatting elements. Visual formatting belongs to the presentation layer and should be achieved through the use of CSS (Cascading Style Sheets). This means that:

- The `style` attribute of HTML tags should not be used, if possible.

- Presentational HTML tags such as `<font>` should not be used at all.

- Tags should be used for their semantic meaning, not because of how browsers render them by default. For instance, developers sometimes use a `<div>` tag where a `<p>` would be more appropriate. It's also favorable to use `<strong>` and `<em>` instead of `<b>` and `<i>` as the latter describe the visual presentation rather than the meaning.

Presentation

A good approach to keep presentation out of the content is to reset, or nullify, all browser defaults; for example using `reset.css` from the Yahoo! UI library. This way the browser's default rendering won't distract you from consciously thinking about the proper semantic tags to use.

Behavior

The third component of a page is the behavior. Behavior should be kept separate from both the content and the presentation. Behavior is usually added by using JavaScript that is isolated to `<script>` tags, and preferably contained in external files. This means not using any inline attributes such as `onclick`, `onmouseover`, and so on. Instead of that, you can use the `addEventListener`/`attachEvent` methods that you have already seen in the previous chapter.

The best strategy for separating behavior from content would be:

- Minimize the number of `<script>` tags

- Avoid inline event handlers

- Do not use CSS expressions

- Dynamically add markup that has no purpose when JavaScript is disabled by the user

- Towards the end of your content, when you are ready to close the `<body>` tag, insert a single external `.js` file

Example of Separating Behavior

Let's say you have a search form on a page and you want to validate the form with JavaScript. So you go ahead and keep the form tags free from any JavaScript and then, immediately before the closing `</body>` tag, you insert a `<script>` tag which links to an external file.

```
<body>
  <form id="myform" method="post" action="server.php">
  <fieldset>
    <legend>Search</legend>
    <input
      name="search"
      id="search"
      type="text"
    />
    <input type="submit" />
  </fieldset>
  </form>
  <script type="text/javascript" src="behaviors.js"></script>
</body>
```

In `behaviors.js` you attach an event listener to the submit event. In your listener, you check to see if the text input field was left blank and if so, stop the form from being submitted. Here's the complete content of `behaviors.js`. It assumes that you've created your `myevent` utility from the exercise at the end of the previous chapter:

```
// init
myevent.addListener('myform', 'submit', function(e){
  // no need to propagate further
  e = myevent.getEvent(e);
  myevent.stopPropagation(e);
  // validate
  var el = document.getElementById('search');
  if (!el.value) { // too bad, field is empty
    myevent.preventDefault(e); // prevent the form submission
    alert('Please enter a search string');
  }
});
```

Namespaces

Global variables should be avoided in order to lower the possibility of variable naming collisions. One way to minimize the number of globals is by namespacing your variables and functions. The idea is simple: you create only one global object and all your other variables and functions become properties of that object.

An Object as a Namespace

Let's create a global object called MYAPP:

```
// global namespace
var MYAPP = MYAPP || {};
```

Now instead of having a global myevent utility (from the previous chapter), you can have it as an event property of the MYAPP object.

```
// sub-object
MYAPP.event = {};
```

Adding the methods to the event utility is pretty much the same as usual:

```
// object together with the method declarations
MYAPP.event = {
  addListener: function(el, type, fn) {
    // .. do the thing
  },
  removeListener: function(el, type, fn) {
    // ...
  },
  getEvent: function(e) {
    // ...
  }
  // ... other methods or properties
};
```

Namespaced Constructors

Using a namespace doesn't prevent you from creating constructor functions. Here is how you can have a DOM utility that has an Element constructor which allows you to create DOM elements more easily.

```
MYAPP.dom = {};
MYAPP.dom.Element = function(type, prop){
  var tmp = document.createElement(type);
  for (var i in prop) {
    tmp.setAttribute(i, prop[i]);
  }
  return tmp;
}
```

Similarly, you can have a Text constructor to create text nodes if you want to:

```
MYAPP.dom.Text = function(txt){
  return document.createTextNode(txt);
}
```

Using the constructors to create a link at the bottom of a page:

```
var el1 = new MYAPP.dom.Element(
    'a',
    {href:'http://phpied.com'}
);
var el2 = new MYAPP.dom.Text('click me');
el1.appendChild(el2);
document.body.appendChild(el1);
```

A namespace() Method

Some libraries, such as YUI, implement a namespace utility method that makes your life easier, so that you can do something like:

```
MYAPP.namespace('dom.style');
```

instead of the more verbose:

```
MYAPP.dom = {};
MYAPP.dom.style = {};
```

Here's how you can create such a namespace() method. First you create an array by splitting the input string using the period (.) as a separator. Then, for every element in the new array, you add a property to your global object if such a property doesn't already exist.

```
var MYAPP = {};
MYAPP.namespace = function(name){
    var parts = name.split('.');
    var current = MYAPP;
    for (var i in parts) {
        if (!current[parts[i]]) {
            current[parts[i]] = {};
        }
        current = current[parts[i]];
    }
}
```

Testing the new method:

```
MYAPP.namespace('event');
MYAPP.namespace('dom.style');
```

The result of the above is the same as if you did:

```
var MYAPP = {
  event: {},
  dom: {
    style: {}
  }
}
```

Init-Time Branching

In the previous chapter, you saw that different browsers often have different implementations for the same or similar functionalities. In such cases, you need to branch your code depending on what's supported by the browser currently executing your script. Depending on your program this branching can happen far too often and, as a result, can slow down the script execution.

You can mitigate this problem by branching some parts of the code during initialization, when the script loads, rather than during runtime. Building upon the ability to define functions dynamically, you can branch and define the same function with a different body depending on the browser. Let's see how.

First, let's define a namespace and placeholder method for the event utility.

```
var MYAPP = {};
MYAPP.event = {
  addListener: null,
  removeListener: null
};
```

At this point, the methods to add or remove a listener are not implemented. Based on the results from feature sniffing, these methods can be defined differently.

```
if (typeof window.addEventListener === 'function') {
    MYAPP.event.addListener = function(el, type, fn) {
        el.addEventListener(type, fn, false);
    };
    MYAPP.event.removeListener = function(el, type, fn) {
        el.removeEventListener(type, fn, false);
    };
} else if (typeof document.attachEvent === 'function'){ // IE
    MYAPP.event.addListener = function(el, type, fn) {
        el.attachEvent('on' + type, fn);
    };
```

```
        MYAPP.event.removeListener = function(el, type, fn) {
            el.detachEvent('on' + type, fn);
        };
    } else { // older browsers
        MYAPP.event.addListener = function(el, type, fn) {
            el['on' + type] = fn;
        };
        MYAPP.event.removeListener = function(el, type, fn) {
            el['on' + type] = null;
        };
    };
```

After this script executes, you have the `addListener()` and `removeListener()` methods defined in a browser-dependent way. Now every time you invoke one of these methods it will not do any more feature sniffing, and as a result will run faster because it is doing less work.

One thing to watch out for when sniffing features is not to assume too much after checking for one feature. In the example above, this rule is broken because the code only checks for `add*` support but then defines both the `add*` and the `remove*` methods. In this case it's probably safe to assume that in a next version of the browser, if IE decides to implement `addEventListener()` it will also implement `removeEventListener()`. But imagine what happens if IE implements `stopPropagation()` but not `preventDefault()` and you haven't checked for these individually. You have assumed that because `addEventListener()` is not defined, the browser is IE and write your code using your knowledge of how IE works. Remember that all of your knowledge is based on the way IE works today, but not necessarily the way it will work tomorrow. So to avoid many rewrites of your code as new browser versions are shipped, it's best to individually check for features you intend to use and don't generalize on what a certain browser supports.

Lazy Definition

The *lazy definition* pattern is very similar to the previous *init-time branching* pattern. The difference is that the branching happens only when the function is called for the first time. When the function is called, it redefines itself with the best implementation. Unlike the init-time branching where the `if` happens once, during loading, here it might not happen at all — in cases when the function is never called. The lazy definition also makes the initialization process lighter, as there's no init-time branching work to be done.

Let's see an example that illustrates this, via the definition of an addListener()
function. The function is first defined with a generic body. It checks which
functionality is supported by the browser when it is called for the first time and then
redefines itself using the most suitable implementation. At the end of the first call,
the function calls itself so that the actual event attaching is performed. The next time
you call the same function it will be defined with its new body and will be ready for
use, so no further branching is necessary.

```
var MYAPP = {};
MYAPP.myevent = {
  addListener: function(el, type, fn){
    if (typeof el.addEventListener === 'function') {
      MYAPP.myevent.addListener = function(el, type, fn) {
          el.addEventListener(type, fn, false);
      };
    } else if (typeof el.attachEvent === 'function'){
      MYAPP.myevent.addListener = function(el, type, fn) {
          el.attachEvent('on' + type, fn);
      };
    } else {
      MYAPP.myevent.addListener = function(el, type, fn) {
          el['on' + type] = fn;
      };
    }
    MYAPP.myevent.addListener(el, type, fn);
  }
};
```

Configuration Object

This pattern is useful when you have a function or method that accepts a lot of
parameters. It's up to you to decide how many constitutes "a lot", but generally a
function with more than three parameters is probably not very convenient to call, as
you have to remember the order of the parameters, and is even more inconvenient
when some of the parameters are optional.

Instead of having many parameters, you can use one parameter and make it an
object. The properties of the object are the actual parameters. This is especially
suitable for passing configuration parameters, because these tend to be numerous
and mostly optional (with smart defaults). The beauty of using a single object as
opposed to multiple parameters is:

- The order doesn't matter
- You can easily skip parameters that you don't want to set

- It makes the function signature easily extendable should future requirements necessitate this

- It makes the code more readable because the config object's properties are present in the calling code, along with their names

Imagine you have a `Button` constructor used to create input buttons. It accepts the text to put inside the button (the `value` attribute of the `<input>` tag) and an optional parameter of the `type` of button.

```
// a constructor that creates buttons
var MYAPP = {};
MYAPP.dom = {};
MYAPP.dom.Button = function(text, type) {
    var b = document.createElement('input');
    b.type = type || 'submit';
    b.value = text;
    return b;
}
```

Using the constructor is simple; you just give it a string. Then you can append the new button to the body of the document:

```
document.body.appendChild(new MYAPP.dom.Button('puuush'));
```

This is all well and works fine, but then you decide you also want to be able to set some of the style properties of the button, such as colors and fonts. You might end up with a definition like:

```
MYAPP.dom.Button = function(text, type, color, border, font) {
    // ....
}
```

Now using the constructor can become a little inconvenient, for example when you want to set the third and fifth parameter, but not the second or the fourth:

```
new MYAPP.dom.Button('puuush', null, 'white', null,
                     'Arial, Verdana, sans-serif');
```

A better approach is to use one config object parameter for all the settings. The function definition can become something like:

```
MYAPP.dom.Button = function(text, conf) {
    var type = conf.type || 'submit';
    var font = conf.font || 'Verdana';
    // ...
}
```

Using the constructor:

```
var config = {
    font: 'Arial, Verdana, sans-serif',
    color: 'white'
};
new MYAPP.dom.Button('puuush', config);
```

Another usage example:

```
document.body.appendChild(
    new MYAPP.dom.Button('dude', {color: 'red'})
);
```

As you can see, it's easy to set only selected parameters and to switch around their order. In addition, it's friendlier and makes the code easier to understand when you see the names of the parameters when you call the method.

Private Properties and Methods

JavaScript doesn't have the notion of *access modifiers*, which set the privileges of the properties in an object. Classical languages often have access modifiers such as:

- Public—all users of an object can access these properties (or methods)
- Private—only the object itself can access these properties
- Protected—only objects inheriting the object in question can access these properties

JavaScript doesn't have a special syntax to denote private properties but, as discussed in Chapter 3, you can use local variables and methods inside a constructor and achieve the same level of protection.

Continuing with the example of the `Button` constructor, you can have a local variable `styles` which contains all the defaults, and a local `setStyle()` function. These are invisible to the code outside of the constructor. Here's how `Button` can make use of the local private properties:

```
var MYAPP = {};
MYAPP.dom = {};
MYAPP.dom.Button = function(text, conf) {
    var styles = {
        font: 'Verdana',
        border: '1px solid black',
        color: 'black',
        background: 'grey'
```

```
    };
    function setStyles() {
        for (var i in styles) {
            b.style[i] = conf[i] || styles[i];

        }
    }
    conf = conf || {};
    var b = document.createElement('input');
    b.type = conf['type'] || 'submit';
    b.value = text;
    setStyles();
    return b;
};
```

In this implementation, styles is a private property and setStyle() is a private method. The constructor uses them internally (and they can access anything inside the constructor), but they are not available to code outside of the function.

Privileged Methods

Privileged methods (this term was coined by Douglas Crockford) are normal public methods that can access private methods or properties. They can act like a bridge in making some of the private functionality accessible but in a controlled manner, wrapped in a privileged method.

Continuing with the previous example, you can create a getDefaults() method that returns styles. In this way the code outside the Button constructor can see the default styles but cannot modify them. In this scenario getDefaults() would be a privileged method.

Private Functions as Public Methods

Let us say you've defined a function that you absolutely need to keep intact, so you make it private. But you also want to provide access to the same function so that outside code can also benefit from it. In this case, you can assign the private function to a publicly available property.

Let's define _setStyle() and _getStyle() as private functions, but then assign them to the public setStyle() and getStyle():

```
var MYAPP = {};
MYAPP.dom = (function(){
  var _setStyle = function(el, prop, value) {
```

```
      console.log('setStyle');
  };
  var _getStyle = function(el, prop) {
      console.log('getStyle');
  };
  return {
    setStyle: _setStyle,
    getStyle: _getStyle,
    yetAnother: _setStyle
  };
})()
```

Now if you call MYAPP.dom.setStyle(), it will invoke the private _setStyle() function. You can also overwrite setStyle() from the outside:

```
MYAPP.dom.setStyle = function(){alert('b')};
```

Now the result will be:

- MYAPP.dom.setStyle points to the new function
- MYAPP.dom.yetAnother still points to _setStyle()
- _setStyle() is always available when any other internal code relies on it to be working as intended, regardless of the outside code

Self-Executing Functions

Another useful pattern that helps you keep the global namespace clean is to wrap your code in an anonymous function and execute that function immediately. This way any variables inside the function are local (as long as you use the var statement) and are destroyed when the function returns, if they aren't part of a closure. This pattern was discussed in more detail in Chapter 3.

```
(function(){
  // code goes here...
})()
```

This pattern is especially suitable for one-off initialization tasks performed when the script loads.

The self-executable pattern can be extended to create and return objects. If the creation of these objects is more complicated and involves some initialization work, then you can do this in the first part of the self-executable function and `return` a single object, which can access and benefit from any private properties in the top portion:

```
var MYAPP = {};
MYAPP.dom = function(){
  // initialization code...
  function _private(){
    // ... body
  }
  return {
    getStyle: function(el, prop) {
      console.log('getStyle');
      _private();
    },
    setStyle: function(el, prop, value) {
      console.log('setStyle');
    }
  };
}();
```

Chaining

Chaining is a pattern that allows you to invoke methods on one line as if the methods are the links in a chain. This could be pretty convenient when calling several related methods. Basically, you invoke the next method on the result of the previous method, without the use of an intermediate variable.

Imagine you've created a constructor that helps you work with DOM elements. The code to create a new `<span>` and add it to the `<body>` could look something like the following:

```
var obj = new MYAPP.dom.Element('span');
obj.setText('hello');
obj.setStyle('color', 'red');
obj.setStyle('font', 'Verdana');
document.body.appendChild(obj);
```

As you know, the constructors return the `this` object they create. You can make your methods such as `setText()` and `setStyle()` also return `this`, which will allow you to call the next method on the instance returned by the previous one. This way you can chain method calls:

```
var obj = new MYAPP.dom.Element('span');
obj.setText('hello')
```

```
        .setStyle('color', 'red')
        .setStyle('font', 'Verdana');
    document.body.appendChild(obj);
```

You might not even need the `obj` variable if you don't plan on using it after the new element has been added to the tree, so the code could look like:

```
    document.body.appendChild(
        new MYAPP.dom.Element('span')
                .setText('hello')
                .setStyle('color', 'red')
                .setStyle('font', 'Verdana')
    );
```

jQuery makes heavy use of the chaining pattern; this is probably one of the most recognizable features of this popular library.

JSON

Let's wrap up the coding patterns section of this chapter with a few words about JSON. JSON is not technically a coding pattern, but you can say that using JSON is a useful pattern.

JSON is a popular lightweight format for exchanging data. It's often preferred over XML when using `XMLHttpRequest()` to retrieve data from the server. JSON stands for JavaScript Object Notation and there's nothing specifically interesting about it other that the fact that it's extremely convenient. The JSON format consists of data, defined using object and array literals. Here is an example of a JSON string that your server could respond with after an XHR request.

```
    {
      'name':   'Stoyan',
      'family': 'Stefanov',
      'books':  ['phpBB2', 'phpBB UG', 'PEAR']
    }
```

An XML equivalent of this would be something like:

```
    <?xml version="1.1" encoding="iso-8859-1"?>
    <response>
      <name>Stoyan</name>
      <family>Stefanov</family>
      <books>
        <book>phpBB2</book>
        <book>phpBB UG</book>
        <book>PEAR</book>
      </books>
    </response>
```

Firstly, you can see how JSON is lighter in terms of the number of bytes. But the main benefit is not the smaller byte size but the fact that it's extremely easy to work with JSON in JavaScript. Let's say you've made an XHR request and have received a JSON string in the `responseText` property of the XHR object. You can convert this string of data into a working JavaScript object by simply using `eval()`:

```
var obj = eval( '(' + xhr.responseText + ')' );
```

Now you can access the data in `obj` as object properties:

```
alert(obj.name); // Stoyan
alert(obj.books[2]); // PEAR
```

The problem with `eval()` is that it is insecure, so it's best if you use a little JavaScript library available from `http://json.org/` to parse the JSON data. Creating an object from a JSON string is still trivial:

```
var obj = JSON.parse(xhr.responseText);
```

Due to its simplicity, JSON has quickly become popular as a language-independent format for exchanging data and you can easily produce JSON on the server side using your preferred language. In PHP, for example, there are the functions `json_encode()` and `json_decode()` that let you serialize a PHP array or object into a JSON string, and vice versa.

Design Patterns

The second part of this chapter presents a JavaScript approach to a subset of the design patterns introduced by the book called *Design Patterns: Elements of Reusable Object-Oriented Software,* an influential book most commonly referred to as the *Book of Four* or the *Gang of Four,* or *GoF* (after its four authors). The patterns discussed in the *GoF* book are divided into three groups:

- *Creational patterns* that deal with how objects are *created* (instantiated)
- *Structural patterns* that describe how different objects can be *composed* in order to provide new functionality
- *Behavioral patterns* that describe ways for objects to *communicate* with each other

There are 23 patterns in the *Book of Four,* and more patterns have been identified since the book's publication. It is way beyond the scope of this book to discuss all of them, so the remainder of the chapter will demonstrate only four of them, along with examples of the implementation of these four in JavaScript. Remember that the patterns are more about interfaces and relationships rather than implementation. Once you have an understanding of a design pattern, it's often not difficult to implement it, especially in a dynamic language such as JavaScript.

The patterns discussed through the rest of the chapter are:

- Singleton
- Factory
- Decorator
- Observer

Singleton

Singleton is a *creational* design pattern meaning that its focus is on creating objects. It is useful when you want to make sure there is only one object of a given kind or class. In a classical language, this would mean that an instance of a class is only created once and any subsequent attempts to create new objects of the same class would return the original instance.

In JavaScript, because there are no classes, a singleton is the default and most natural pattern. Every object is a single object. If you don't copy it and don't use it as a prototype of another object, it will remain the only object of its kind.

The most basic implementation of the singleton in JavaScript is the object literal:

```
var single = {};
```

Singleton 2

If you want to use class-like syntax and still implement the singleton, things can become a bit more interesting. Let's say you have a constructor called `Logger()` and you want to be able to do something like:

```
var my_log = new Logger();
my_log.log('some event');
// ... 1000 lines of code later ...
var other_log = new Logger();
other_log.log('some new event');
alert(other_log === my_log); // true
```

The idea is that although you use `new`, only one instance needs to be created, and this instance is then returned in consecutive calls.

Global Variable

One approach would be to use a global variable to store the single instance. Your constructor could look like this:

```
function Logger() {
  if (typeof global_log === "undefined") {
    global_log = this;
  }
  return global_log;
}
```

Using this constructor gives the expected result:

```
var a = new Logger();
var b = new Logger();
alert(a === b); // true
```

The drawback is, of course, the use of a global variable. It can be overwritten at any time, even accidentally, and you lose the instance. The opposite — your global variable overwriting someone else's — is also possible.

Property of the Constructor

As you know, functions are objects and they have properties. You can assign the single instance to a property of the constructor function.

```
function Logger() {
  if (typeof Logger.single_instance === "undefined") {
    Logger.single_instance = this;
  }
  return Logger.single_instance;
}
```

If you write `var a = new Logger()`, a will point to the newly created `Logger.single_instance` property. A subsequent call `var b = new Logger()` will result in b pointing to the same `Logger.single_instance` property, which is exactly what you wanted.

This approach certainly solves the global namespace issue, because no global variables are created. The only drawback is that the property of the `Logger` constructor is publicly visible, so it can be overwritten at any time. In such cases, the single instance can be lost or modified.

In a Private Property

The solution to the problem of overwriting the publicly-visible property is to not use a public property, but a private one. You already know how to protect variables with a closure, so as an exercise you can implement this approach to the singleton pattern.

Factory

The factory is another creational design pattern as it deals with creating objects. The factory is useful when you have similar types of objects and you don't know in advance which one you want to use. Based on user input or other criteria, your code determines the type of object it needs on the fly.

Let's say you have three different constructors which implement similar functionality. The objects they create all take a URL but do different things with it. One creates a text DOM node; the second creates a link and the third, an image.

```
var MYAPP = {};
MYAPP.dom = {};
MYAPP.dom.Text = function() {
  this.insert = function(where) {
    var txt - document.createTextNode(this.url);
    where.appendChild(txt);
  };
};
MYAPP.dom.Link = function() {
  this.insert = function(where) {
    var link = document.createElement('a');
    link.href = this.url;
    link.appendChild(document.createTextNode(this.url));
    where.appendChild(link);
  };
};
MYAPP.dom.Image = function() {
  this.insert = function(where) {
    var im = document.createElement('img');
    im.src = this.url;
    where.appendChild(im);
  };
};
```

The way to use the three different constructors is exactly the same: you set the `url` property and then call the `insert()` method.

```
var o = new MYAPP.dom.Image();
o.url = 'http://images.packtpub.com/images/PacktLogoSmall.png';
o.insert(document.body);
var o = new MYAPP.dom.Text();
o.url = 'http://images.packtpub.com/images/PacktLogoSmall.png';
o.insert(document.body);
var o = new MYAPP.dom.Link();
o.url = 'http://images.packtpub.com/images/PacktLogoSmall.png';
o.insert(document.body);
```

Imagine your program doesn't know in advance which type of object is required. The user decides during runtime by clicking a button for example. If `type` contains the required type of object, you'll probably need to use an `if` or a `switch`, and do something like this:

```
var o;
if (type === 'Image') {
  o = new MYAPP.dom.Image();
}
if (type === 'Link') {
  o = new MYAPP.dom.Link();
}
if (type === 'Text') {
  o = new MYAPP.dom.Text();
}
o.url = 'http://...'
o.insert();
```

This works fine, but if you have a lot of constructors, the code might become too lengthy. Also, if you are creating a library or a framework, you might not even know the exact names of the constructor functions in advance. In such cases, it's useful to have a factory function that takes care of creating an object of the dynamically determined type.

Let's add a factory method to the `MYAPP.dom` utility:

```
MYAPP.dom.factory = function(type) {
  return new MYAPP.dom[type];
}
```

Now you can replace the three `if`s with the simpler:

```
var o = MYAPP.dom.factory(type);
o.url = 'http://...'
o.insert();
```

The example `factory()` method above was simple, but in a real life scenario you'll probably want to do some validation against the `type` value and optionally do some setup work common to all object types.

Decorator

The *Decorator* design pattern is a *structural* pattern; it doesn't have much to do with how objects are created but rather how their functionality is extended. Instead of using inheritance where you extend in a linear way (parent-child-grandchild), you can have one base object and a pool of different decorator objects that provide extra functionality. Your program can pick and choose which decorators it wants and in which order. For a different program, you might have a different set of requirements and pick different decorators out of the same pool. Take a look at how the usage part of the decorator pattern could be implemented:

```
var obj = {
  function: doSomething(){
    console.log('sure, asap');
  },
  //  ...
};
obj = obj.getDecorator('deco1');
obj = obj.getDecorator('deco13');
obj = obj.getDecorator('deco5');
obj.doSomething();
```

You can see how you can start with a simple object that has a `doSomething()` method. Then you can pick some of the decorator objects (identified by name) you have lying around. All decorators provide a `doSomething()` method which first calls the same method of the previous decorator and then proceeds with its own code. Every time you add a decorator, you overwrite the base `obj` with an improved version of it. At the end, when you are finished adding decorators, you call `doSomething()`. As a result all of the `doSomething()` methods of all the decorators are executed in sequence. Let's see an example.

Decorating a Christmas Tree

Let's illustrate the decorator pattern with an example: decorating a Christmas tree. You start with the `decorate()` method.

```
var tree = {};
tree.decorate = function() {
  alert('Make sure the tree won\'t fall');
};
```

Now let's implement a `getDecorator()` method which will be used to add extra decorators. The decorators will be implemented as constructor functions, and they'll all inherit from the base `tree` object.

```
tree.getDecorator = function(deco){
  tree[deco].prototype = this;
  return new tree[deco];
};
```

Now let's create the first decorator, `RedBalls()`, as a property of `tree` (in order to keep the global namespace cleaner). The `RedBall` objects also provide a `decorate()` method, but they make sure they call their parent's `decorate()` first.

```
tree.RedBalls = function() {
  this.decorate = function() {
    this.RedBalls.prototype.decorate();
    alert('Put on some red balls');
  }
};
```

Similarly, adding a `BlueBalls()` and `Angel()` decorators:

```
tree.BlueBalls = function() {
  this.decorate = function() {
    this.BlueBalls.prototype.decorate();
    alert('Add blue balls');
  }
};
tree.Angel = function() {
  this.decorate = function() {
    this.Angel.prototype.decorate();
    alert('An angel on the top');
  }
};
```

Now let's add all of the decorators to the base object:

```
tree = tree.getDecorator('BlueBalls');
tree = tree.getDecorator('Angel');
tree = tree.getDecorator('RedBalls');
```

Finally, running the `decorate()` method:

```
tree.decorate();
```

This single call results in the following alerts (in this order):

- **Make sure the tree won't fall**
- **Add blue balls**
- **An angel on the top**
- **Put some red balls**

As you see, this functionality allows you to have as many decorators as you like, and to choose and combine them in any way you like.

Observer

The observer pattern (also known as the subscriber-publisher pattern) is a behavioral pattern, which means that it deals with how different objects interact and communicate with each other. When implementing the observer pattern you have the following objects:

- One or more publisher objects that announce when they do something important, and

- One or more subscribers that are tuned in to one or more publishers and listen to what the publishers announce, then act appropriately

The observer pattern may sound familiar to the browser events discussed in the previous chapter, and rightly so, because the browser events are one example application of this pattern. The browser is the publisher: it announces the fact that an event (such as onclick) has happened. Your event listener functions that are subscribed to (listen to) this type of event will be notified when the event happens. The browser-publisher sends an event object to all of the subscribers, but in your custom implementation you don't have to use event objects, you can send any type of data you find appropriate.

There are two subtypes of the observer pattern: push and pull. Push is where the publishers are responsible for notifying each subscriber, and pull is where the subscribers monitor for changes in a publisher's state.

Let's take a look at an example implementation of the push model. Let's keep the observer-related code into a separate object and then use this object as a mixin, adding its functionality to any other object that decides to be a publisher. In this way any object can become a publisher and any function object can become a subscriber. The `observer` object will have the following properties and methods:

- An array of `subscribers` that are just callback functions
- `addSubscriber()` and `removeSubscriber()` methods that add to and remove from the `subscribers` array
- A `publish()` method that takes data and calls all subscribers, passing the data to them
- A `make()` method that takes any object and turns it into a publisher by adding all of the above methods to it

Here's the observer mixin object which contains all the subscription-related methods and can be used to turn any object into a publisher.

```
var observer = {
  addSubscriber: function(callback) {
    this.subscribers[this.subscribers.length] = callback;
  },
  removeSubscriber: function(callback) {
    for (var i = 0; i < this.subscribers.length; i++) {
      if (this.subscribers[i] === callback) {
        delete(this.subscribers[i]);
      }
    }
  },
  publish: function(what) {
    for (var i = 0; i < this.subscribers.length; i++) {
      if (typeof this.subscribers[i] === 'function') {
        this.subscribers[i](what);
      }
    }
  },
  make: function(o) { // turns an object into a publisher
    for(var i in this) {
      o[i] = this[i];
      o.subscribers = [];
    }
  }
};
```

Now let's create some publishers. A publisher can be any object; its only duty is to call the `publish()` method whenever something important occurs. Here's a `blogger` object which calls `publish()` every time a new blog posting is ready.

```
var blogger = {
  writeBlogPost: function() {
    var content = 'Today is ' + new Date();
    this.publish(content);
  }
};
```

Another object could be the *LA Times* newspaper which calls `publish()` when a new newspaper issue is out.

```
var la_times = {
  newIssue: function() {
    var paper = 'Martians have landed on Earth!';
    this.publish(paper);
  }
};
```

Turning these simple objects into publishers is pretty easy:

```
observer.make(blogger);
observer.make(la_times);
```

Now let's have two simple objects `jack` and `jill`:

```
var jack = {
  read: function(what) {
    console.log('I just read that ' + what)
  }
};
var jill = {
  gossip: function(what) {
    console.log('You didn\'t hear it from me, but ' + what)
  }
};
```

`jack` and `jill` can subscribe to the `blogger` object by providing the callback methods they want to be called when something is published.

```
blogger.addSubscriber(jack.read);
blogger.addSubscriber(jill.gossip);
```

What happens now when the `blogger` writes a new post? The result is that `jack` and `jill` get notified:

```
>>> blogger.writeBlogPost();
```

I just read that Today is Sun Apr 06 2008 00:43:54 GMT-0700 (Pacific Daylight Time)

You didn't hear it from me, but Today is Sun Apr 06 2008 00:43:54 GMT-0700 (Pacific Daylight Time)

At any time, `jill` may decide to cancel her subscription. Then when writing another blog post, the unsubscribed object is no longer notified:

```
>>> blogger.removeSubscriber(jill.gossip);
>>> blogger.writeBlogPost();
```

I just read that Today is Sun Apr 06 2008 00:44:37 GMT-0700 (Pacific Daylight Time)

`jill` may decide to subscribe to *LA Times*, as an object can be a subscriber to many publishers.

```
>>> la_times.addSubscriber(jill.gossip);
```

Then when LA Times publishes a new issue, `jill` gets notified and `jill.gossip()` is executed.

```
>>> la_times.newIssue();
```

You didn't hear it from me, but Martians have landed on Earth!

Summary

In this final chapter, you learned about some common JavaScript coding patterns and learned how to make your programs cleaner, faster, and better at working with other programs and libraries. Then you saw a discussion and sample implementations of some of the design patterns from the *Book of Four*. You can see how JavaScript is a fully-featured dynamic object-oriented programming language and that implementing classical patterns in a dynamic language is pretty easy. The patterns are, in general, a large topic and you can join the author of this book in a further discussion of the JavaScript patterns at the web site `JSPatterns.com`.

You now have sufficient knowledge to be able to create scalable and reusable high-quality JavaScript applications and libraries using the concepts of Object-Oriented Programming. *Bon voyage!*

A
Reserved Words

This Appendix provides two lists of reserved keywords. The first one is the current list of reserved words, and the second is the list of words reserved for future implementations.

You cannot use reserved words as variable names.

```
var break = 1; // syntax error
```

If you use these words as object properties, you have to quote them.

```
var o = {break: 1};    // OK in Firefox, error in IE
var o = {'break': 1};  // OK
alert(o.break);        // error in IE
alert(o['break']);     // OK
```

Keywords

- break
- case
- catch
- continue
- default
- delete
- do
- else
- finally
- for
- function

- if
- in
- instanceof
- new
- return
- switch
- this
- throw
- try
- typeof
- var
- void
- while
- with

Future Reserved Words

- abstract
- boolean
- byte
- char
- class
- const
- debugger
- double
- enum
- export
- extends
- final
- float
- goto
- implements
- import
- int

- interface
- long
- native
- package
- private
- protected
- public
- short
- static
- super
- synchronized
- throws
- transient
- volatile

B

Built-in Functions

This Appendix contains a list of the built-in functions (methods of the global object), discussed in Chapter 3.

Function	Description

parseInt()	Takes two parameters: an input object and radix; then tries to return an integer representation of the input. Doesn't handle exponents in the input. The default radix is 10 (a decimal number). Returns NaN on failure. Omitting the radix may lead to unexpected results (for example for inputs such as 08), so it's best to always specify it.
	
	`>>> parseInt('10e+3')`
	
	10
	
	`>>> parseInt('FF')`
	
	NaN
	
	`>>> parseInt('FF', 16)`
	
	255

parseFloat()	Takes a parameter and tries to return a floating-point number representation of it. Understands exponents in the input.
	
	`>>> parseFloat('10e+3')`
	
	10000
	
	`>>> parseFloat('123.456test')`
	
	123.456

Function	Description

isNaN()	Abbreviated from "Is Not a Number". Accepts a parameter and returns true if the parameter is not a valid number, false otherwise. Attempts to convert the input to a number first.
	
	>>> isNaN(NaN)
	
	true
	
	>>> isNaN(123)
	
	false
	
	>>> isNaN(parseInt('FF'))
	
	true
	
	>>> isNaN(parseInt('FF', 16))
	
	false

isFinite()	Returns true if the input is a number (or can be converted to a number), but is not the number Infinity or -Infinity. Returns false for infinity or non-numeric values.
	
	>>> isFinite(1e+1000)
	
	false
	
	>>> isFinite(-Infinity)
	
	false
	
	>>> isFinite("123")
	
	true

encodeURIComponent()	Converts the input into a URL-encoded string. For more details on how URL encoding works, consult the Wikipedia article: http://en.wikipedia.org/wiki/Url_encode >>>encodeURIComponent ('http://phpied.com/') **"http%3A%2F%2Fphpied.com%2F"** >>> encodeURIComponent ('some script?key=v@lue') **"some%20script%3Fkey%3Dv%40lue"**
decodeURIComponent()	Takes an URL-encoded string and decodes it. >>> decodeURIComponent('%20%40') **" @"**

Function	Description

`encodeURI()`	URL-encodes the input, but assumes a full URL is given, so returns a valid URL by not encoding the protocol (for example `http://`) and host name (for example `www.phpied.com`).
	
	`>>> encodeURI('http://phpied.com/')`
	
	"http://phpied.com/"
	
	`>>> encodeURI('some script?key=v@lue')`
	
	"some%20script?key=v@lue"

`decodeURI()`	Opposite of `encodeURI()`. `>>> decodeURI("some%20script?key=v@lue")` **"some script?key=v@lue"**

`eval()`	Accepts a string of JavaScript code and executes it. Returns the result of the last expression in the input string.
	
	To be avoided where possible.
	
	`>>> eval('1+2')`
	
	3
	
	`>>> eval('parseInt("123")')`
	
	123
	
	`>>> eval('new Array(1,2,3)')`
	
	[1, 2, 3]
	
	`>>> eval('new Array(1,2,3); 1+1;')`
	
	2

Built-in Objects

This Appendix lists the built-in constructor functions outlined in the ECMAScript standard, together with the properties and methods of the objects created by these constructors.

Object

`Object()` is a constructor that creates objects, for example:

```
>>> var o = new Object();
```

This is the same as using the object literal:

```
>>> var o = {}; // recommended
```

You can pass anything to the constructor and it will try to guess what it is and use a more appropriate constructor. For example, passing a string to `new Object()` will be the same as using the `new String()` constructor. This is not a recommended practise, but still possible.

```
>>> var o = new Object('something');
>>> o.constructor
```

String()

```
>>> var o = new Object(123);
>>> o.constructor
```

Number()

All other objects, built-in or custom, inherit from Object. So the properties and methods discussed below apply to all types of objects.

Members of the Object Constructor

Property/Method	Description

Object.prototype	The prototype of all objects (also an object itself). Anything you add to this prototype will be inherited by all other objects.
	
	`>>> var s = new String('noodles');`
	`>>> Object.prototype.custom = 1;`
	1
	`>>> s.custom`
	1

Members of the Objects Created by the Object Constructor

Property/Method	Description

constructor	Points back to Object
	
	`>>> Object.prototype.`
	    `constructor === Object`
	true
	`>>> var o = new Object();`
	`>>> o.constructor === Object`
	true

toString(radix)	Returns a string representation of the object. If the object happens be a Number object, then the radix parameter defines the base of the returned number. The default radix is 10.
	
	`>>> var o = {prop: 1};`
	`>>> o.toString()`
	"[object Object]"
	`>>> var n = new Number(255);`
	`>>> n.toString()`
	"255"
	`>>> n.toString(16)`
	"ff"

Property/Method	Description
toLocaleString()	Same as toString() but matching the current locale. Meant to be implemented by objects such as Date() and provide locale-specific values, such as different date formatting.

valueOf()	Returns the this object itself, but for other types of objects may return a different value. For example, Number objects return a primitive number and Date objects return a timestamp.
	
	`>>> var o = {};`
	`>>> typeof o.valueOf()`
	"object"
	`>>> var n = new Number(101);`
	`>>> typeof n.valueOf()`
	"number"
	`>>> var d = new Date();`
	`>>> typeof d.valueOf()`
	"number"
	`>>> d.valueOf()`
	1208158875493

hasOwnProperty(prop)	Returns true if a property is an own property of the object or false if it was inherited from the prototype chain. Also returns false if the property doesn't exist.
	
	`>>> var o = {prop: 1};`
	`>>> o.hasOwnProperty('prop')`
	true
	`>>> o.hasOwnProperty('toString')`
	false

isPrototypeOf(obj)	Returns true if an object is used as a prototype of another object. Any object from the prototype chain can be tested, not only the direct ancestor.
	
	`>>> var s = new String('');`
	`>>> Object.prototype.isPrototypeOf(s)`
	true
	`>>> String.prototype.isPrototypeOf(s)`
	true
	`>>> Array.prototype.isPrototypeOf(s)`
	false

Property/Method	Description

`propertyIsEnumerable` `(prop)`	Returns **true** if a property shows up in a for-in loop.
	
	`>>> var a = [1,2,3];`
	`>>> a.propertyIsEnumerable('length')`
	false
	`>>> a.propertyIsEnumerable(0)`
	true

Array

The `Array` constructor creates array objects:

```
>>> var a = new Array(1,2,3);
```

This is the same as the array literal:

```
>>> var a = [1,2,3]; //recommended
```

When you pass only one numeric value to the `Array` constructor, it's assumed to be the array length. An array with this length will be created, and filled with `undefined` elements.

```
>>> var a = new Array(3);
>>> a.length
```

3

```
>>> a
```

[undefined, undefined, undefined]

This can sometimes lead to some unexpected behavior. For example, the following use of the array literal is valid:

```
>>> var a = [3.14]
>>> a
```

[3.14]

However, passing the floating-point number to the `Array` constructor is an error:

```
>>> var a = new Array(3.14)
```

invalid array length

Members of the Array Objects

Property/Method	Description
length	The number of elements in the array. `>>> [1,2,3,4].length` **4**
concat(i1, i2, i3,...)	Merges arrays together. `>>> [1,2].concat([10,20], [300,400])` **[1, 2, 10, 20, 300, 400]**

join(separator)	Turns an array into a string. The separator parameter is a string and the default value is a comma.
	
	`>>> [1,2,3].join()`
	
	"1,2,3"
	
	`>>> [1,2,3].join('|')`
	
	"1|2|3"
	
	`>>> [1,2,3].join(' is less than ')`
	
	"1 is less than 2 is less than 3"

pop()	Removes the last element of the array and returns it.
	
	`>>> var a = ['une', 'deux', 'trois'];`
	
	`>>> a.pop()`
	
	"trois"
	
	`>>> a`
	
	["une", "deux"]

push(i1, i2, i3,...)	Appends elements to the end of the array and returns the length of the modified array.
	
	`>>> var a = [];`
	
	`>>> a.push('zig', 'zag', 'zebra','zoo');`
	
	4

reverse()	Reverses the elements of the array and returns the modified array.
	
	`>>> var a = [1,2,3];`
	
	`>>> a.reverse()`
	
	[3, 2, 1]
	
	`>>> a`
	
	[3, 2, 1]

Property/Method	Description

shift()	Like pop() but removes the first element, not the last.
	
	``
	>>> var a = [1,2,3];
	>>> a.shift();
	``
	1
	``
	>>> a
	``
	[2, 3]

slice (start_index, end_index)	Extracts a piece of the array without modifying the source array.
	
	``
	>>> var a = ['apple', 'banana',
	            'js', 'css', 'orange'];
	>>> a.slice(2,4)
	``
	["js", "css"]
	``
	>>> a
	``
	["apple", "banana", "js", "css", "orange"]

sort(callback)	Sorts an array. Optionally accepts a callback function for custom sorting. The callback function receives two array elements as arguments and should return 0 if they are equal, 1 if the first is greater and -1 if the second is greater.
	
	An example of a custom sorting function that does a proper *numeric* sort (since the default is *character* sorting):
	
	``
	function customSort(a, b){
	   if (a > b) return 1;
	   if (a < b) return -1;
	   return 0;
	}
	``
	Example use of sort():
	
	``
	>>> var a = [101, 99, 1, 5];
	>>> a.sort();
	``
	[1, 101, 5, 99]
	``
	>>> a.sort(customSort);
	``
	[1, 5, 99, 101]
	``
	>>> [7,6,5,9].sort(customSort);
	``
	[5, 6, 7, 9]

Property/Method	Description

`splice(start, delete_count, i1, i2, i3,...)`	This is probably the most powerful of the array functions. It can remove and add elements at the same time. The first parameter is where to start removing, the second is how many items to remove and the rest of the parameters are new elements to be inserted in the place of the removed ones.
	
	`>>> var a = ['apple', 'banana',`
	`                'js', 'css', 'orange'];`
	`>>> a.splice(2, 2, 'pear', 'pineapple');`
	["js", "css"]
	`>>> a`
	["apple", "banana", "pear", "pineapple", "orange"]

`unshift(i1, i2, i3,...)`	Like `push()` but adds the elements at the beginning of the array as opposed to the end. Like `shift()` but adds to the array as opposed to removing from it. Returns the length of the modified array.
	
	`>>> var a = [1,2,3];`
	`>>> a.unshift('one', 'two');`
	5
	`>>> a`
	["one", "two", 1, 2, 3]

Function

JavaScript functions are objects. They can be defined using the `Function` constructor, like so:

```
>>> var sum = new Function('a', 'b', 'return a + b;');
```

This is equivalent to the function literal:

```
>>> var sum = function(a, b){return a + b;};
```

or the more common:

```
>>> function sum(a, b){return a + b;}
```

The use of the `Function` constructor is discouraged in favor of the function literals.

Members of the Function Objects

Property/Method	Description

apply(this_obj, params_array)	Allows you to call another function while overwriting its `this` value. The first parameter that `apply()` accepts is the object to be bound to `this` inside the function and the second is an array of parameters to be passed to the function being called.
	
	```\nfunction whatIsIt(){\n return this.toString();\n}\n>>> var myObj = {};\n>>> whatIsIt.apply(myObj);\n```
	"[object Object]"
	```\n>>> whatIsIt.apply(window);\n```
	"[object Window]"

call(this_obj, p1, p2, p3, ...)	Same as `apply()` but accepts parameters one by one, as opposed to as one array.

length	The number of parameters the function expects.
	
	```\n>>> alert.length\n```
	1
	```\n>>> parseInt.length\n```
	2

Boolean

The `Boolean` constructor creates boolean objects (not to be confused with boolean primitives). The boolean objects are not very useful and are listed here for the sake of completeness.

```
>>> var b = new Boolean();
>>> b.valueOf()
```

false

```
>>> b.toString()
```

"false"

A boolean object is not the same as a boolean primitive value. As you know, all objects are truthy:

```
>>> b === false
```

false

```
>>> typeof b
```

"object"

Boolean objects don't have any properties other than the ones inherited from `Object`.

Number

Creates number objects:

```
>>> var n = new Number(101);
>>> typeof n
```

"object"

```
>>> n.valueOf();
```

101

`Number` objects are not primitive objects, but if you use a number method on a primitive number, the primitive will be converted to a `Number` object behind the scenes and the code will work.

```
>>> var n = 123;
>>> typeof n;
```

"number"

```
>>> n.toString()
```

"123"

Members of the Number Constructor

Property/Method	Description

Number.MAX_VALUE	A constant property (cannot be changed) that contains the maximum allowed number.
	
	`>>> Number.MAX_VALUE`
	
	1.7976931348623157e+308
	
	`>>> Number.MAX_VALUE = 101;`
	
	Number.MAX_VALUE is read-only

Number.MIN_VALUE	The smallest number you can work with in JavaScript. `>>> Number.MIN_VALUE` **5e-324**

Number.NaN	Contains the *Not A Number* number.
	
	`>>> Number.NaN`
	
	NaN
	
	NaN is not equal to anything including itself.
	
	`>>> Number.NaN === NaN`
	
	false
	
	`Number.NaN` is more reliable than simply using NaN, because the latter can be overwritten by mistake.
	
	`>>> NaN = 1; // don't do this!`
	
	1
	
	`>>> NaN`
	
	1
	
	`>>> Number.NaN`
	
	NaN

Property/Method	Description
Number.POSITIVE_INFINITY	Contains the Infinity number. This is more reliable than the global Infinity value (property of the global object) because it is read-only.
Number.NEGATIVE_INFINITY	Has the value -Infinity. See above.

Members of the Number Objects

Property/Method	Description

toFixed(fractionDigits)	Fixed-point representation of a number object as a string. Rounds the returned value.
	
	>>> var n = new Number(Math.PI);
	>>> n.valueOf();
	3.141592653589793
	>>> n.toFixed(3)
	"3.142"

toExponential(fractionDigits)	Exponential notation of a number object as a string. Rounds the returned value.
	
	>>> var n = new Number(56789);
	>>> n.toExponential(2)
	"5.68e+4"

toPrecision(precision)	String representation of a number object, either exponential or fixed-point, depending on the number object.
	
	>>> var n = new Number(56789);
	>>> n.toPrecision(2)
	"5.7e+4"
	>>> n.toPrecision(5)
	"56789"
	>>> n.toPrecision(4)
	"5.679e+4"
	>>> var n = new Number(Math.PI);
	>>> n.toPrecision(4)
	"3.142"

String

The `String()` constructor creates string objects. Primitive strings are turned into objects behind the scenes if you call a method on them as if they were objects.

Creating a string object and a string primitive:

```
>>> var s_obj = new String('something');
>>> var s_prim = 'something';
>>> typeof s_obj
```

"object"

```
>>> typeof s_prim
```

"string"

The object and the primitive are not equal when compared by type with `===`:

```
>>> s_obj === s_prim
```

false

```
>>> s_obj == s_prim
```

true

`length` is a property of string objects:

```
>>> s_obj.length
```

9

If you access `length` on a non-object but a primitive string, the primitive is converted to an object behind the scenes and the operation is successful:

```
>>> "something".length
```

9

Members of the String Constructor

Property/Method	Description

`String.fromCharCode` `(code1, code2, code3, ...)`	Returns a string created using the input character codes:
	`>>> String.fromCharCode`
	`          (115, 99, 114, 105, 112, 116);`
	"script"

Members of the String Objects

Property/Method	Description
length	The number of characters in the string. `>>> new String('four').length` **4**
charAt(pos)	Returns the character at the specified position. Positions start at 0. `>>> "script".charAt(0);` **"s"**
charCodeAt(pos)	Returns the code of the character at the specified position. `>>> "script".charCodeAt(0);` **115**
concat(str1, str2, ...)	Return a new string glued from the input pieces. `>>> "".concat('zig', '-', 'zag');` **"zig-zag"**

indexOf(needle, start)	If the needle matches a part of the string, the position of the match is returned. The optional second parameter tells where the search should start from. Returns -1 if no match is found.
	
	`>>> "javascript".indexOf('scr')`
	
	4
	
	`>>> "javascript".indexOf('scr', 5)`
	
	-1

lastIndexOf(needle, start)	Same as indexOf() but starts the search from the end of the string. The last occurence of "a": `>>> "javascript".lastIndexOf('a')` **3**

localeCompare(needle)	Compares two strings in the current locale. Returns 0 if the two strings are equal, 1 if the needle gets sorted before the string object, -1 otherwise.
	
	`>>> "script".localeCompare('crypt')`
	
	1
	
	`>>> "script".localeCompare('sscript')`
	
	-1
	
	`>>> "script".localeCompare('script')`
	
	0

Property/Method	Description
match(regexp)	Accepts a regular expression object and returns an array of matches. `>>> "R2-D2 and C-3PO".match(/[0-9]/g)` **["2", "2", "3"]**

replace(needle, replacement)	Allows you to replace the matching results of a regexp pattern. The replacement can also be a callback function. Capturing patterns are available as $1, $2,...$9.
	
	`>>> "R2-D2".replace(/2/g, '-two')`
	"R-two-D-two"
	`>>> "R2-D2".replace(/(2)/g, '$1$1')`
	"R22-D22"

search(regexp)	Returns the position of the first regular expression match. `>>> "C-3PO".search(/[0-9]/)` **2**

slice(start, end)	Returns the part of a string identified by start and end position. If start is negative, then the start position is length + start, similarly if the end parameter is negative, the end position is length + end.
	
	`>>> "R2-D2 and C-3PO".slice(4,13)`
	"2 and C-3"
	`>>> "R2-D2 and C-3PO".slice(4,-1)`
	"2 and C-3P"

split(separator, limit)	Turns a string into an array. The second parameter, limit, is optional. The separator can also be a regular expression.
	
	`>>> "1,2,3,4".split(',')`
	["1", "2", "3", "4"]
	`>>> "1,2,3,4".split(',', 2)`
	["1", "2"]

substring(start, end)	Similar to slice(). When start or end are negative or invalid, they are considered 0. If they are greater than the string length, they are considered to be the length. If end > start, their values are swapped.
	
	`>>> "R2-D2 and C-3PO".substring(4, 13)`
	"2 and C-3"
	`>>> "R2-D2 and C-3PO".substring(13, 4)`
	"2 and C-3"

Property/Method	Description
toLowerCase() toLocaleLowerCase()	Transforms the string to lower case. >>> "JAVA".toLowerCase() **"java"**
toUpperCase() toLocaleUpperCase()	Transforms the string to upper case. >>> "script".toUpperCase() **"SCRIPT"**

Date

The Date constructor can be used with several types of input:

- You can pass values for year, month, date of the month, hour, minute, second and millisecond, like so:

```
>>> new Date(2011, 0, 1, 13, 30, 35, 500)
```

Sat Jan 01 2011 13:30:35 GMT-0800 (Pacific Standard Time)

- You can skip any of the input parameters, in which case they are assumed to be 0. Note that month values are from 0 (January) to 11 (December), hours are from 0 to 23, minutes and seconds 0 to 59, and milliseconds 0 to 999.

- You can pass a timestamp:

```
>>> new Date(1293917435500)
```

Sat Jan 01 2011 13:30:35 GMT-0800 (Pacific Standard Time)

- If you don't pass anything, the current date/time is assumed:

```
>>> new Date()
```

Fri Apr 18 2008 01:13:00 GMT-0700 (Pacific Daylight Time)

- If you pass a string, it's parsed in attempt to extract a possible date value:

```
>>> new Date('May 4, 2008')
```

Sun May 04 2008 00:00:00 GMT-0700 (Pacific Daylight Time)

Members of the Date Constructor

Property/Method	Description

`Date.parse(string)`	Similar to passing a string to `new Date()`, this method parses the input string in attempt to extract a valid date value. Returns a timestamp on success, NaN on failure:
	
	`>>> Date.parse('May 4, 2008')`
	1209884400000
	`>>> Date.parse('4th')`
	NaN

`Date.UTC(year, month, date, hours, minutes, seconds, ms)`	Returns a timestamp but in UTC (Coordinated Universal Time), not in local time.
	
	`>>> Date.UTC`
	`    (2011, 0, 1, 13, 30, 35, 500)`
	1293888635500

Members of the Date Objects

Property/Method	Description/Example

`toUTCString()`	Same as `toString()` but in universal time. Here's how Pacific Standard (PST) local time differs from UTC:
	
	`>>> var d = new Date(2010, 0, 1);`
	`>>> d.toString()`
	"Fri Jan 01 2010 00:00:00 GMT-0800 (Pacific Standard Time)"
	`>>> d.toUTCString()`
	"Fri, 01 Jan 2010 08:00:00 GMT"

`toDateString()`	Returns only the date portion of `toString()`: `>>> new Date(2010, 0, 1).toDateString();` **"Fri Jan 01 2010"**
`toTimeString()`	Returns only the time portion of `toString()`: `>>> new Date(2010, 0, 1).toTimeString();` **"00:00:00 GMT-0800 (Pacific Standard Time)"**

Property/Method	Description/Example

`toLocaleString()`
`toLocaleDateString()`
`toLocaleTimeString()`
	Equivalent to `toString()`, `toDateString()`, and `toTimeString()` respectively, but in a friendlier format, according to the current user's locale.
	
	`>>> new Date(2010, 0, 1).toString();`
	
	"Fri Jan 01 2010 00:00:00 GMT-0800 (Pacific Standard Time)"
	
	`>>> new Date(2010, 0, 1).toLocaleString();`
	
	"Friday, January 01, 2010 12:00:00 AM"

`getTime()`
`setTime(time)`
	Get or set the time (using a timestamp) of a date object. The following example creates a date and moves it one day forward:
	
	`>>> var d = new Date(2010, 0, 1);`
	
	`>>> d.getTime();`
	
	1262332800000
	
	`>>> d.setTime(d.getTime()`
	`            + 1000 * 60 * 60 * 24);`
	
	1262419200000
	
	`>>> d.toLocaleString()`
	
	"Saturday, January 02, 2010 12:00:00 AM"

`getFullYear()`
`getUTCFullYear()`
`setFullYear(year, month, date)`
`setUTCFullYear(year, month, date)`
	Get/Set a full year using local or UTC time. There is also `getYear()` but it is not Y2K compliant, so `getFullYear()` should be used.
	
	`>>> var d = new Date(2010, 0, 1);`
	
	`>>> d.getYear()`
	
	110
	
	`>>> d.getFullYear()`
	
	2010
	
	`>>> d.setFullYear(2011)`
	
	1293868800000
	
	`>>> d`
	
	Sat Jan 01 2011 00:00:00 GMT-0800 (Pacific Standard Time)

Property/Method	Description/Example

getMonth()
getUTCMonth()
setMonth(month, date)
setUTCMonth(month, date)
	Get/Set month, starting from 0 (January):
	`>>> var d = new Date(2010, 0, 1);`
	`>>> d.getMonth()`
	0
	`>>> d.setMonth(11)`
	1291190400000
	`>>> d.toLocaleDateString()`
	"Wednesday, December 01, 2010"

getDate()
getUTCDate()
setDate(date)
setUTCDate(date)
	Get/Set date of the month.
	`>>> var d = new Date(2010, 0, 1);`
	`>>> d.toLocaleDateString()`
	"Friday, January 01, 2010"
	`>>> d.getDate();`
	1
	`>>> d.setDate(31);`
	1264924800000
	`>>> d.toLocaleDateString()`
	"Sunday, January 31, 2010"

Property/Method	Description/Example

getHours()
 getUTCHours()
 setHours(hour, min, sec, ms)
 setUTCHours(hour, min, sec, ms)
 getMinutes()
 getUTCMinutes()
 setMinutes(min, sec, ms)
 setUTCMinutes(min, sec, ms)
 getSeconds()
 getUTCSeconds()
 setSeconds(sec, ms)
 setUTCSeconds(sec, ms)
 getMilliseconds()
 getUTCMilliseconds()
 setMilliseconds(ms)
 setUTCMilliseconds (ms)
	Get/Set hour, minutes, seconds, milliseconds, all starting from 0.
	
	 `>>> var d = new Date(2010, 0, 1);`
	 `>>> d.getHours() + ':' + d.getMinutes()`
	 "0:0"
	 `>>> d.setMinutes(59)`
	 1262336399000
	 `>>> d.getHours() + ':' + d.getMinutes()`
	 "0:59"

getTimezoneOffset()	Returns the difference between local and universal (UTC) time, measured in minutes. For example the difference between PST (Pacific Standard Time) and UTC:
	
	 `>>> new Date().getTimezoneOffset()`
	 420
	 `>>> 420/60`
	 7

Property/Method	Description/Example

getDay()
getUTCDay()
	Returns the day of the week, starting from 0 (Sunday):
	`>>> var d = new Date(2010, 0, 1);`
	`>>> d.toLocaleDateString()`
	"Friday, January 01, 2010"
	`>>> d.getDay()`
	5
	`>>> var d = new Date(2010, 0, 3);`
	`>>> d.toLocaleDateString()`
	"Sunday, January 03, 2010"
	`>>> d.getDay()`
	0

Math

Math is a little different from the other built-in objects, because it cannot be used as a constructor to create objects. It is just a collection of functions and constants. Some examples, to illustrate the difference, are given below:

```
>>> typeof String.prototype
```

"object"

```
>>> typeof Date.prototype
```

"object"

```
>>> typeof Math.prototype
```

"undefined"

```
>>> typeof Math
```

"object"

```
>>> typeof String
```

"function"

Members of the Math Object

Property/Method	Description
	These are some useful math constants, all read-only. Here are their values:
Math.E	`>>> Math.E` **2.718281828459045**
Math.LN10	`>>> Math.LN10` **2.302585092994046**
Math.LN2	`>>> Math.LN2` **0.6931471805599453**
Math.LOG2E	`>>> Math.LOG2E` **1.4426950408889634**
Math.LOG10E	`>>> Math.LOG10E` **0.4342944819032518**
Math.PI	`>>> Math.PI` **3.141592653589793**
Math.SQRT1_2	`>>> Math.SQRT1_2` **0.7071067811865476**
Math.SQRT2	`>>> Math.SQRT2` **1.4142135623730951**
Math.acos(x) Math.asin(x) Math.atan(x) Math.atan2(y, x) Math.cos(x) Math.sin(x) Math.tan(x)	Trigonometric functions
	round() gives you the nearest integer, ceil() rounds up and floor() rounds down:
Math.round(x)	`>>> Math.round(5.5)` **6**
Math.floor(x)	`>>> Math.floor(5.5)` **5**
Math.ceil(x)	`>>> Math.ceil(5.1)` **6**

Property/Method	Description
	max() returns the largest and min() returns the smallest of the numbers passed to them as arguments. If at least one of the input parameters is NaN, the result is also NaN.
Math.max(num1, num2, num3, ...)	>>> Math.max(2, 101, 4.5) **101**
Math.min(num1, num2, num3, ...)	>>> Math.min(2, 101, 4.5) **2**
	Absolute value.

Math.abs(x)	>>> Math.abs(-101)
	101
	>>> Math.abs(101)
	101

Math.exp(x)	Exponential function: Math.E to the power of x
Math.log(x)	Natural logarithm of x.
	Square root of x.

Math.sqrt(x)	>>> Math.sqrt(9)
	3
	>>> Math.sqrt(2) === Math.SQRT2
	true

	x to the power of y.
Math.pow(x, y)	>>> Math.pow(3, 2) **9**
	Random number between 0 and 1 (including 0).
Math.random()	>>> Math.random() **0.8279076443185321**

RegExp

You can create a regular expression object by using the RegExp() constructor and passing the expression pattern as the first parameter and the pattern modifiers as the second.

```
>>> var re = new RegExp('[dn]o+dle', 'gmi');
```

This matches "noodle", "doodle", "doooodle", and so on. It's equivalent to using the regular expression literal:

```
>>> var re = ('/[dn]o+dle/gmi'); // recommended
```

Chapter 4 and Appendix D contain more information on regular expressions and patterns.

Members of RegExp Objects

Property/Method	Description
global	Read-only, true if the g modifier was set when creating the regexp object.
ignoreCase	Read-only. true if the i modifier was set when creating the regexp object.
multiline	Read-only. true if the m modifier was set when creating the regexp object
lastIndex	Contains the position in the string where the next match should start. test() and exec() set this position after a successful match. Only relevant when the g (global) modifier was used.

```
>>> var re = /[dn]o+dle/g;
>>> re.lastIndex
```
0
```
>>> re.exec("noodle doodle");
```
["noodle"]
```
>>> re.lastIndex
```
6
```
>>> re.exec("noodle doodle");
```
["doodle"]
```
>>> re.lastIndex
```
13
```
>>> re.exec("noodle doodle");
```
null
```
>>> re.lastIndex
```
0

source	Read-only. Returns the regular expression pattern (without the modifiers).

```
>>> var re = /[nd]o+dle/gmi;
>>> re.source
```
"[nd]o+dle"

Property/Method	Description
exec(string)	Matches the input string with the regular expression. On a successful match returns an array containing the match and any capturing groups. When the g modifier is used, it matches the first occurrence and sets the lastIndex property. Returns **null** when there's no match.
	>>> var re = /([dn])(o+)dle/g;
	>>> re.exec("noodle doodle");
	["noodle", "n", "oo"]
	>>> re.exec("noodle doodle");
	["doodle", "d", "oo"]
test(string)	Same as exec() but only returns **true** or **false**.
	>>> /noo/.test('Noodle')
	false
	>>> /noo/i.test('Noodle')
	true

Error Objects

Error objects are created either by the environment (the browser) or by your code.

```
>>> var e = new Error('jaavcsritp is _not_ how you spell it');
>>> typeof e
```

"object"

Other than the Error constructor, six additional ones exist and they all inherit Error:

- EvalError

- RangeError

- ReferenceError

- SyntaxError

- TypeError

- URIError

Members of the Error Objects

Property	Description
name	The name of the error constructor used to create the object:
	>>> var e = new EvalError('Oops');
	>>> e.name
	"EvalError"
message	Additional error information:
	>>> var e = new Error('Oops... again');
	>>> e.message
	"Oops... again"

Regular Expressions

When you use regular expressions (discussed in Chapter 4), you can match literal strings, for example:

```
>>> "some text".match(/me/)
```

["me"]

But the true power of regular expressions comes from matching patterns, not literal strings. The following table describes the different syntax you can use in your patterns, and provides some examples of their use.

Pattern	Description
[abc]	Matches a class of characters. ```>>> "some text".match(/[otx]/g)``` **["o", "t", "x", "t"]**

[a-z]	A class of characters defined as a range. For example [a-d] is the same as [abcd], [a-z] matches all lowercase characters, [a-zA-Z0-9_] matches all characters, numbers and the underscore character.
	
	```>>> "Some Text".match(/[a-z]/g)```
	
	["o", "m", "e", "e", "x", "t"]
	
	```>>> "Some Text".match(/[a-zA-Z]/g)```
	
	["S", "o", "m", "e", "T", "e", "x", "t"]

[^abc]	Matches everything that is *not* matched by the class of characters. ```>>> "Some Text".match(/[^a-z]/g)``` **["S", " ", "T"]**

Pattern	Description

a|b	Matches a or b. The pipe character means OR, and it can be used more than once.
	
	`>>> "Some Text".match(/t|T/g);`
	["T", "t"]
	`>>> "Some Text".match(/t|T|Some/g);`
	["Some", "T", "t"]

a(?=b)	Matches a only if followed by b.
	
	`>>> "Some Text".match(/Some(?=Tex)/g);`
	null
	`>>> "Some Text".match(/Some(?= Tex)/g);`
	["Some"]

a(?!b)	Matches a only when *not* followed by b.
	
	`>>> "Some Text".match(/Some(?! Tex)/g);`
	null
	`>>> "Some Text".match(/Some(?!Tex)/g);`
	["Some"]

\	Escape character used to help you match the special characters used in patterns as literals.
	
	`>>> "R2-D2".match(/[2-3]/g)`
	["2", "2"]
	`>>> "R2-D2".match(/[2\-3]/g)`
	["2", "-", "2"]

\n	New line
\r	Carriage return
\f	Form feed
\t	Tab
\v	Vertical tab

Pattern	Description
\s	White space, or any of the five escape sequences above. `>>> "R2\n D2".match(/\s/g)` **["\n", " "]**
\S	Opposite of the above; matches everything but white space. Same as `[^\s]`: `>>> "R2\n D2".match(/\S/g)` **["R", "2", "D", "2"]**
\w	Any letter, number, or underscore. Same as `[A-Za-z0-9_]`. `>>> "Some text!".match(/\w/g)` **["S", "o", "m", "e", "t", "e", "x", "t"]**
\W	Opposite of \w. `>>> "Some text!".match(/\W/g)` **[" ", "!"]**
\d	Matches a number, same as `[0-9]`. `>>> "R2-D2 and C-3PO".match(/\d/g)` **["2", "2", "3"]**
\D	Opposite of \d; matches non-numbers, same as `[^0-9]` or `[^\d]`. `>>> "R2-D2 and C-3PO".match(/\D/g)` **["R", "-", "D", " ", "a", "n", "d", " ", "C", "-", "P", "O"]**

\b	Matches a word boundary such as space or punctuation.
	Matching R or D followed by 2:
	
	`>>> "R2D2 and C-3PO".match(/[RD]2/g)`
	
	["R2", "D2"]
	
	Same as above but only at the end of a word:
	
	`>>> "R2D2 and C-3PO".match(/[RD]2\b/g)`
	
	["D2"]
	
	Same pattern but the input has a dash, which is also an end of a word:
	
	`>>> "R2-D2 and C-3PO".match(/[RD]2\b/g)`
	
	["R2", "D2"]

Pattern	Description

\B	The opposite of \b.
	
	>>> "R2-D2 and C-3PO".match(/[RD]2\B/g)
	
	null
	
	>>> "R2D2 and C-3PO".match(/[RD]2\B/g)
	
	["R2"]

[\b]	Matches the backspace character
\0	The null character
\u0000	Matches a Unicode character, represented by a four-digit hexadecimal number. >>> "СТОЯН".match(/\u0441\u0442\u043E/) **["сто"]**
\x00	Matches a character code represented by a two-digit hexadecimal number. >>> "dude".match(/\x64/g) **["d", "d"]**

^	The beginning of the string to be matched. If you set the m modifier (multi-line), it matches the beginning of each line.
	
	>>> "regular\nregular\nexpression".match(/r/g);
	
	["r", "r", "r", "r", "r"]
	
	>>> "regular\nregular\nexpression".match(/^r/g);
	
	["r"]
	
	>>> "regular\nregular\nexpression".match(/^r/mg);
	
	["r", "r"]

$	Matches the end of the input or, when using the multi-line modifier, the end of each line.
	
	>>> "regular\nregular\nexpression".match(/r$/g);
	
	null
	
	>>> "regular\nregular\nexpression".match(/r$/mg);
	
	["r", "r"]

.	Matches any character except for the new line and the linefeed.
	
	>>> "regular".match(/r./g);
	
	["re"]
	
	>>> "regular".match(/r.../g);
	
	["regu"]

Pattern	Description
*	Matches the preceding pattern if it occurs 0 or more times. For example / . * / will match anything including nothing (an empty input).

	`>>> "".match(/.*/)`
	[""]
	`>>> "anything".match(/.*/)`
	["anything"]
	`>>> "anything".match(/n.*h/)`
	["nyth"]

?	Matches the preceding pattern if it occurs 0 or 1 times.
	`>>> "anything".match(/ny?/g)` **["ny", "n"]**
+	Matches the preceding pattern if it occurs at least once (or more times).

	`>>> "anything".match(/ny+/g)`
	["ny"]
	`>>> "R2-D2 and C-3PO".match(/[a-z]/gi)`
	["R", "D", "a", "n", "d", "C", "P", "O"]
	`>>> "R2-D2 and C-3PO".match(/[a-z]+/gi)`
	["R", "D", "and", "C", "PO"]

{n}	Matches the preceding pattern if it occurs exactly n times.

	`>>> "regular expression".match(/s/g)`
	["s", "s"]
	`>>> "regular expression".match(/s{2}/g)`
	["ss"]
	`>>> "regular expression".match(/\b\w{3}/g)`
	["reg", "exp"]

Pattern	Description
{min,max}	Matches the preceding pattern if it occurs between min and max number of times. You can omit max, which will mean no maximum, but only a minimum. You cannot omit min.

An example where the input is "doodle" with the "o" repeated 10 times:

```
>>> "doooooooooodle".match(/o/g)
```

["o", "o", "o", "o", "o", "o", "o", "o", "o", "o"]

```
>>> "doooooooooodle".match(/o{2}/g)
```

["oo", "oo", "oo", "oo", "oo"]

```
>>> "doooooooooodle".match(/o{2,}/g)
```

["oooooooooo"]

```
>>> "doooooooooodle".match(/o{2,6}/g)
```

["oooooo", "oooo"]

Pattern	Description
(pattern)	When the pattern is in parentheses, it is remembered so that it can be used for replacements. This is also known as capturing patterns.

The captured matches are available as $1, $2,... $9

Matching all "r" occurrences and repeating them:

```
>>> "regular expression".replace(/(r)/g, '$1$1')
```

"rregularr exprression"

Matching "re" and turning it to "er":

```
>>> "regular expression".replace
        (/(r)(e)/g, '$2$1')
```

"ergular experssion"

Pattern	Description
(?:pattern)	Non-capturing pattern, not remembered and not available in $1, $2...

Here's an example of how "re" is matched, but the "r" is not remembered and the second pattern becomes $1:

```
>>> "regular expression".replace
        (/(?:r)(e)/g, '$1$1')
```

"eegular expeession"

Make sure you pay attention when a special character can have two meanings, as is the case with ^, ?, and \b.

Index

Thank you for buying
Object-Oriented JavaScript

About Packt Publishing

Packt, pronounced 'packed', published its first book "*Mastering phpMyAdmin for Effective MySQL Management*" in April 2004 and subsequently continued to specialize in publishing highly focused books on specific technologies and solutions.

Our books and publications share the experiences of your fellow IT professionals in adapting and customizing today's systems, applications, and frameworks. Our solution based books give you the knowledge and power to customize the software and technologies you're using to get the job done. Packt books are more specific and less general than the IT books you have seen in the past. Our unique business model allows us to bring you more focused information, giving you more of what you need to know, and less of what you don't.

Packt is a modern, yet unique publishing company, which focuses on producing quality, cutting-edge books for communities of developers, administrators, and newbies alike. For more information, please visit our website: www.packtpub.com.

Writing for Packt

We welcome all inquiries from people who are interested in authoring. Book proposals should be sent to authors@packtpub.com. If your book idea is still at an early stage and you would like to discuss it first before writing a formal book proposal, contact us; one of our commissioning editors will get in touch with you.

We're not just looking for published authors; if you have strong technical skills but no writing experience, our experienced editors can help you develop a writing career, or simply get some additional reward for your expertise.

Learning the Yahoo! User Interface library

ISBN: 978-1-847192-32-5   Paperback: 380 pages

Develop your next generation web applications with the YUI JavaScript development library.

Understand the principles of Active Directory design

1. Improve your coding and productivity with the YUI Library

2. Gain a thorough understanding of the YUI tools

3. Learn from detailed examples for common tasks

Learning jQuery

ISBN: 978-1-847192-50-9   Paperback: 380 pages

jQuery: Better Interaction Design and Web Development with Simple JavaScript Techniques

1. Create better, cross-platform JavaScript code

2. Detailed solutions to specific client-side problems

Please check **www.PacktPub.com** for information on our titles

Made in the USA
Lexington, KY
23 March 2010